P9-AOA-823

THE
MYTHMAKER

PAUL
AND THE INVENTION
OF CHRISTIANITY

THE MYTHMAKER

PAUL AND THE INVENTION OF CHRISTIANITY

HYAM MACCOBY

1817

HARPER & ROW, PUBLISHERS, New York
Cambridge, Philadelphia, San Francisco,
London, Mexico City, São Paulo, Singapore, Sydney

THE MYTHMAKER: PAUL AND THE INVENTION OF CHRISTIANITY. Copyright © 1986 by Hyam Maccoby. All rights reserved. Printed in the United States of America. No part of this book may be used or reproduced in any manner whatsoever without written permission except in the case of brief quotations embodied in critical articles and reviews. For information address Harper & Row, Publishers, Inc., 10 East 53rd Street, New York, N.Y. 10022.

FIRST U.S. EDITION

Library of Congress Cataloging-in-Publication Data

Maccoby, Hyam, 1924–
   The mythmaker.

   Bibliography: p.
   Includes index.
   1. Paul, the Apostle, Saint. 2. Jesus Christ—Person and offices. 3. Christianity—Origin. I. Title.
BS2506.M28   1986   225.9'24   85-45680
ISBN 0-06-015582-5

86 87 88 89 90 RRD 10 9 8 7 6 5 4 3 2 1

For Cynthia

CONTENTS

ACKNOWLEDGEMENTS

I should like to thank Dr Francis T. Glasson, with whom I have discussed various issues relevant to this book over a considerable period. His remarks were most thought-provoking, even when I did not agree with them.

I should like to thank also Professor E. P. Sanders for his generous and stimulating comments. I am also most grateful to Professor A. R. C. Leaney, Professor P. R. Ackroyd, Canon J. W. Packer and Rabbi Jonathan Sacks for their encouragement of the rabbinical aspects of my work.

Special thanks are due to Mr Jack Eisner for the generosity and warmth of his support.

I have been greatly heartened by the deep understanding of the origins of the Jewish-Christian conflict shown by Professor Roy Eckhart and Dr Robert Everett, and by their courageous support.

I am most grateful to Professor Yehuda Bauer for his encouragement of my work, and to the International Centre for the Study of Antisemitism, at the Hebrew University of Jerusalem, for supporting its continuance with a grant.

I should like to thank also my colleagues and students at the Leo Baeck College for their unfailing encouragement and companionship in scholarly enquiry.

The poet Samuel Menashe has been an indefatigable and inspiring friend and adviser, and I am glad to express here my deep gratitude to him.

My chief thanks, however, must go to my dear wife, Cynthia, whose keen criticism and advice has contributed to every page of this book, and whose constant, loving support has made its completion possible.

H.M.

PREFACE

As a Talmudic scholar, I have found that knowledge of the Talmud and other rabbinical works has opened up the meaning of many puzzling passages in the New Testament. In my earlier book on Jesus, *Revolution in Judaea*, I showed how, in the Synoptic Gospels, Jesus speaks and acts as a Pharisee, though the Gospel editors have attempted to conceal this by representing him as opposing Pharisaism even when his sayings were most in accordance with Pharisee teaching. In the present book, I have used the rabbinical evidence to establish an opposite contention: that Paul, whom the New Testament wishes to portray as having been a trained Pharisee, never was one. The consequences of this for the understanding of early Christianity are immense.

In addition to the rabbinical writings, I have made great use of the ancient historians, especially Josephus, Epiphanius and Eusebius. Their statements must be weighed in relation to their particular interests and bias; but when such bias has been identified and discounted, there remains a residue of valuable information. Exactly the same applies to the New Testament itself. Its information is often distorted by the bias of the author or editor, but a knowledge of the nature of this bias makes possible the emergence of the true shape of events.

For an explanation of my stance in relation to the various schools of New Testament interpretation of modern times, the reader is referred to the Note on Method, p. 206.

In using the Epistles as evidence of Paul's life, views and 'mythology', I have confined myself to those Epistles which are accepted by the great majority of New Testament scholars as the genuine work of Paul. Disputed Epistles, such as Colossians, however pertinent to my argument, have been ignored.

When quoting from the New Testament, I have usually used the New English Bible version, but, from time to time, I have used the

Authorized Version or the Revised Version, when I thought them preferable in faithfulness to the original. While the New English Bible is in general more intelligible to modern readers than the older versions, its concern for modern English idiom sometimes obscures important features of the original Greek; and its readiness to paraphrase sometimes allows the translator's presuppositions to colour his translation. I have pointed out several examples of this in the text.

In considering the background of Paul, I have returned to one of the earliest accounts of Paul in existence, that given by the Ebionites, as reported by Epiphanius. This account has been neglected by scholars for quite inadequate and tendentious reasons. Robert Graves and Joshua Podro in *The Nazarene Gospel Restored* did take the Ebionite account seriously; but, though they made some cogent remarks about it, their treatment of the matter was brief. I hope that the present book will do more to alter the prevailing dismissive attitude towards the evidence of this fascinating and important ancient community.

PART I

SAUL

CHAPTER 1

THE PROBLEM OF PAUL

At the beginning of Christianity stand two figures: Jesus and Paul. Jesus is regarded by Christians as the founder of their religion, in that the events of his life comprise the foundation story of Christianity; but Paul is regarded as the great interpreter of Jesus' mission, who explained, in a way that Jesus himself never did, how Jesus' life and death fitted into a cosmic scheme of salvation, stretching from the creation of Adam to the end of time.

How should we understand the relationship between Jesus and Paul? We shall be approaching this question not from the standpoint of faith, but from that of historians, who regard the Gospels and the rest of the New Testament as an important source of evidence requiring careful sifting and criticism, since their authors were propagating religious beliefs rather than conveying dispassionate historical information. We shall also be taking into account all relevant evidence from other sources, such as Josephus, the Talmud, the Church historians and the Gnostic writings.

What would Jesus himself have thought of Paul? We must remember that Jesus never knew Paul; the two men never once met. The disciples who knew Jesus best, such as Peter, James and John, have left no writings behind them explaining how Jesus seemed to them or what they considered his mission to have been. Did they agree with the interpretations disseminated by Paul in his fluent, articulate writings? Or did they perhaps think that this newcomer to the scene, spinning complicated theories about the place of Jesus in the scheme of things, was getting everything wrong? Paul claimed that his interpretations were not just his own invention, but had come to him by personal inspiration; he claimed that he had personal acquaintance with the resurrected Jesus, even though he had never met him during his lifetime. Such acquaintance, he claimed, gained through visions and transports, was actually superior to acquaintance with Jesus during his lifetime, when Jesus was much more reticent about his purposes.

We know about Paul not only from his own letters but also from the book of Acts, which gives a full account of his life. Paul, in fact, is the hero of Acts, which was written by an admirer and follower of his, namely, Luke, who was also the author of the Gospel of that name. From Acts, it would appear that there was some friction between Paul and the leaders of the 'Jerusalem Church', the surviving companions of Jesus; but this friction was resolved, and they all became the best of friends, with common aims and purposes. From certain of Paul's letters, particularly Galatians, it seems that the friction was more serious than in the picture given in Acts, which thus appears to be partly a propaganda exercise, intended to portray unity in the early Church. The question recurs: what would Jesus have thought of Paul, and what did the Apostles think of him?

We should remember that the New Testament, as we have it, is much more dominated by Paul than appears at first sight. As we read it, we come across the Four Gospels, of which Jesus is the hero, and do not encounter Paul as a character until we embark on the post-Jesus narrative of Acts. Then we finally come into contact with Paul himself, in his letters. But this impression is misleading, for the earliest writings in the New Testament are actually Paul's letters, which were written about AD 50–60, while the Gospels were not written until the period AD 70–110. This means that the theories of Paul were already before the writers of the Gospels and coloured their interpretations of Jesus' activities. Paul is, in a sense, present from the very first word of the New Testament. This is, of course, not the whole story, for the Gospels are based on traditions and even written sources which go back to a time before the impact of Paul, and these early traditions and sources are not entirely obliterated in the final version and give valuable indications of what the story was like before Paulinist editors pulled it into final shape. However, the dominant outlook and shaping perspective of the Gospels is that of Paul, for the simple reason that it was the Paulinist view of what Jesus' sojourn on Earth had been about that was triumphant in the Church as it developed in history. Rival interpretations, which at one time had been orthodox, opposed to Paul's very individual views, now became heretical and were crowded out of the final version of the writings adopted by the Pauline Church as the inspired canon of the New Testament.

This explains the puzzling and ambiguous role given in the Gospels to the companions of Jesus, the twelve disciples. They are shadowy figures, who are allowed little personality, except of a schematic kind. They are also portrayed as stupid; they never quite understand what Jesus is up to. Their importance in the origins of Christianity is played down in a remarkable way. For example, we find immediately after Jesus' death that the leader of the Jerusalem Church is Jesus' brother James. Yet in the Gospels, this James does not appear at all as having anything to do with Jesus' mission and story. Instead, he is given a brief mention as one of the brothers of Jesus who allegedly *opposed* Jesus during his lifetime and regarded him as mad. How it came about that a brother who had been hostile to Jesus in his lifetime suddenly became the revered leader of the Church immediately after Jesus' death is not explained, though one would have thought that some explanation was called for. Later Church legends, of course, filled the gap with stories of the miraculous conversion of James after the death of Jesus and his development into a saint. But the most likely explanation is, as will be argued later, that the erasure of Jesus' brother James (and his other brothers) from any significant role in the Gospel story is part of the denigration of the early leaders who had been in close contact with Jesus and regarded with great suspicion and dismay the Christological theories of the upstart Paul, flaunting his brand new visions in interpretation of the Jesus whom he had never met in the flesh.

Who, then, was Paul? Here we would seem to have a good deal of information; but on closer examination, it will turn out to be full of problems. We have the information given by Paul about himself in his letters, which are far from impersonal and often take an autobiographical turn. Also we have the information given in Acts, in which Paul plays the chief role. But the information given by any person about himself always has to be treated with a certain reserve, since everyone has strong motives for putting himself in the best possible light. And the information given about Paul in Acts also requires close scrutiny, since this work was written by someone committed to the Pauline cause. Have we any other sources for Paul's biography? As a matter of fact, we have, though they are scattered in various unexpected places, which it will be our task to explore: in a fortuitously preserved extract from the otherwise lost writings of the Ebionites, a sect of great importance for our quest; in a disguised attack on Paul included in a text of orthodox Christian authority; and in an Arabic manuscript, in which a text of the early Jewish Christians, the opponents of Paul, has been preserved by an unlikely chain of circumstances.

Let us first survey the evidence found in the more obvious and well-known sources. It appears from Acts that Paul was at first called 'Saul', and that his birthplace was Tarsus, a city in Asia Minor (Acts 9: 11, and 21: 39, and 22: 3). Strangely enough, however, Paul himself, in his letters, never mentions that he came from Tarsus, even when he is at his most autobiographical. Instead, he gives the following information about his origins: 'I am an Israelite myself, of the stock of Abraham, of the tribe of Benjamin' (Romans 11: 2); and '. . . circumcised on my eighth day, Israelite by race, of the tribe of Benjamin, a Hebrew born and bred; in my attitude to the law, a Pharisee. . . .' (Philippians 3: 5). It seems that Paul was not anxious to impart to the recipients of his letters that he came from somewhere so remote as Tarsus from Jerusalem, the powerhouse of Pharisaism. The impression he wished to give, of coming from an unimpeachable Pharisaic background, would have been much impaired by the admission that he in fact came from Tarsus, where there were few, if any, Pharisee teachers and a Pharisee training would have been hard to come by.

We encounter, then, right at the start of our enquiry into Paul's background, the question: was Paul really from a genuine Pharisaic family, as he says to his correspondents, or was this just something that he said to increase his status in their eyes? The fact that this question is hardly ever asked shows how strong the influence of traditional religious attitudes still is in Pauline studies. Scholars feel that, however objective their enquiry is supposed to be, they must always preserve an attitude of deep reverence towards Paul, and never say anything to suggest that he may have bent the truth at times, though the evidence is strong enough in various parts of his life-story that he was not above deception when he felt it warranted by circumstances.

It should be noted (in advance of a full discussion of the subject) that modern scholarship has shown that, at this time, the Pharisees were held in high repute throughout the Roman and Parthian empires as a dedicated group who upheld religious ideals in the face of tyranny, supported leniency and mercy in the application of laws, and championed the rights of the poor against the oppression of the rich. The undeserved reputation for hypocrisy which is attached to the name 'Pharisee' in medieval and modern times is due to the campaign against the Pharisees in the Gospels – a campaign dictated by politico-religious considerations at the time when the Gospels were given their final editing, about forty to eighty years after the death of Jesus. Paul's desire to be thought of as a person of Pharisee upbringing should thus be understood in the light of the actual reputation of the Pharisees in Paul's lifetime; Paul was claiming a high honour, which would much enhance his status in the eyes of his correspondents.

Before looking further into Paul's claim to have come from a Pharisee background, let us continue our survey of what we are told about Paul's career in the more accessible sources. The young Saul, we are told, left Tarsus and came to the Land of Israel, where he studied in the Pharisee academy of Gamaliel (Acts 22: 3). We know from other sources about Gamaliel, who is a highly respected figure in the rabbinical writings such as the Mishnah, and was given the title 'Rabban', as the leading sage of his day. That he was the leader of the whole Pharisee party is attested also by the New Testament itself, for he plays a prominent role in one scene in the book of Acts (chapter 5) – a role that, as we shall see later, is hard to reconcile with the general picture of the Pharisees given in the Gospels.

Yet Paul himself, in his letters, never mentions that he was a pupil of Gamaliel, even when he is most concerned to stress his qualifications as a Pharisee. Here again, then, the question has to be put: was Paul ever really a pupil of Gamaliel or was this claim made by Luke as an embellishment to his narrative? As we shall see later, there are certain considerations which make it most unlikely, quite apart from Paul's significant omission to say anything about the matter, that Paul was ever a pupil of Gamaliel's.

We are also told of the young Saul that he was implicated, to some extent, in the death of the martyr Stephen. The people who gave false evidence against Stephen, we are told, and who also took the leading part in the stoning of their innocent victim, 'laid their coats at the feet of a young man named Saul'. The death of Stephen is described, and it is added, 'And Saul was among those who approved of his murder' (Acts 8: 1). How much truth is there in this detail? Is it to be regarded as historical fact or as dramatic embellishment, emphasizing the contrast between Paul before and after conversion? The death of Stephen is itself an episode that requires searching analysis, since it is full of problems and contradictions. Until we have a better idea of why and by whom Stephen was killed and what were the views for which he died, we can only note the alleged implication of Saul in the matter as a subject for further investigation. For the moment, we also note that the alleged implication of Saul heightens the impression that adherence to Pharisaism would mean violent hostility to the followers of Jesus.

The next thing we are told about Saul in Acts is that he was 'harrying the Church; he entered house after house, seizing men and women, and sending them to prison' (Acts 8: 3). We are not told at this point by what authority or on whose orders he was carrying out this persecution. It was clearly not a matter of merely individual action on

7

his part, for sending people to prison can only be done by some kind of official. Saul must have been acting on behalf of some authority, and who this authority was can be gleaned from later incidents in which Saul was acting on behalf of the High Priest. Anyone with knowledge of the religious and political scene at this time in Judaea feels the presence of an important problem here: the High Priest was not a Pharisee, but a Sadducee, and the Sadducees were bitterly opposed to the Pharisees. How is it that Saul, allegedly an enthusiastic Pharisee ('a Pharisee of the Pharisees'), is acting hand in glove with the High Priest? The picture we are given in our New Testament sources of Saul, in the days before his conversion to Jesus, is contradictory and suspect.

The next we hear of Saul (chapter 9) is that he 'was still breathing murderous threats against the disciples of the Lord. He went to the High Priest and applied for letters to the synagogues at Damascus authorizing him to arrest anyone he found, men or women, who followed the new way, and bring them to Jerusalem.' This incident is full of mystery. If Saul had his hands so full in 'harrying the church' in Judaea, why did he suddenly have the idea of going off to Damascus to harry the Church there? What was the special urgency of a visit to Damascus? Further, what kind of jurisdiction did the Jewish High Priest have over the non-Jewish city of Damascus that would enable him to authorize arrests and extraditions in that city? There is, moreover, something very puzzling about the way in which Saul's relation to the High Priest is described: as if he is a private citizen who wishes to make citizen's arrests according to some plan of his own, and approaches the High Priest for the requisite authority. Surely there must have been some much more definite official connection between the High Priest and Saul, not merely that the High Priest was called upon to underwrite Saul's project. It seems more likely that the plan was the High Priest's and not Saul's, and that Saul was acting as agent or emissary of the High Priest. The whole incident needs to be considered in the light of probabilities and current conditions.

The book of Acts then continues with the account of Saul's conversion on the road to Damascus through a vision of Jesus and the succeeding events of his life as a follower of Jesus. The pre-Christian period of Saul's life, however, does receive further mention later in the book of Acts, both in chapter 22 and chapter 26, where some interesting details are added, and also some further puzzles.

In chapter 22, Saul (now called Paul), is shown giving his own account of his early life in a speech to the people after the Roman commandant had questioned him. Paul speaks as follows:

8

I am a true-born Jew, a native of Tarsus in Cilicia. I was brought up in this city, and as a pupil of Gamaliel I was thoroughly trained in every point of our ancestral law. I have always been ardent in God's service, as you all are today. And so I began to persecute this movement to the death, arresting its followers, men and women alike, and putting them in chains. For this I have as witnesses the High Priest and the whole Council of Elders. I was given letters from them to our fellow-Jews at Damascus, and had started out to bring the Christians there to Jerusalem as prisoners for punishment; and this is what happened. . . .

Paul then goes on to describe his vision of Jesus on the road to Damascus. Previously he had described himself to the commandant as 'a Jew, a Tarsian from Cilicia, a citizen of no mean city'.

It is from this passage that we learn of Paul's native city, Tarsus, and of his alleged studies under Gamaliel. Note that he says that, though born in Tarsus, he was 'brought up in this city' (i.e. Jerusalem) which suggests that he spent his childhood in Jerusalem. Does this mean that his parents moved from Tarsus to Jerusalem? Or that the child was sent to Jerusalem on his own, which seems unlikely? If Paul spent only a few childhood years in Tarsus, he would hardly describe himself proudly as 'a citizen of no mean city' (Tarsus). Jews who had spent most of their lives in Jerusalem would be much more prone to describe themselves as citizens of Jerusalem. The likelihood is that Paul moved to Jerusalem when he was already a grown man, and he left his parents behind in Tarsus, which seems all the more probable in that they receive no mention in any account of Paul's experiences in Jerusalem. As for Paul's alleged period of studies under Gamaliel, this would have had to be in adulthood, for Gamaliel was a teacher of advanced studies, not a teacher of children. He would accept as a pupil only someone well grounded and regarded as suitable for the rabbinate. The question, then, is where and how Paul received this thorough grounding, if at all. As pointed out above and argued fully below, there are strong reasons to think that Paul never was a pupil of Gamaliel.

An important question that also arises in this chapter of Acts is that of Paul's Roman citizenship. This is mentioned first in chapter 16. Paul claims to have been *born* a Roman citizen, which would mean that his father was a Roman citizen. There are many problems to be discussed in this connection, and some of these questions impinge on Paul's claim to have had a Pharisaic background.

A further account of Paul's pre-Christian life is found in chapter 26 of Acts, in a speech addressed by Paul to King Agrippa. Paul says:

My life from my youth up, the life I led from the beginning among my people and in Jerusalem, is familiar to all Jews. Indeed they have known me long enough and could testify, if they only would, that I belonged to the strictest group in our religion: I lived as a Pharisee. And it is for a hope kindled by God's promise to our forefathers that I stand in the dock today. Our twelve tribes hope to see the fulfilment of that promise. . . . I myself once thought it my duty to work actively against the name of Jesus of Nazareth; and I did so in Jerusalem. It was I who imprisoned many of God's people by authority obtained from the chief priests; and when they were condemned to death, my vote was cast against them. In all the synagogues I tried by repeated punishment to make them renounce their faith; indeed my fury rose to such a pitch that I extended my persecution to foreign cities. On one such occasion I was travelling to Damascus with authority and commission from the chief priests. . . .

Again the account continues with the vision on the road to Damascus.

This speech, of course, cannot be regarded as the authentic words addressed by Paul to King Agrippa, but rather as a rhetorical speech composed by Luke, the author of Acts, in the style of ancient historians. Thus the claim made in the speech that Paul's career as a Pharisee of high standing was known to 'all Jews' cannot be taken at face value. It is interesting that Paul is represented as saying that he 'cast his vote' against the followers of Jesus, thus helping to condemn them to death. This can only refer to the voting of the Sanhedrin or Council of Elders, which was convened to try capital cases; so what Luke is claiming here for his hero Paul is that he was at one time a member of the Sanhedrin. This is highly unlikely, for Paul would surely have made this claim in his letters, when writing about his credentials as a Pharisee, if it had been true. There is, however, some confusion both in this account and in the accounts quoted above about whether the Sanhedrin, as well as the High Priest or 'chief priests', was involved in the persecution of the followers of Jesus. Sometimes the High Priest alone is mentioned, sometimes the Sanhedrin is coupled with him, as if the two are inseparable. But we see on two occasions cited in Acts that the High Priest was outvoted by the Pharisees in the Sanhedrin; on both occasions, the Pharisees were *opposing* an attempt to persecute the followers of Jesus; so the representation of High Priest and Sanhedrin as having identical aims is one of the suspect features of these accounts.

It will be seen from the above collation of passages in the book of Acts concerning Paul's background and early life, together with Paul's own references to his background in his letters, that the same strong picture emerges: that Paul was at first a highly trained Pharisee rabbi, learned in all the intricacies of the rabbinical commentaries on scripture and legal traditions (afterwards collected in the rabbinical compilations, the Talmud and Midrash). As a Pharisee, Paul was strongly opposed to the new sect which followed Jesus and which believed that he had been resurrected after his crucifixion. So opposed was Paul to this sect that he took violent action against it, dragging its adherents to prison. Though this strong picture has emerged, some doubts have also arisen, which, so far, have only been lightly sketched in: how is it, for example, that Paul claims to have voted against Christians on trial for their lives before the Sanhedrin, when in fact, in the graphically described trial of Peter before the Sanhedrin (Acts 5), the Pharisees, led by Gamaliel, voted for the *release* of Peter? What kind of Pharisee was Paul, if he took an attitude towards the early Christians which, on the evidence of the same book of Acts, was untypical of the Pharisees? And how is it that this book of Acts is so inconsistent within itself that it describes Paul as violently opposed to Christianity *because* of his deep attachment to Pharisaism, and yet also describes the Pharisees as being friendly towards the early Christians, standing up for them and saving their lives?

It has been pointed out by many scholars that the book of Acts, on the whole, contains a surprising amount of evidence favourable to the Pharisees, showing them to have been tolerant and merciful. Some scholars have even argued that the book of Acts is a pro-Pharisee work; but this can hardly be maintained. For, outweighing all the evidence favourable to the Pharisees is the material relating to Paul, which is, in all its aspects, unfavourable to the Pharisees; not only is Paul himself portrayed as being a virulent persecutor *when he was a Pharisee*, but Paul declares that he himself was punished by flogging five times (II Corinthians 11: 24) by the 'Jews' (usually taken to mean the Pharisees). So no one really comes away from reading Acts with any good impression of the Pharisees, but rather with the negative impressions derived from the Gospels reinforced.

Why, therefore, is Paul always so concerned to stress that he came from a Pharisee background? A great many motives can be discerned, but there is one that needs to be singled out here: the desire to stress the alleged continuity between Judaism and Pauline Christianity. Paul wishes to say that whereas, when he was a Pharisee, he mistakenly regarded the early Christians as heretics who had departed from true Judaism, after his conversion he took the opposite view, that Christianity was the true Judaism. All his training as a Pharisee, he wishes to say – all his study of scripture and tradition – really leads to the acceptance of Jesus as the Messiah prophesied in the Old

Testament. So when Paul declares his Pharisee past, he is not merely proclaiming his own sins – 'See how I have changed, from being a Pharisee persecutor to being a devoted follower of Jesus!' – he is also proclaiming his credentials – 'If someone as learned as I can believe that Jesus was the fulfilment of the Torah, who is there fearless enough to disagree?'

On the face of it, Paul's doctrine of Jesus is a daring departure from Judaism. Paul was advocating a doctrine that seemed to have far more in common with pagan myths than with Judaism: that Jesus was a divine-human person who had descended to Earth from the heavens and experienced death for the express purpose of saving mankind. The very fact that the Jews found this doctrine new and shocking shows that it plays no role in the Jewish scripture, at least not in any way easily discernible. Yet Paul was not content to say that his doctrine was new; on the contrary, he wished to say that every line of the Jewish scripture was a foreshadowing of the Jesus-event as he understood it, and that those who understood the scripture in any other way were failing in comprehension of what Judaism had always been about. So his insistence on his Pharisaic upbringing was part of his insistence on continuity.

There were those who accepted Paul's doctrine, but *did* regard it as a radical new departure, with nothing in the Jewish scriptures fore-shadowing it. The best known figure of this kind was Marcion, who lived about a hundred years after Paul, and regarded Paul as his chief inspiration. Yet Marcion refused to see anything Jewish in Paul's doctrine, but regarded it as a new revelation. He regarded the Jewish scriptures as the work of the Devil and he excluded the Old Testament from his version of the Bible.

Paul himself rejected this view. Though he regarded much of the Old Testament as obsolete, superseded by the advent of Jesus, he still regarded it as the Word of God, prophesying the new Christian Church and giving it authority. So his picture of himself as a Pharisee symbolizes the continuity between the old dispensation and the new: a figure who comprised in his own person the turning-point at which Judaism was transformed into Christianity.

Throughout the Christian centuries, there have been Christian scholars who have seen Paul's claim to a Pharisee background in this light. In the medieval Disputations convened by Christians to convert Jews, arguments were put forward purporting to show that not only the Jewish scriptures but even the rabbinical writings, the Talmud and the Midrash, supported the claims of Christianity that Jesus was the

Messiah, that he was divine and that he had to suffer death for mankind.[1] Though Paul was not often mentioned in these Disputations, the project was one of which he would have approved. In modern times, scholars have laboured to argue that Paul's doctrines about the Messiah and divine suffering are continuous with Judaism as it appears in the Bible, the Apocrypha and Pseudepigrapha, and in the rabbinical writings (the best-known effort of this nature is *Paul and Rabbinic Judaism*, by W. D. Davies).

So Paul's claim to expert Pharisee learning is relevant to a very important and central issue – whether Christianity, in the form given to it by Paul, is really continuous with Judaism or whether it is a new doctrine, having no roots in Judaism, but deriving, in so far as it has an historical background, from pagan myths of dying and resurrected gods and Gnostic myths of heaven-descended redeemers. Did Paul truly stand in the Jewish tradition, or was he a person of basically Hellenistic religious type, but seeking to give a colouring of Judaism to a salvation cult that was really opposed to everything that Judaism stood for?

CHAPTER 2

THE STANDPOINT OF THIS BOOK

As against the conventional picture of Paul, outlined in the last chapter, the present book has an entirely different and unfamiliar view to put forward. This view of Paul is not only unfamiliar in itself, but it also involves many unfamiliar standpoints about other issues which are relevant and indeed essential to a correct assessment of Paul; for example:

Who and what were the Pharisees? What were their religious and political views as opposed to those of the Sadducees and other religious and political groups of the time? What was their attitude to Jesus? What was their attitude towards the early Jerusalem Church?

Who and what was Jesus? Did he really see himself as a saviour who had descended from heaven in order to suffer crucifixion? Or did he have entirely different aims, more in accordance with the Jewish thoughts and hopes of his time? Was the historical Jesus quite a different person from the Jesus of Paul's ideology, based on Paul's visions and trances?

Who and what were the early Church of Jerusalem, the first followers of Jesus? Have their views been correctly represented by the later Church? Did James and Peter, the leaders of the Jerusalem Church, agree with Paul's views (as orthodox Christianity claims) or did they oppose him bitterly, regarding him as a heretic and a betrayer of the aims of Jesus?

Who and what were the Ebionites, whose opinions and writings were suppressed by the orthodox Church? Why did they denounce Paul? Why did they combine belief in Jesus with the practice of Judaism?

14

Why did they believe in Jesus as Messiah, but not as God? Were they a later 'Judaizing' group, or were they, as they claimed to be, the remnants of the authentic followers of Jesus, the church of James and Peter?

The arguments in this book will inevitably become complicated, since every issue is bound up with every other. It is impossible to answer any of the above questions without bringing all the other questions into consideration. It is, therefore, convenient at this point to give an outline of the standpoint to which all the arguments of this book converge. This is not an attempt to pre-judge the issue. The following summary of the findings of this book may seem dogmatic at this stage, but it is intended merely as a guide to the ramifications of the ensuing arguments and a bird's eye view of the book, and as such will stand or fall with the cogency of the arguments themselves. The following, then, are the propositions argued in the present book:

1 Paul was never a Pharisee rabbi, but was an adventurer of undistinguished background. He was attached to the Sadducees, as a police officer under the authority of the High Priest, before his conversion to belief in Jesus. His mastery of the kind of learning associated with the Pharisees was not great. He deliberately misrepresented his own biography in order to increase the effectiveness of his missionary activities.

2 Jesus and his immediate followers were Pharisees. Jesus had no intention of founding a new religion. He regarded himself as the Messiah in the normal Jewish sense of the term, i.e. a human leader who would restore the Jewish monarchy, drive out the Roman invaders, set up an independent Jewish state, and inaugurate an era of peace, justice and prosperity (known as 'the kingdom of God') for the whole world. Jesus believed himself to be the figure prophesied in the Hebrew Bible who would do all these things. He was not a militarist and did not build up an army to fight the Romans, since he believed that God would perform a great miracle to break the power of Rome. This miracle would take place on the Mount of Olives, as prophesied in the book of Zechariah. When this miracle did not occur, his mission had failed. He had no intention of being crucified in order to save mankind from eternal damnation by his sacrifice. He never regarded himself as a divine being, and would have regarded such an idea as pagan and idolatrous, an infringement of the first of the Ten Commandments.

3 The first followers of Jesus, under James and Peter, founded the

Jerusalem Church after Jesus's death. They were called the Nazarenes, and in all their beliefs they were indistinguishable from the Pharisees, except that they believed in the resurrection of Jesus, and that Jesus was still the promised Messiah. They did not believe that Jesus was a divine person, but that, by a miracle from God, he had been brought back to life after his death on the cross, and would soon come back to complete his mission of overthrowing the Romans and setting up the Messianic kingdom. The Nazarenes did not believe that Jesus had abrogated the Jewish religion, or Torah. Having known Jesus personally, they were aware that he had observed the Jewish religious law all his life and had never rebelled against it. His sabbath cures were not against Pharisee law. The Nazarenes were themselves very observant of Jewish religious law. They practised circumcision, did not eat the forbidden foods and showed great respect to the Temple. The Nazarenes did not regard themselves as belonging to a new religion; their religion was Judaism. They set up synagogues of their own, but they also attended non-Nazarene synagogues on occasion, and performed the same kind of worship in their own synagogues as was practised by all observant Jews. The Nazarenes became suspicious of Paul when they heard that he was preaching that Jesus was the founder of a new religion and that he had abrogated the Torah. After an attempt to reach an understanding with Paul, the Nazarenes (i.e. the Jerusalem Church under James and Peter) broke irrevocably with Paul and disowned him.

4 Paul, not Jesus, was the founder of Christianity as a new religion which developed away from both normal Judaism and the Nazarene variety of Judaism. In this new religion, the Torah was abrogated as having had only temporary validity. The central myth of the new religion was that of an atoning death of a divine being. Belief in this sacrifice, and a mystical sharing of the death of the deity, formed the only path to salvation. Paul derived this religion from Hellenistic sources, chiefly by a fusion of concepts taken from Gnosticism and concepts taken from the mystery religions, particularly from that of Attis. The combination of these elements with features derived from Judaism, particularly the incorporation of the Jewish scriptures, re-interpreted to provide a background of sacred history for the new myth, was unique; and Paul alone was the creator of this amalgam. Jesus himself had no idea of it, and would have been amazed and shocked at the role assigned to him by Paul as a suffering deity. Nor did Paul have any predecessors among the Nazarenes, though later mythography tried to assign this role to Stephen, and modern scholars have

discovered equally mythical predecessors for Paul in a group called the 'Hellenists'. Paul, as the personal begetter of the Christian myth, has never been given sufficient credit for his originality. The reverence paid through the centuries to the great Saint Paul has quite obscured the more colourful features of his personality. Like many evangelical leaders, he was a compound of sincerity and charlatanry. Evangelical leaders of his kind were common at this time in the Greco-Roman world (e.g. Simon Magus, Apollonius of Tyana).

5 A source of information about Paul that has never been taken seriously enough is a group called the Ebionites. Their writings were suppressed by the Church, but some of their views and traditions were preserved in the writings of their opponents, particularly in the huge treatise on *Heresies* by Epiphanius. From this it appears that the Ebionites had a very different account to give of Paul's background and early life from that found in the New Testament and fostered by Paul himself. The Ebionites testified that Paul had *no* Pharisaic background or training; he was the son of Gentiles, converted to Judaism, in Tarsus, came to Jerusalem when an adult, and attached himself to the High Priest as a henchman. Disappointed in his hopes of advancement, he broke with the High Priest and sought fame by founding a new religion. This account, while not reliable in all its details, is substantially correct. It makes far more sense of all the puzzling and contradictory features of the story of Paul than the account of the official documents of the Church.

6 The Ebionites were stigmatized by the Church as heretics who failed to understand that Jesus was a divine person and asserted instead that he was a human being who came to inaugurate a new earthly age, as prophesied by the Jewish prophets of the Bible. Moreover, the Ebionites refused to accept the Church doctrine, derived from Paul, that Jesus abolished or abrogated the Torah, the Jewish law. Instead, the Ebionites observed the Jewish law and regarded themselves as Jews. The Ebionites were not heretics, as the Church asserted, nor 're-Judaizers', as modern scholars call them, but the authentic successors of the immediate disciples and followers of Jesus, whose views and doctrines they faithfully transmitted, believing correctly that they were derived from Jesus himself. They were the same group that had earlier been called the Nazarenes, who were led by James and Peter, who had known Jesus during his lifetime, and were in a far better position to know his aims than Paul, who met Jesus only in dreams and visions. Thus the opinion held by the Ebionites about Paul is of extraordinary interest and deserves respectful consideration, instead of dismissal as

'scurrilous' propaganda – the reaction of Christian scholars from ancient to modern times.

The above conspectus brings into sharper relief our question, was Paul a Pharisee? It will be seen that this is not merely a matter of biography or idle curiosity. It is bound up with the whole question of the origins of Christianity. A tremendous amount depends on this question, for, if Paul was not a Pharisee rooted in Jewish learning and tradition, but instead a Hellenistic adventurer whose acquaintance with Judaism was recent and shallow, the construction of myth and theology which he elaborated in his letters becomes a very different thing. Instead of searching through his system for signs of continuity with Judaism, we shall be able to recognize it for what it is – a brilliant concoction of Hellenism, superficially connecting itself with the Jewish scriptures and tradition, by which it seeks to give itself a history and an air of authority.

Christian attitudes towards the Pharisees and thus towards the picture of Paul as a Pharisee have always been strikingly ambivalent. In the Gospels, the Pharisees are attacked as hypocrites and would-be murderers: yet the Gospels also convey an impression of the Pharisees as figures of immense authority and dignity. This ambivalence reflects the attitude of Christianity to Judaism itself; on the one hand, an allegedly outdated ritualism, but on the other, a panorama of awesome history, a source of authority and blessing, so that at all costs the Church must display itself as the new Israel, the true Judaism. Thus Paul, as Pharisee, is the subject of alternating attitudes. In the nineteenth century, when Jesus was regarded (by Renan, for example) as a Romantic liberal, rebelling against the authoritarianism of Pharisaic Judaism, Paul was deprecated as a typical Pharisee, enveloping the sweet simplicity of Jesus in clouds of theology and difficult formulations. In the twentieth century, when the concern is more to discover the essential Jewishness of Christianity, the Pharisee aspect of Paul is used to connect Pauline doctrines with the rabbinical writings – again Paul is regarded as never losing his essential Pharisaism, but this is now viewed as good, and as a means of rescuing Christianity from isolation from Judaism. To be Jewish and yet not to be Jewish, this is the essential dilemma of Christianity, and the figure of Paul, abjuring his alleged Pharisaism as a hindrance to salvation and yet somehow clinging to it as a guarantee of authority, is symbolic.

CHAPTER 3

THE PHARISEES

If we are to answer the question of whether or not Paul was a Pharisee, or even to understand the significance of his claim to have been one, it is necessary to have a fuller account of who the Pharisees were and what they stood for. Here we must not rely on the Gospel picture of the Pharisees, which is strongly hostile. The Gospels portray the Pharisees as the chief opponents of Jesus, criticizing him for curing people on the sabbath, and even plotting to kill him because of these cures. The Gospels also represent Jesus as criticizing the Pharisees most strongly, calling them hypocrites and oppressors. Because of this Gospel picture, the word 'Pharisee' has come to be synonymous with 'hypocrite' in the Western mind, and the defects attributed to the Pharisees – self-righteousness, meanness, authoritarian severity and exclusiveness – have contributed to the anti-Semitic stereotype and have been assigned to Jews generally.[1]

In recent years, many Christian scholars have come to realize that this Gospel picture of the Pharisees is propaganda, not fact.[2] Our main source of authentic information about the Pharisees is their own voluminous literature, including prayers, hymns, books of wisdom, law books, sermons, commentaries on the Bible, mystical treatises, books of history and many other genres. Far from being arid ritualists, they were one of the most creative groups in history.

Moreover, the Pharisees, far from being rigid and inflexible in applying religious laws, were noted (as the first-century historian Josephus points out[3], and as is amply confirmed in the Pharisee law books) for the leniency of their legal rulings, and for the humanity and flexibility with which they sought to adapt the law of the Bible to changing conditions and improved moral conceptions. They were able to do this because, though they regarded the Bible as the inspired word of God, they did not take a literalist view of the *interpretation* of the Bible.

19

Their word for religious teaching was *Torah*, and they believed that as well as the Written Torah, there was also an Oral Torah, which took the Written Torah as its base and expanded it by way of definition, commentary, questioning and exegesis, so that it became a living reality. Some of the Oral Law, they believed, was just as old as the Written Law, having been given to Moses by God; but this ancient origin was claimed only for certain basic elements of the Oral Law. Most of it had arisen in the course of time in response to new historical conditions; for example, it was not claimed that the prayers of the liturgy, such as the Eighteen Benedictions, were composed by Moses or by any of the prophets of the Hebrew Bible; it was acknowledged that these prayers were composed by leading Pharisees, who from time to time added or subtracted from these prayers, or even to the calendar of feasts or fasts, as seemed appropriate.

Since the Pharisees acknowledged a human element in religious teaching – an element for which no divine inspiration could be claimed – they acknowledged also the right to disagreement or difference of opinion. Thus the Pharisees' writings are remarkable for the variety of differing opinions that they record: the Mishnah and the Talmud are largely records of these disagreements on every legal topic under the sun. To take a subject at random, we see at the beginning of Tractate Sanhedrin (which discusses the structure of the legal system itself):

> Cases concerning offences punishable by scourging are decided by a tribunal of three. In the name of Rabbi Ishmael they said: By twenty-three. The intercalating of the month and the intercalating of the year are decided upon by a tribunal of three. So Rabbi Meir. But Rabban Simeon ben Gamaliel says: The matter is begun by three, discussed by five, and decided upon by seven; but if it is decided upon by three the intercalation is valid.

The personages involved in this exchange of views belong to about a hundred years after the time of Jesus, but their movement was continuous with that of the Pharisees of Jesus' and Paul's time. One of the personages mentioned was a direct descendant of the Gamaliel who figures in the New Testament book of Acts as the leader of the Pharisees in the time of Paul.

The Pharisees argued amongst themselves not only about matters of religious law but also about matters of theology. However, it was in matters of law that they felt that some decision had to be reached and, since they had no method for deciding such matters other than by discussion and debate, the decisions were made by a majority vote. Once a majority decision had been reached, the dissenting rabbis were required to toe the line and accept the result of the vote, not because they were regarded as refuted, but because of the principle of the rule of law, which was conceived in exactly the same terms as in parliamentary democracies today, where the opposition party may argue as strongly as it likes before a vote is taken and talk just as strongly about the unwisdom of the decision after the vote, but must still accept the decision as the law of the land until it has an opportunity to reverse the decision by another majority vote. Among the Pharisees, a majority vote was regarded with such seriousness that there was a legend amongst them that God had once attempted to intervene to reverse one of these majority decisions (by telling them through a 'voice from Heaven' that the minority opinion was correct), but had been told that He was out of order, since He Himself had given the sages the power of decision by vote, and He Himself had said in his Torah that 'it [the Torah] is not in Heaven' (Deuteronomy 30: 12), by which the sages understood that the Torah was to be applied and administered by the processes of human intellect, not by miracles or divine intervention. God's reaction to this, the legend continues, was to laugh, and say, 'My children have defeated me!'[4]

Thus the assemblies of the sages (as the Pharisee leaders were called before the destruction of the Jerusalem Temple in AD 70, after which they became known as 'rabbis') made decisions, but did not invest these decisions with divine authority. The opinions of dissenting minorities were carefully recorded and included in the records such as the Mishnah, so that (as the Mishnah itself explains in Eduyot 1: 5) it may become the basis of new decision in the future, if required (just as today the opinions of dissenting judges are recorded in the High Court and are cited as support if an attempt is made at a later date to bring in a new ruling).

Thus the Pharisees avoided the option, open to all religions based on a scripture believed to be divinely inspired, of adding the infallibility of the Church to the infallibility of scripture. Instead they developed the concept of a scriptural canon which was the centre of human attention and was constantly being scrutinized in the light of the human intellect; and, even more important, they had the idea that God Himself wished this process of human reasoning to go on without interruption by Himself, and that He approved the struggles of the human mind to interpret His design for the universe, even if these efforts were not free of error: 'According to the effort is the reward.'[5] Thus the Pharisees were able to disagree with each other without quarrelling and without persecution of dissenting views; for difference of opinion was itself an

21

essential ingredient of their concept of the religious life, rather than a danger to it. They did, however, occasionally resort to disciplinary measures against rabbis (such as the great Rabbi Eliezer), not because of their dissentient views, but because of their refusal to accept a majority vote that had gone against them.

It was only in the sphere of religious law, though, that such disciplinary measures (consisting essentially of social ostracism of the offender for a period) were taken. In the sphere of theology, where there was no urgent need for a practical decision, no such measures were taken. A wide variety of views was tolerated by the sages and their successors, the rabbis, without any accusations of heresy. Thus, in the matter of the belief in the coming of the Messiah, or the definition of the nature of his reign, it was possible for a respected rabbi to take the view that there would be no personal Messiah in the future at all, since all the biblical Messianic prophecies had been fulfilled in the person of Hezekiah. This was an unusual, even eccentric, view, but the rabbi in question[6] was not regarded as in any way a heretic. This contrasts strongly with the heresy hunts and bitter factionalism of Christianity, which burnt people at the stake for having unusual views about the nature of Christ (a name that is only the Greek form of the Hebrew word *Messiah*). The Pharisees distinguished between what they called *halakhah* ('going') and *aggadah* ('telling'), and whilst they demanded conformity, after full discussion, in *halakhah*, they allowed full scope to individual styles of thought in *aggadah*, which they regarded as poetry rather than as theology.

Though not addicted to heresy hunting, the Pharisees did regard certain groups as heretical, largely because these groups did not accept the concept of the Oral Law. The most powerful group regarded as heretical by the Pharisees was that of the Sadducees, of whom frequent mention is made in the Gospels, where they are described as opponents of the Pharisees, without any clear exposition of the point of conflict involved. The relation between the Pharisees and the Sadducees is of the utmost importance in understanding both Jesus and Paul, and the times in which they lived.

The essential point at issue between the Pharisees and the Sadducees was the validity of the Oral Law, but this point was far from academic, for it led to enormous differences of outlook on social and political questions, as well as in the practice of religion. Rejecting the Oral Law, the Sadducees saw no need for a class of interpreters, sages or rabbis engaged in expounding the scriptures in accordance with new ideas and circumstances. The difference between the Sadducees and the

Pharisees is thus brought out clearly in the type of religious leader which they respectively revered. The Sadducees turned for leadership to the priests and especially the High Priest, while the Pharisees were led by very different personalities, whose character was determined by the demands of the Oral Law. The priests were a hereditary caste, descended from Aaron, the brother of Moses. They had a special function to perform in the service of the Temple, and were supported by the tithes levied from the whole population, though not compulsorily. To look to the priesthood for leadership was thus to put the Temple into the centre of one's religious life. Three institutions thus comprised the focus of Sadducee religion: the Bible, the Temple and the priesthood.

For the Pharisees, on the other hand, the priests and the Temple had only a secondary importance. They regarded the priests not as leaders or spiritual guides, but merely as ceremonial functionaries, who had the job of keeping the Temple sacrifices going and administering the maintenance of the Temple generally. Even the High Priest was regarded as a mere functionary and had no authority to pronounce on matters of religion. It was a Pharisee saying that 'a learned bastard takes precedence over an ignorant High Priest'[7], and most High Priests were in fact regarded by the Pharisees as ignorant.

Instead of the priests, the Pharisees looked for guidance to their own leaders, the *hakhamim* (sages), who were not a hereditary class but came from every level of society, including the poorest. The *hakhamim* or rabbis were really lay leaders, who achieved their authority by their ability to master the extensive materials that comprised a Pharisee's education. This included not only the whole Hebrew Bible, which was regarded as merely the first step in education, but also the whole superstructure of law, history, science and homiletic exegesis (*midrash*) which had accumulated in the Pharisee academies. A Pharisee leader had to be both an expert lawyer and an inspiring preacher, for the Bible itself contains both the outline of an entire legal constitution and a conspectus of history with a theory of the spiritual mission of the Jewish people and its place in God's purposes for humanity. Thus a Pharisee sage might one day be acting as a judge in a complicated case involving the laws of damages, and the next day he might be preaching in the synagogue about God's love for the repentant sinner, using for his sermon not only instances drawn from the Bible but also moving, simple parables drawn from his own imagination or from the Pharisee stock of homiletic material. In performing these tasks, the sages did not at this stage of history become a professional class; the general pattern

23

was that each sage had his own profession by which he made his living, some of these professions being humble in status, and he gave his services to the community without pay or, at the most, with compensation for the hours lost from his own profession.

In consequence of the shift of authority from the priests to the sages, the place of the Temple itself was different in the world of the Pharisees from that which it occupied for the Sadducees. The Temple was not a place of study, but of ceremonial and sacrifice, and, while the Pharisees acknowledged the importance of animal and vegetable sacrifices (since the Bible had instituted them), they did not consider these ceremonies as central to their religious life, which focused rather on the acquisition of knowledge about how people should live together in society, and on the carrying into practice the principles of justice and love. The institution in which this process of communal education was pursued was not the Temple, but the synagogue. The Pharisees were the creators of congregationalism: the fostering of the local religious community.

This decentralization and diffusion of religion into manifold local centres was typical of Pharisaism, and this meant that the common people regarded the priesthood in Jerusalem as rather remote and unreal figures compared with their local sage, to whom they could come with their problems and who gave them regular instruction in the synagogue. He came from their own ranks, and claimed no aristocratic superiority over them; nor did he claim any magical or mystical authority, but only a wider range of learning, which he encouraged them to acquire, since learning was regarded as the duty of every Jew and as the basis of all useful and virtuous living. Thus the Pharisees were not only the founders of congregationalism, but also the founders of the idea and practice of universal education, though here they claimed to be merely fulfilling the injunctions of the Bible itself, which stresses the duty of education in many passages.[8]

In combating the authority of the priesthood, the Pharisees did not regard themselves as innovators or revolutionaries, but rather as the upholders of authentic Judaism. In the Bible the chief teaching role in religion is given not to the priests, but to the prophets, who had no hereditary claims and might come from any section of the people. Moses, the founder of Israelite religion, did not make himself High Priest, but gave this role to his brother Aaron, a relative nonentity. The rabbis thus regarded themselves as the heirs of the prophets and especially of Moses, and as having the teaching role that had always been carefully distinguished, in Jewish practice and religion, from the

24

sacerdotal role. The rabbis did not, however, claim to have prophetic gifts themselves; they thought that prophecy had ceased with the last of the biblical prophets, and would only be renewed in the Messianic age. Their task, as they conceived it, was to interpret the inspired words of scripture by a corporate effort, not unlike that of modern science, in which each rabbi contributed his own stock of thoughts and interpretations to a common pool. Consequently they developed methods of logical analysis and argument by analogy which produced in the Talmud one of the greatest achievements of the human intellect, discussing with the greatest intelligence and professional ability matters of morality, business ethics and legal administration in a manner far in advance of their age.

The Sadducees, on the other hand, regarded themselves as defending the *status quo* against the innovations of the Pharisees. The Bible, the priesthood and the Temple were the institutions which they honoured: the Bible needed no complicated apparatus of interpretation, the priesthood needed no officious class of lay scholars to supplement it, and the Temple provided all the atonement required without a proliferation of synagogues for prayer, study and preaching. Many modern scholars have taken the Sadducees as the representatives of ancient Judaism, standing out against Pharisee innovation; but this picture has serious defects. The Sadducees were indeed defending the *status quo*, but it was a *status quo* of fairly recent duration, dating from the third century BC, when Judaea was ruled by the Ptolemaic Greeks of Egypt. Under this regime, the High Priest was given central status and power by the Greek overlords, successors in the region to the power of Alexander the Great. The High Priesthood in this era was made the instrument of foreign rule, a role which it was to retain into the era of the Romans. When the Pharisees arose as a distinctive movement, around the period (c. 160 BC) of Jewish rebellion against foreign rule (which had meanwhile passed from the Ptolemaic Greeks of Egypt to the Seleucid Greeks of Syria), they were opposed to the priesthood not only for religious, but also for political reasons. They wished to free the Jews from the stranglehold of the priesthood not only in order to return to the old prophetic ideal of lay leadership, but also in order to return the priesthood to its proper biblical role as a guild of ceremonial officials, rather than a centre of political power.

The political opposition of the Pharisees to the High Priesthood continued even after the victory of the Jews over their foreign Greek rulers; for the Hasmonean dynasty, which then took power over their fellow Jews, combined the monarchy with the High Priesthood, thus increasing further the political power of the High Priesthood. The Pharisees bitterly opposed this constitutional development, and consequently suffered persecution from the Hasmonean kings. The record of the Pharisees as opponents of power is utterly unknown to those who base their ideas of the Pharisees on the biased and inadequate picture of them given in the Gospels. Far from being oppressors, the Pharisees were continually the party of opposition. A far better picture of them, from the political standpoint, can be gained from the writings of Josephus, who in fact opposed them as trouble-makers and thorns in the flesh of the political authorities.[9]

It should be noted that, though the religious position of the Sadducees gave the highest role of authority to the priests, it would not be true to say that the priesthood on the whole supported the Sadducee standpoint. Most of the rank-and-file priests were Pharisees and were thus opponents, both politically and religiously, of the High Priest. Like the majority of the Jewish people, these ordinary priests accepted the Pharisee leaders, the sages, as their spiritual guides, and did not presume to offer themselves as rival authorities merely on account of their Aaronic descent. They accepted that, as priests, they were merely Temple officials and not religious teachers; some of them even entered the Pharisee academies and trained to be sages themselves – for no one was debarred from becoming a sage, not even a priest.

Among the priests, it was chiefly a few families of great wealth and political influence with the reigning power who were Sadducees. The Sadducee party, indeed, formed a small minority among the Jewish people, comprising wealthy landowners as well as wealthy priests. People such as these were the natural allies of whatever authority happened to be in power, whether Ptolemaic Greeks, Seleucid Greeks, Hasmoneans, Herodians or Romans. The Sadducees were thus cut off from the sources of popular unrest. The Temple, as the visible centre of Judaism, could be taken over by any ruling power and provided with a regime of collaborators. But the real centres of Jewish religious authority, the synagogues in which the Pharisee leaders presided, were too humble and too decentralized to be taken over, even if the Roman authorities had known that this was where the road to control of the Jews lay. In the time of Jesus and Paul, the occupying power was the Romans, who actually appointed the High Priests, just as Herod had done before them. They imagined that by appointing some subservient quisling to the post of High Priest, they had assumed control of the Jewish religion, little realizing that Judaism was a religion in which the apparent spiritual head, the High Priest, was in reality of little account, being personally despised by the majority of the Jews, and even in his official capacity regarded as having no real authority.

It is impossible to understand the events of the time of Jesus and Paul without a clear understanding of the equivocal role and position of the High Priest in Jewish society – on the one hand, a figure of gorgeous pomp leading the splendid ceremonial of the Temple and, on the other, a person of no authority. The ordinary reader of the Gospels assumes, naturally enough, that the High Priest was a figure corresponding, in the Jewish religion, to the Pope in the Catholic Church or the Archbishop of Canterbury in the Church of England. This mistake arises from the fact that in the Christian religion the ceremonial role has always been combined with the teaching role: the Christian priest performs the mass and also teaches the people through sermons and lessons. Christians are thus unfamiliar with the fact that in Judaism these two roles have always been distinct: the man who performs the sacrifices does not pronounce on theology or religious law, or adopt the role of inspirer or prophet. The Jewish division of roles has been of inestimable benefit to the survival of the Jewish religion, for it has meant that the corruption or destruction of the apparent centres of the religion has had little effect on its continuance. The High Priesthood frequently became hopelessly corrupt, but as long as there were movements like Pharisaism to revive the sources of authority among the laity, the religion was not seriously affected. Even the destruction of the Temple, which in the eyes of non-Jewish observers spelled the death of Judaism, had no such result, since the vitality of the religion did not depend on the Temple worship or on its practitioners.

The corruption of the High Priesthood in the time of Jesus and Paul is also attested by the literature of the Dead Sea sect or Essenes. This sect, however, was very different from the Pharisees in their reaction to their perception of corruption in the Temple and the High Priesthood. The Pharisees were able to co-operate with the High Priesthood precisely because they did not regard it as important. Since, to them, the High Priest was a ceremonial functionary, not a figure of spiritual power, it did not matter to them how inadequate he might be as a person, as long as he performed his ceremonial duties with a modicum of efficiency. Thus they saw to it that the High Priest was supervised by Pharisees in the performance of his duties, both to guard against his ignorance of the law and also to guard against any attempt on his part to introduce Sadducee practices into the order of the Temple service; once these precautions had been taken, they were satisfied, for the Temple service would be valid whatever the moral or theoretical shortcomings of the officiator. (In practice, the High Priest almost always submitted to this Pharisee supervision, because of the pressure of public opinion.[10])

The Dead Sea Scroll sect, however, took the office of the High Priest far more seriously than this and consequently, when they became convinced that the High Priesthood had become hopelessly corrupt, they withdrew from Jewish society altogether and formed a monastic community, dreaming and praying for the Last Days, when a pure Temple service would be restored. The Dead Sea Scroll sect actually had a far higher estimation of the role of the Temple and the priesthood than did the Pharisees, and recent scholarship[11] indicates that they were probably a breakaway branch of the Sadducees (they called themselves the 'sons of Zadok'). They represent the religious ideals of the Sadducee sect before it became politicized and corrupt – a sect which genuinely believed in the central importance of Bible, Temple and priesthood, and opposed the lay movement of the Pharisees.

When we read in the New Testament of incidents in which the High Priest figures, either in relation to Jesus or in relation to Paul, we have to rid ourselves of preconceptions about the role of the High Priest and try to understand the issues in the light of the historical facts. In particular, a flood of light can be thrown on the New Testament story by bearing in mind the deep antagonism between the Pharisee movement and the High Priest of that period, not only a Sadducee, but an appointee of the Romans and a quisling collaborator with Roman power.

CHAPTER 4

WAS JESUS A PHARISEE?

In the light of the previous chapter, it may well be asked, 'if the Pharisees were indeed such an enlightened, progressive movement, why did Jesus criticize them so severely?' The answer has already been suggested: that Jesus did not in historical fact criticize the Pharisees in the way represented in the Gospels; he was indeed himself a Pharisee. The whole picture of Jesus at loggerheads with the Pharisees is the creation of a period some time after Jesus' death, when the Christian Church was in conflict with the Pharisees because of its claim to have superseded Judaism. The Gospels are a product of this later period; or rather, the Gospels consist of materials, some of them deriving from an earlier period, which were edited in an anti-Pharisee sense. Thus it is possible to refute the anti-Pharisee picture in the Gospels themselves, which even after their re-editing retain many details from the earlier accounts which show that Jesus was not in conflict with the Pharisees and was a Pharisee himself.

The process of re-editing is not just a hypothesis; it can be plainly seen within the Gospels by comparing the way in which the various Gospels treat the same incident. The fact that there are four Gospels, instead of just one, makes the task of reconstructing the original story much easier, especially when one bears in mind the results of modern scholarship, which have shown in what order the Gospels were written. According to the most firmly based scholarship Mark is the earliest Gospel, so we can often be enlightened just by comparing the version of Mark with that of any later Gospel.

To give just one preliminary example, we find in Mark an account of a conversation between Jesus and a certain 'lawyer' (a term used as an alternative to 'Pharisee' both in the Gospels and in later Christian literature):

> Then one of the lawyers, who had been listening to these discussions and had noted how well he answered, came forward and asked him, 'Which commandment is first of all?' Jesus answered, 'The first is "Hear O Israel: the Lord our God is the only Lord; love the Lord your God with all your heart, with all your soul, with all your mind, and with all your strength." The second is this: "Love your neighbour as yourself." There is no other commandment greater than these.' The lawyer said to him, 'Well said, Master. You are right in saying that God is one and beside him there is no other. And to love him with all your heart, all your understanding, and all your strength, and to love your neighbour as yourself – that is far more than any burnt offerings or sacrifices.' When Jesus saw how sensibly he answered, he said to him, 'You are not far from the kingdom of God.' (Mark 12: 28–34)

The version of this story found in the later Gospel, Matthew, is as follows:

> Hearing that he had silenced the Sadducees, the Pharisees met together; and one of their number tested him with this question: 'Master, which is the greatest commandment in the Law?' He answered, ' "Love the Lord your God with all your heart, with all your soul, with all your mind." That is the greatest commandment. It comes first. The second is like it: "Love your neighbour as yourself." Everything in the Law and the prophets hangs on these two commandments.' (Matthew 22: 34–40)

In this second version of the story, the friendliness of the exchange has been obliterated. The Pharisee questioner is not motivated by admiration, as in the first version ('noted how well he answered'), but merely wishes to 'test' Jesus, i.e. try to catch him out. In the first version, the Pharisee questioner is given a lengthy reply to Jesus, praising him and adding a remark of his own about the superiority of love to sacrifices, and to this Jesus replies with courteous respect, saying that his questioner is 'not far from the kingdom of God'. All this is omitted in the second version, which is just one more story about an envious Pharisee being silenced by the superior wisdom of Jesus.

It should be noted, too, that Jesus' singling out of these two verses from the Hebrew Bible (one from Deuteronomy and the other from Leviticus) as the greatest of the commandments was not an original idea of his own, but an established part of Pharisee thinking. The central feature of the liturgy created by the Pharisees (and still used by Jews today) is what is called the *shema*, which is the very passage from Deuteronomy cited by Jesus: 'Hear O Israel: the Lord our God is the only Lord; love the Lord your God with all your heart, with all your soul, and with all your strength.' This injunction was regarded by the Pharisees as so important that they declared that merely to recite these verses twice a day was sufficient to discharge the basic duty of prayer.[1] Interestingly, too, in view of Jesus' final comment to the 'lawyer', the rabbis regarded these verses as having a strong connection with the 'kingdom of God' (a phrase not coined by Jesus, but part of Pharisaic phraseology). They declared that to recite these verses comprised 'the acceptance of the yoke of the kingdom of God'. It should be noted that in Pharisaic thinking, 'the kingdom of God' had two meanings: it meant the *present* kingdom or reign of God, or it could mean the *future* reign of God over the whole world in the Messianic age. It is possible to discern in Jesus' frequent use of the same expression the same twofold meaning: sometimes he means a future state of affairs which he has come to prophesy (e.g. 'Repent, for the kingdom of God is near'), and sometimes he is referring to the present kingship of God, which every mortal is obliged to acknowledge (e.g. 'The kingdom of God is among you'). In the present passage, it seems to be the second meaning that is paramount.

The other verse quoted by Jesus from Leviticus, 'Love your neighbour as yourself,' was also regarded by the Pharisees as of central importance, and was treated by the two greatest figures of Pharisaism, Hillel[2] and Rabbi Akiba,[3] as the great principle of Judaism on which everything else depended. This did not mean, of course, that the rest of the law was to be ignored or swept away, just because this was the most important principle of it; on the contrary, the law was regarded as the working out and practical implementation of the principle of love of neighbour, giving guidance about how love of neighbour could be expressed in the complexities of daily life; a principle without such elaboration would be as much use as the axioms of Euclid without the propositions. Later Christian writers, misunderstanding this point, thought that, when Jesus singled out love of God and love of neighbour, he was thereby dismissing the rest of the Torah. There is no reason whatever to think that this was Jesus' meaning, especially as he was in such cordial agreement with the Pharisee lawyer (at least in the earlier and more authentic account of Mark).

The apparently disparaging remark of the 'lawyer' about the sacrifices should also not be misunderstood. He did not mean that he thought that sacrifices or the Temple worship in general should be abolished, only that the words of the Hebrew prophets should be borne in mind, warning against regarding the sacrifices as a magical means of producing atonement, rather than as symbols of true repentance and reconciliation with God. The most awesome day of the Jewish year was the Day of Atonement, when sacrifices were offered in the Temple and the scapegoat was sent into the wilderness; yet it was Pharisee doctrine that none of these awe-inspiring ceremonies had any effect unless true repentance had occurred and restitution had been made for any harm done to one's fellow man. So the Pharisee was not opposing the offering of sacrifices (which were prescribed in holy writ), but putting them into their proper place, just as the Pharisees in general supported the Temple worship and the priesthood in their duties, but strongly opposed any tendency to regard all this as the be all and end all of Jewish religion, as the Sadducees tended to do. Here again, there is no reason whatever to suppose that Jesus' attitude towards the Temple worship was any different.

The analysis of this incident about Jesus and the 'lawyer' thus shows two things: that there was no disagreement between Jesus and the Pharisees, and that there is a process of editing going on in the Gospels to make it appear that there was. For the later Gospel version turns an amicable conversation into a hostile confrontation. This does not mean that we may turn to the Gospel of Mark, the earliest Gospel, for an unbiased picture of the Pharisees; on the contrary, the Gospel of Mark is full of bias against the Pharisees, but, as the earliest Gospel, it has not carried through the process of anti-Pharisee re-editing with quite such thoroughness as the succeeding Gospels, so that more of the original story is still apparent.

Here we hit upon an important principle of interpretation of the Gospels: when we come across a passage that goes against the grain of the narrative, we may be confident that this is part of the original, authentic narrative that has survived the operations of the censor. Since the general trend is anti-Pharisee, so that the narrative becomes more and more anti-Pharisee as it is successively re-edited, any passages friendly to the Pharisees cannot be late additions to the text (for the motivation of the editor is to cut out such passages, not to add to them); instead they must be survivals that have escaped the eye of the editor. This does not mean that a later Gospel must always, and in relation to every incident, be more thoroughly edited and less authentic than an earlier Gospel, for the various Gospels are not presenting the same material taken from only one source. Each Gospel contains material for which it is not indebted to a previous Gospel and which it is handling as a first-time editor; these different sources of material have been labelled by modern scholars with capital letters such as Q, L, etc.

Consequently, when such an independent source is in question, a later Gospel may retain authentic early material not contained in an earlier Gospel. Any scientific study of the Gospels must always bear the above considerations in mind. It follows that, when we speak of a later Gospel taking the bias or tendency further, we mean that this occurs when both Gospels are handling material taken from the same source. This is the case in the example given above, where it is clear that the report of the incident of Jesus and the 'lawyer' occurs first in Mark, and when it later occurs in Matthew, it is an adapted version produced by the author of Matthew on the basis of the report in Mark, which the author of Matthew had before him when he wrote his Gospel.

This is, of course, only a preliminary example. Now follows a more extended argument to show that Jesus was no antagonist of Pharisaism, but was himself a Pharisee. This argument is not a digression from the subject of Paul, the main concern of this book, for the question of whether Jesus was a Pharisee is most relevant to the question of whether Paul was a Pharisee. For the picture in the Gospels of Jesus being hounded by the Pharisees is what gives credence to the later picture, in Acts, of Paul (or rather Saul) the Pharisee hounding the successors of Jesus, the 'Jerusalem Church'. If Jesus was never hounded by the Pharisees and was himself a Pharisee, it becomes all the more incredible that Paul, when he hounded the 'Jerusalem Church', was actually a Pharisee. The lenient and tolerant attitude of Gamaliel, the leader of the Pharisees in Paul's time, towards the 'Jerusalem Church' then becomes intelligible as merely a continuation of the friendliness of the Pharisees towards Jesus himself. The contention of this book is that Jesus, usually represented as anything but a Pharisee, was one, while Paul, always represented as a Pharisee in his un-regenerate days, never was. In the course of the argument, it will become plain why this strange reversal of the facts was brought about by the New Testament writers.

An important ground of conflict between Jesus and the Pharisees, according to the Gospels, was Jesus' insistence on healing on the sabbath, which was allegedly against Pharisee law. The Gospels allege that the Pharisees not only criticized Jesus for healing on the sabbath, but schemed to bring about his death for this reason (Mark 3: 6; Matthew 12: 14). Jesus is also credited with certain arguments which he put to the Pharisees to defend his practice of sabbath healing: for example, that since circumcision was permitted on the sabbath, why should healing be forbidden (John 7: 23)? It is an amazing fact that, when we consult the Pharisee law books to find out what the Pharisees

33

actually taught about healing on the sabbath, we find that they did *not* forbid it, and they even used the very same arguments that Jesus used to show that it was permitted. Moreover, Jesus' celebrated saying, 'The sabbath was made for man, not man for the sabbath,' which has been hailed so many times as an epoch-making new insight proclaimed by Jesus, is found almost word for word in a Pharisee source, where it is used to support the Pharisee doctrine that the saving of life has precedence over the law of the sabbath. So it seems that whoever it was that Jesus was arguing against when he defended his sabbath healing, it cannot have been the Pharisees.

An indication of who these opponents really were can be found in one of the sabbath stories. Here it is stated that, in anger at Jesus' sabbath healing, the Pharisees 'began plotting against him with the partisans of Herod to see how they could make away with him' (Mark 3: 6). The partisans of Herod (i.e. Herod Antipas, ruler, by Roman appointment, of Galilee) were the most Hellenized of all the Jews and the most politicized, in the sense that their motivation was not in the least religious, but was actuated only by considerations of power. An alliance between the Pharisees (who were the centre of opposition to the Roman occupation) and the Herodians is quite impossible. But an alliance between the Herodians and the Sadducees was not only possible but actual. The Sadducees, as explained above, though ostensibly a religious party, were so concerned to preserve the *status quo* that they had become henchmen of Rome, their leader, the High Priest, being a Roman appointee, entrusted with the task of serving the interests of the occupation. It seems most probable, then, that, by an editorial intervention, the name 'Pharisees' was substituted here for the original 'Sadducees', and this is probably the case, too, in the other stories in which Jesus is inexplicably arguing a Pharisee viewpoint about the sabbath *against* the Pharisees. The Sadducees, we know, had a stricter viewpoint about the sabbath than the Pharisees, and (though this cannot be documented, since no Sadducee documents have survived) it may well be that, unlike the Pharisees, they forbade healing on the sabbath. This, at any rate, is a hypothesis that makes sense, whereas the stories as they stand, with Pharisees wishing to kill Jesus for preaching Pharisee doctrine, make no sense.

Since Jesus certainly came into conflict with the High Priest of his day, who was a Sadducee, it would be quite natural for stories to be preserved in which Jesus figures as an opponent of Sadducee religious doctrines, even though, as we shall see, the *chief* point of conflict between Jesus and the Sadducees was political rather than religious. In the Pharisee literature many stories are found about Pharisee teachers who engaged in argument with Sadducees. A frequent topic of these debates was the question of the resurrection of the dead, in which the Pharisees believed, and the Sadducees disbelieved. As it happens, such a story has been preserved in the Gospels about Jesus (Mark 12: 18–27 and parallels). The answers given to the Sadducees by Jesus are typical of those given by Pharisees in their debates. Even among non-Jews it was too well known that the Pharisees believed in resurrection for these stories to be re-edited as confrontations between Jesus and the Pharisees, so they were left unaltered – interesting evidence of the status of Jesus as a Pharisee, though, of course, the Gospels represent Jesus as arguing, not as a Pharisee, but simply as one whose views happened for once to coincide with those of the Pharisees.

What was the motive for the re-editing of stories about conflict between Jesus and the Sadducees so that he was portrayed as in conflict with the Pharisees instead? The reason is simple. The Pharisees were known to be the chief religious authorities of the Jews, not the Sadducees. In fact, at the time that the Gospels were edited, the Sadducees had lost any small religious importance that they had once had, and the Pharisees were the sole repository of religious authority. As we shall see shortly in more detail, it was of the utmost importance to the Gospel editors to represent Jesus as having been a rebel against Jewish religion, not against the Roman occupation. The wholesale re-editing of the material in order to give a picture of conflict between Jesus and the Pharisees was thus essential. Also, since it was known that the Sadducees were collaborators with Rome, any substantial picture of opposition by Jesus to the Sadducees, even on purely religious grounds, would have given an impression of Jesus as an opponent of Rome – just the impression that the Gospel editors wished to avoid.

That there was in reality no conflict between Jesus and the Pharisees is shown by certain telltale features which have been allowed to remain in the narrative. An important example is: 'At that time a number of Pharisees came to him and said, "You should leave this place and go on your way; Herod is out to kill you" ' (Luke 13: 31). This passage has puzzled all the commentators. Why should the Pharisees, who, in previous stories, have been represented as longing for Jesus' death because of his sabbath healings, come forward to give him a warning intended to save his life? Some pious Christian commentators, anxious to preserve the picture of malevolent Pharisees, have concocted an elaborate scenario in which the Pharisees were playing a double game:

knowing that there was more danger for Jesus in Jerusalem than in Galilee, they gave Jesus a spurious warning about Herod in order to induce him to flee to his death in Jerusalem. Apart from the fact that this is mere fantasy, it is hardly likely that, if the Pharisees had previously shown themselves to be Jesus' deadly enemies, they could expect Jesus to accept a message from them as actuated by the friendliest of motives.

This story indeed is valuable evidence of friendly relations between Jesus and the Pharisees; to give such a warning, the Pharisees must have regarded Jesus as one of their own. The very fact that this story is so inconsistent with the general picture of Jesus' relations with the Pharisees in the Gospels guarantees its historical truth; such a story could not have been added at a late stage in the editing of the material, but must be a survival from an early stage which by some oversight was not edited out.

An important indication that the stories about Pharisee opposition to Jesus on the question of sabbath healing are not to be taken at face value is the fact that there is no mention of this charge at Jesus' trial. If Jesus, as the Gospels represent, actually incurred a capital charge in Pharisee eyes because of his sabbath activities, why was this not brought against him at a time when he was on trial for his life? Why, in fact, is there no mention of *any* charges brought specifically by the Pharisees at Jesus' trial? As we shall see in the next chapter, Jesus' trial was not on religious charges at all, but on political charges, though the Gospels, pursuing their general aim of depoliticizing Jesus' aims, try to give the political charges a religious flavour. Yet, if the trial really had been a religious one, who better than the Pharisees, the alleged bitter religious enemies of Jesus, to play the most prominent part in the proceedings? The question really ought to be shifted to the opposite extreme and put in this form: why was it that the Pharisees did not *defend* Jesus at his trial, in the same way that Gamaliel, the leader of the Pharisees, defended Jesus' disciple Peter when the latter was put on trial before the religious Sanhedrin? The answer is that the Pharisees were not even present at Jesus' trial, which was not before the religious Sanhedrin, but before the political tribunal in which the High Priest, as representative and henchman of the Romans, presided over a court of his own minions.

If the matter of sabbath healing cannot be substantiated as a ground of conflict between Jesus and the Pharisees, what about the other features of Jesus' teaching which the Gospels represent as revolutionary and offensive to the Jewish religious authorities of the time?

What about Jesus' claim to be the Messiah? Was not this blasphemous in the eyes of the Pharisees? What about Jesus' threat to destroy the Temple – an allegation brought against him at his trial? What about his aspiration to reform or even abrogate the law of Moses? The answer is that none of these matters constituted any threat to the religious view of the Pharisees, and on examination we shall find that on all these matters Jesus' view was pure Pharisaism and one that confirms that he was himself a member of the Pharisee movement.

Jesus' claim to be the Messiah was not in any way blasphemous in the eyes of the Pharisees or, indeed, of any other Jews, for the title 'Messiah' carried no connotation of deity or divinity. The word 'Messiah' simply means 'anointed one', and it is a title of kingship; every Jewish king of the Davidic dynasty had this title. To claim to be the Messiah meant simply to claim the throne of Israel, and while this was a reckless and foolhardy thing to do when the Romans had abolished the Jewish monarchy, it did not constitute any offence in Jewish law. On the contrary, the Jews all lived in hope of the coming of the Messiah, who would rescue them from the sufferings of foreign occupation and restore to them their national independence. Anyone who claimed to be the promised Messiah (prophesied by the prophets of the Hebrew Bible) who would restore the beloved dynasty of David would be sure of a sympathetic following. Jesus was by no means the only person during this period to make a Messianic claim, and not one of these claimants was accused of blasphemy. These Messianic claimants were not all of the same type: some were warriors, like Bar Kokhba or Judas of Galilee, while some were non-militarist enthusiasts, like Theudas or 'the Egyptian' (both mentioned in the New Testament as well as in Josephus [4]), who gathered a crowd of believers and waited confidently for a miracle by which the Romans would be overthrown. Jesus was of the latter type, as I have argued in full elsewhere; like 'the Egyptian', he expected the great miracle to take place on the Mount of Olives, as prophesied by Zechariah.[5] Some Messiahs had the limited aim of merely liberating the Jews from Rome, while others, of whom Jesus was one, expected this liberation to be the precursor of an era of peace and liberation for the whole world, when, in the words of the prophets, the swords would be beaten into ploughshares, and the wolf would lie down with the lamb. But none of these aspirations had any tinge of blasphemy; on the contrary, they were an integral part of Judaism, in which the Messianic hope was the logical outcome of belief in the One God, whose reign would one day extend over all humanity.

In later Christianity, however, after the death of Jesus, the Greek translation of the Hebrew word *Messiah* (i.e. 'Christ') had come to mean a deity or divine being. Consequently, Christians reading this meaning back into Jesus' lifetime, found it easy to believe that Jesus' claim to Messiahship would have shocked his fellow Jews and made him subject to a charge of blasphemy. The Gospels, indeed, credit Jesus with a concept of his own Messiahship that was different from that of his fellow Jews; but even if this were the case, since he used the word 'Messiah' about himself, his fellow Jews would have no reason to believe that he meant anything abnormal by it, especially as, according to the Gospels, he was so reticent about the alleged special meaning that he attached to this word that even his own disciples did not understand his meaning. Consequently, no charge of blasphemy could arise from a concept that was never divulged. In historical scholarship, however, the idea of an undivulged Messianic concept ('the Messianic secret') is merely an attempt by later Christians to attribute to Jesus an idea that in reality did not arise until after his death.

It is interesting, again, that in the Synoptic Gospels it is never the Pharisees who accuse Jesus of blasphemy on Messianic grounds, but only the High Priest. This indicates that the charge against Jesus for claiming to be the Messiah was not a religious charge at all, but a political one. It was no infringement of Pharisee law to claim to be the Messiah, but since 'Messiah' means 'king', and since the Romans had abolished the Jewish monarchy, anyone who claimed to be the Messiah was acting subversively towards the Roman occupation, and, as the Roman-appointed quisling whose task was to guard against anti-Roman activities, the High Priest would be bound to take an interest in any Messianic claimants with a view to handing them over to the Romans for punishment. The Gospels, however, in pursuance of their policy of representing Jesus as a rebel against Jewish religion, depict the High Priest as concerned about blasphemy rather than rebellion.

Similarly, the charge against Jesus that he threatened to destroy the Temple and rebuild it was brought against him only at his trial, and the Pharisees are not associated with this charge. This is indeed a political, not a religious charge, for the Temple built by Herod was not expected by the Pharisees to last into the Messianic age. Jesus very probably did declare his intention of destroying the Temple and rebuilding it, for this is just what anyone seriously claiming to be the Messiah would do. The Pharisees had no superstitious veneration for the Temple, and would not be horrified at the idea that Jesus intended to build a new one, like his ancestor Solomon. The only people who would be seriously upset by such an intention would be the High Priest and his entourage, who could expect to see themselves swept away by the projected Messianic regime. Indeed, at the time of the Jewish War in AD 66, the first thing that the rebels against Rome did was to dismiss the High Priest and appoint a new one from a family uncontaminated by collaboration with Rome. Yet again, this charge is represented in the Gospels as a religious charge of blasphemy instead of as a political charge of rebellion against the *status quo*, in which the High Priest and the Temple were instruments of Rome.

As for the alleged reforms of Judaism which Jesus is represented as advocating, none of these, on examination, proves to be in breach of Pharisee ideas. Thus we are told that Jesus opposed the concept of 'an eye for an eye', found in the legal code of the Hebrew Bible, substituting the law of love for the law of revenge. This is a travesty of the situation in Pharisaism. The Pharisees did not regard the expression 'an eye for an eye' as a literal legal prescription. They poured scorn on such an idea as quaint and uncivilized (asking, for example, 'What happens if a one-eyed man knocks out someone's eye?'). They regarded the expression 'an eye for an eye' as meaning that in principle any injury perpetrated against one's fellow man should be compensated for in accordance with the seriousness of the injury. Indeed, the legal code of the Hebrew Bible itself provides for such compensation, when it states that loss of employment and doctor's bills must be paid for by the person responsible for an injury (Exodus 21: 19). So clearly the Pharisees were not putting any strained interpretation on the Hebrew Bible when they understood the expression 'an eye for an eye' to refer to monetary compensation rather than savage retribution. As for Jesus' further recommendation that one should not seek compensation if injured, but should offer the other cheek, he certainly did not extend this idea to freedom from any obligation to compensate for injuries that one may have committed. As a counsel of perfection[6] (not as a practical law), the idea of refusing to receive compensation was an option in Pharisaic thought too; but this did not mean that injuries could be committed with impunity without any remedy in law; on the contrary, the very person who was ready to waive his own legal right to compensation would be the first to uphold the right of others, especially if he himself had injured them. This is an area in which confusion of thought is rife, and Jesus is credited with upholding a definition of the 'law of love' which is mere nonsense, and would result in a society in which oppression and violence would reign unchecked. The Pharisees too believed in the 'law of love', as is shown by their doctrine that love of God and love of fellow man are the basic principles of the Torah; but love of one's fellow man is shown more by a determination to secure his rights than by a blanket abolition of all rights. There is no reason to suppose that Jesus held such a foolish doctrine, or that his views were different from those of other Pharisees.

As for Jesus' individual 'reforms' of Jewish laws, these were non-existent. We find in Mark 7: 19 an expression which has been translated to mean that Jesus 'declared all foods clean', but this translation has been much disputed, and many scholars regard the phrase as an editorial addition anyway. In another passage, we find Jesus explicitly endorsing the Jewish laws of purity, when he tells the leper he has cured, 'Go and show yourself to the priest, and make the offering laid down by Moses for your cleansing' (Mark 1: 43).

True, we find Jesus speaking in the tone of a reformer in the Sermon on the Mount, when he says, 'You have learned that our forefathers were told. . . . But what I tell you is this.' Here he seems to assume a tone of authority and an independence of previous teaching which would justify the description of a 'reformer'. However, since the whole episode of the Sermon on the Mount is Matthew's invention (the sayings being found scattered over various episodes in the other Gospels, except in Luke, where the sermon is transferred to a plain and the grandiose note of authority is missing), the simplest explanation is that the reformer's tone has been imported into the story by later Christian editors, to whom the idea that Jesus taught with the same kind of authority as other Pharisee teachers was unpalatable.

An interesting episode that seems to support the picture of Jesus as a ruthless reformer of the Torah and as unconcerned with the observance of its laws is the corn-plucking incident, which first occurs in Mark 2:

> One sabbath he was going through the cornfields; and his disciples as they went, began to pluck ears of corn. The Pharisees said to him, 'Look, why are they doing what is forbidden on the sabbath?' He answered, 'Have you never read what David did when he and his men were hungry and had nothing to eat? He went into the House of God, in the time of Abiathar the High Priest, and ate the consecrated loaves, though no one but a priest is allowed to eat them, and even gave them to his men.'
>
> He also said to them, 'The sabbath is made for the sake of man and not man for the sabbath: therefore the Son of Man is sovereign even over the sabbath.'

This incident cannot be explained as having been originally an altercation with the Sadducees, for the Pharisees did indeed forbid the plucking of corn on the sabbath, together with all other forms of agricultural labour. So Jesus, by allowing his disciples to pluck ears of corn on the sabbath, was flouting a clear Pharisee law, or so it appears.

An indication that all is not as it appears, however, is Jesus' saying at the end: 'The sabbath is made for the sake of man and not man for the sabbath.' This, as previously mentioned, is a Pharisee maxim[7], and it gives the key to the whole incident. For the Pharisees used this maxim to show that *in circumstances of danger to human life* the sabbath laws could be, and had to be, ignored. In the story as it stands, there was no danger to human life to excuse the disciples from ignoring the sabbath law; but, as we examine the story further, we find more and more indications that the circumstances did indeed involve extreme danger.

Jesus in his explanation to the Pharisees cites, in true Pharisee fashion, an episode from scripture as the ground of his attitude to the corn-plucking. This is the case of David and his violation of the sanctity of the shewbread; and this case is explained in the Pharisee literature[8] (with good support from the actual text) as having been one of extreme danger to life, since David and his men were dying of starvation in their flight from King Saul. That is why, in Pharisee theory, David and his men were justified in eating the holy shewbread, though in circumstances where there was no danger to human life this was regarded as a heinous sin. Since the case of David was one of extreme emergency, it would seem to be an absurd instance for Jesus to give unless the circumstances of himself and his disciples were equally desperate at the time of the corn-plucking incident. If, as the narrative seems to indicate, they were engaged merely in a leisurely stroll through the cornfields on the sabbath, and the disciples idly plucked and munched the corn for want of anything better to do, the David incident would have been quite irrelevant (apart from having nothing to do with the sabbath). If we restore the element of emergency to the narrative, however, it suddenly makes perfect sense.

Jesus and his followers, in flight from Herod Antipas and the Romans, at the last extremity of exhaustion and hunger arrive at a cornfield. It is the sabbath day, but Jesus, judging the situation to be, like the case of David, an emergency in which all ritual observances, whether of the sabbath or the Temple, are abrogated by Pharisee law, allows his disciples to satisfy their hunger by plucking corn. Later, when questioned about the incident by some Pharisee friends, he explains how he came to rule that the sabbath law should be broken.

This explanation also throws light on another puzzling point. To pluck ears of corn from a field was not only a breach of the sabbath law, but also a breach of the law against theft. Some Christian scholars have tried to cover this point by referring to the law in Deuteronomy 23: 25–6: 'When thou comest into the standing corn of thy neighbour, then thou mayest pluck the ears with thine hand.' This, however, as the Pharisee literature shows (e.g. Mishnah Bava Metzia 7: 2) applies only to workmen who are working in a field for the owner; life would soon become impossible for farmers if every casual passer-by were allowed to take his fill of corn. But in cases of danger to life, the laws of theft were regarded as null and void – in fact, Pharisee law regards it as a duty to steal in order to save life.[9] Jesus, therefore, was quite entitled, in Pharisee thinking, to disregard the law of theft as well as the law of the sabbath in such circumstances.

Why then, was the element of emergency removed from the story as we have it in the Gospels, thus reducing the whole episode to nonsense? The answer is: for the same reason that the element of emergency has been removed from the whole of the Gospels, which portray Judaea and Galilee as peaceful areas under benign Roman rule, instead of what they were in historical reality at this time, areas of bitter unrest and constant rebellion against the savage oppression of the Romans and the depredations of the tax-farmers (or publicans). If the sense of emergency had been retained in the story, not only would it have to be revealed that Jesus was not flouting Pharisee law but also that he was a hunted man, wanted by Herod and the Romans, and in rebellion against them.

Thus the corn-plucking incident, so far from telling against the view that Jesus was a Pharisee, cannot be understood except on the hypothesis that Jesus was one. His use of biblical precedent and of a Pharisee maxim in order to establish that exceptional circumstances warranted a breach of the law are entirely in accordance with Pharisee practice and principles, and do not justify an interpretation in terms of rebellion against the law. Jesus' final remark, '. . . therefore the Son of Man is sovereign even over the sabbath,' is generally held to mean that Jesus was declaring his lofty independence from Jewish law and his right to abrogate its provisions at will. This, however, is not necessarily the meaning of the sentence. The expression 'son of man' in Aramaic simply means 'man' or 'human being'. The meaning could therefore be, 'Human beings are more important than the sabbath,' a sentiment with which all Pharisees would agree. Many of the puzzling 'Son of Man' sayings in the New Testament can be explained on similar lines, though a residue remains in which Jesus uses the expression 'Son of Man' as a title expressive of his own role. As a title, it by no means implies divine status, but rather prophetic status; it is used throughout the book of Ezekiel in this sense.

The alleged conflict between Jesus and the Pharisees on the question of his association with 'sinners and publicans' also requires some comment. The mistake usually made is to think that these people were not really sinners in any serious sense, but were merely lacking in respectability or apt to neglect the laws of ritual purity. In fact, neither respectability nor ritual purity were the issues; the 'publicans' were gangsters, torturers and murderers who assisted the Roman tax-farmers in extorting goods and money from their fellow Jews to the point where many committed suicide or became outlaws rather than face penury or slavery. Jesus, however, fully confident in his nationwide campaign of 'repentance', preparatory to a Messianic miracle of national redemption from Rome, approached these desperate sinners not because he loved their company, but in the hope of converting them from their evil ways. Those 'publicans' or tax-gatherers who were touched by Jesus' appeal did not remain publicans. An example is Zacchaeus (Luke 19), who renounced his whole way of life and undertook to restore all the loot he had gathered and also give half his possessions to charity. This is just the mode of restitution prescribed for repentant tax-gatherers in the Pharisee work the Tosefta. Some scholars have alleged that the Pharisees held out no hope of repentance to tax-gatherers. This is not true, but they certainly regarded repentance and restitution as very difficult for them.[10] It may be that, in this instance, there was a genuine point of disagreement between Jesus and the other Pharisees, Jesus being confident of converting the tax-gatherers, while other Pharisee teachers thought that association with gangsters would be more likely to affect the would-be converter for the worse than the gangsters for the better.

It should be remembered that Jesus would have been a most unusual Pharisee if he had never disagreed with other Pharisees. As explained earlier, amicable disagreement was an essential ingredient in Pharisaism, and the Pharisee literature is full of disagreements between the various sages of the movement. In some cases, the New Testament has created conflict between Jesus and the Pharisees, not by altering 'Sadducees' to 'Pharisees' or by removing some essential element from the story, but simply by turning what was originally a friendly argument into a hostile confrontation.

Thus in various ways, Jesus has been isolated in the Gospels from the movement to which he belonged, the Pharisees. Yet, despite every effort to turn him into an isolated figure, his identity as a Pharisee

43

remains indelibly stamped on him by his style of preaching. His use of parables (often thought by people unfamiliar with Pharisee literature to be a mark of his uniqueness) was typical of Pharisee preaching; and even his quaint expressions such as 'a camel going through the eye of a needle', or 'take the beam out of your own eye' are Pharisee locutions found in the Talmud. This is true, of course, only of the Jesus found in the Synoptic Gospels (i.e. Mark, Matthew and Luke). In the Fourth Gospel, that of John, Jesus has become unrecognizable. He uses no parables, nor any idiosyncratic rabbinical expressions; instead he spouts grandiose Hellenistic mysticism and proclaims himself a divine personage. Here the authentic Jesus has been lost in the post-Jesus myth. It is not here that we find the genuine Jesus, rooted in the Jewish religion of his time, and pursuing aims that were intelligible to his fellow Jews.

CHAPTER 5

WHY WAS JESUS
CRUCIFIED?

If Jesus was a Pharisee, made no claim that was blasphemous, and never attempted to abolish the sabbath or any other accepted Jewish religious institution, why was he crucified? This question has proved most puzzling and embarrassing to Christian scholars who have acquired enough knowledge of Pharisaism to realize that the traditional story of conflict between Jesus and the religious authorities will not do. Some have tried to find a solution in the divisions which existed *within* the Pharisee party, for example, between the House of Hillel and the House of Shammai. According to this view, Jesus *was* a Pharisee, but fell foul of the stricter wing of the Pharisees, the Shammaiites. But the arguments and disagreements that took place between these Pharisee factions were carried on at an amicable level and were decided by majority vote, which sometimes went in favour of the Hillelites and sometimes in favour of the Shammaiites. It is unthinkable that the Shammaiites would attempt to bring about the death of a prominent Hillelite. Moreover, it does not even appear that Jesus did belong to the Hillelite or more liberal wing of the Pharisees, for his strict view on divorce seems much more in accordance with the views of the House of Shammai.

Another view is that Jesus belonged to a section of the Pharisees called the Hasidim, who practised a supererogatory code of conduct and were known as healers and wonder-workers; men such as Hanina ben Dosa, Honi the Circle-maker and Abba Hilkiah. As a 'charismatic' Pharisee, it is suggested, Jesus may have fallen foul of the 'legalistic' Pharisees.[1] Again, there is no reason to believe that there was any serious conflict between 'charismatic' and 'legalistic' Pharisees; on the contrary the evidence suggests that they held each other in the highest regard. Jesus may well have belonged to the Hasidim, who, indeed, of all the Pharisees show the strongest similarity in type to Jesus, but this would only have made him more respected by the main body of the Pharisees.

Other scholars have made desperate attempts to find some point on which Jesus' views might have roused the ire of the Pharisees: one scholar has even suggested that the root of the trouble was that Jesus preached in the open air.[2] Such far-fetched suggestions show how difficult it is to find any plausible reason why Jesus should have offended the Pharisees by his teaching.

It is important for the argument of this book that we should have a clear idea of why Jesus died in historical fact, for Paul, our main theme, made the crucifixion of Jesus into the centre of his thinking. Paul's view of Jesus has coloured the story told in the Gospels and has thus influenced the imagination of all Western civilization. To search for the historical facts of Jesus' death is thus to uncover the real world in which Paul's thinking had its origin and to explain the motivation of Paul in transforming a historical event into a cosmic myth. Blaming the Pharisees or Jewish religion generally for Jesus' death was one of the by-products of this transformation of a man into a myth. The picture of the early Paul (or Saul) as a persecuting Pharisee has powerfully reinforced this aspect of the matter.

Jesus was a man who was born into Jewish society in Galilee; he was not a divine being who descended from outer space in order to suffer death on behalf of mankind. If we want to know why Jesus was killed, we have to ask why a Jew from Galilee in those times might meet his end on a Roman cross.

Many Jews from Galilee died in the same way during this period. Judas of Galilee was a Jewish patriot who led an armed rebellion against the Romans. Many hundreds of his supporters were crucified by the Romans. At one time, while Jesus was a boy, four thousand Jews were crucified by the Romans for an insurrection against Roman taxes. Crucifixion was the cruel form of execution which the Romans used for rebels against their rule. Galilee was always a centre of rebellion[3], partly because it was not under direct Roman rule and, therefore, like Vichy France during the last World War, gave some scope for the organization of resistance.

The presumption is, therefore, that Jesus the Galilean who died on the cross did so for the same reason as the others: because he was a threat to the Roman occupation. The Gospels indeed tell us that this was the charge made against him. The actual charge, according to

Luke was as follows: 'We found this fellow perverting the nation, and, forbidding to give tribute to Caesar, saying that he himself is Christ a King' (Luke 23: 2). On his cross, the charge for which he was executed was affixed, according to Roman usage: it was that he had claimed to be 'King of the Jews', a capital offence at a time when the Romans had abolished the Jewish monarchy. To 'pervert the nation' meant to disturb them from their allegiance to Rome. The use of the term 'Christ' (or 'Messiah') here in its original political sense is interesting, for it shows that despite Christian editing of the Gospels, which ensured that the term was de-politicized in almost every instance, editorial vigilance could occasionally slip.

But the Gospels put all their energy into saying that, though Jesus was executed on a political charge, this was a *false* charge. The real reason why Jesus was brought to his death, the Gospels allege, was not political but religious. The political charge, they say, was pursued with vigour; John even has the Jews saying to Pilate, 'If you let this man go, you are no friend to Caesar; any man who claims to be a king is defying Caesar' (John 19: 12). But the Gospels allege that there was really no substance in it, for Jesus had no political aims whatever, was indeed a pacifist, had no desire to end Roman rule, and, when he claimed to be 'King of the Jews', did so in some innocuous spiritual sense that did not in any way conflict with the Roman occupation.

According to this account, Jesus was framed; he was innocent of the political charges for which he was executed. But also, it should be noticed, the Romans in this account were innocent of his death. They were tricked, bamboozled and blackmailed into executing Jesus. The scene in which Pontius Pilate, the Roman Governor of Judaea, washes his hands, saying, 'My hands are clean of this man's blood,' symbolizes the innocence of Rome (Matthew 27: 24). The full blame for the death of Jesus is thus laid on the Jews, who are even made to accept the blame in the same scene with the words, 'His blood be on us and on our children.' The transfer of guilt from the Romans to the Jews could not be more graphically performed.

Everything depends, then, on whether the picture of Jesus as a rebel against Jewish religion can be substantiated. Only if it can be plausibly shown that Jesus' claim to be the Messiah was blasphemous in Jewish law, or that his sabbath healing was offensive to the Pharisees, or his threat to destroy the Temple was shocking to them can we say that the charge on which Jesus was executed — the political charge of posing a threat to the Roman occupation — was incorrect, the real reason being the hostility of the Jewish religious authorities, who sought to make away with him by falsely denouncing him to the Roman Governor as a political troublemaker. If none of the religious charges can be substantiated, then the Jewish religious authorities had no reason to hand him over to the Romans. The only charge remaining is the ostensible charge itself, that of political subversion, and this must be the real reason for Jesus' death.

In fact, as we have seen in the last chapter, the desperate attempts of the Gospels to show that Jesus was in some way a rebel against Jewish religion are utterly implausible in the light of any genuine understanding of Jewish religion at the time. Only one of the Gospels, that of John, portrays Jesus as expressing ideas that would indeed have shocked the Jewish religious authorities and Jews generally – but John's is the latest and least authentic of the Gospels, and lacks all the Jewish flavouring found in the other Gospels authenticating their picture of Jesus as a Jewish teacher. In the Synoptic Gospels, Jesus is indeed portrayed as shocking the Pharisees, but only with ideas and expressions that would not in fact have been shocking to them, and which they would have heartily approved. Jesus' genuine opinions and teaching have still been preserved in these earlier Gospels; it is only their impact that has been falsified.

We are left then with the political charge of rebellion against Rome. Here we must make the all-important distinction between the Pharisees and the High Priest. The High Priest would indeed have been alarmed and hostile to Jesus, because of his claim to Messiahship and his threat to the Temple, for the High Priest was appointed by the Romans to look after their interests. Claiming to be the Messiah meant claiming to be King of the Jews. If it had meant that Jesus regarded himself as God, the High Priest would have regarded Jesus as merely a harmless lunatic; but it meant something much more urgent and practical than that – it signalled revolt. Jesus' threat to the Temple was not subversive of Jewish religion, but it was a real threat to the quisling regime of the High Priest.

The Pharisees, on the other hand, would have had no objection on political grounds to Jesus' claim to Messiahship. The Pharisees were the party of resistance against Rome. It was from their ranks that the Zealots came, the brave guerrilla fighters who looked to Judas of Galilee as their leader. Most of the Pharisees took a more moderate view, thinking that the rule of the Romans was probably destined to stay for quite a long time, but they continued to hope for liberation and therefore regarded any Messianic attempt with sympathy. Their attitude is perfectly summed up in the speech of Gamaliel (Acts 5):

'. . . if this idea of theirs or its execution is of human origin, it will collapse; but if it is from God, you will never be able to put them down, and you risk finding yourselves at war with God.' This wait-and-see policy in relation to every Messianic attempt was cautious and sensible, but at root sympathetic, for the Pharisees were the party of patriotism and would have liked nothing better than to see a successful Messianic movement, as is shown by their support for Bar Kokhba a hundred years later.

The reason for Jesus' crucifixion, then, was simply that he was a rebel against Rome. He was not framed on a political charge by the Jews; rather it was the Jews who were framed by the Gospels, whose concern was to shift the blame for the crucifixion from the Romans (and their Jewish henchmen, the High Priest and his entourage) to the Jews and their religion.

This does not mean, of course, that Jesus was a secular political rebel, like Che Guevara in modern times. Such a conception of politics is quite anachronistic. Jesus' main concern was religion, not politics. He preached as a rabbi, proclaimed the coming Kingdom of God like a prophet, and eventually announced himself King in the religious tradition of David, Solomon and Hezekiah. In Judaism, it is impossible to separate religion and politics, because in Judaism the main concern is with this world, rather than the next. As the Psalmist says, 'The heavens are for the Lord, and the earth for the children of men,' which means that it is the task of humanity to make the world a better place – to make it full of justice, love, mercy and peace – not to escape from it into a 'better world' beyond the skies. Jesus followed the tradition of Moses, who was both a prophet and a liberator; but Jesus came into conflict with an inexorable empire that crushed him.

CHAPTER 6

WAS PAUL A PHARISEE?

It was Paul who detached Jesus from his mission of liberation and turned him into an otherworldly figure whose mission had no relevance to politics or to the sufferings of his fellow Jews under the Romans. This transformation had the effect of making the Jews, instead of the Romans, responsible for Jesus' crucifixion. Because Jesus had been raised above politics, the Jews became the victims in a real political as well as religious sense, when they became the pariahs of Christendom, deprived of political and economic rights and subject to constant persecution.

Who, then, was Paul? What kind of man was he who could so change the meaning of Jesus' life and death that it became the basis of a new religion in whose central myth the Jews were the villains, instead of the heroes, of sacred history? Jesus had preached the coming of the Kingdom of God and had envisaged himself as the King of Israel in a world of international peace, in which the Roman Empire and other military empires had disappeared. He had never declared himself to be a divine figure or claimed that his death would atone for the sins of mankind; his failure to overcome the Romans by a great miracle from God was the end of all his hopes, as his despairing cry on the cross shows. Jesus' scenario of the future contained the Jews as the people of God, restored to independence in their Holy Land, and acting as a nation of priests for the whole world in the Kingdom of God. Paul's new scenario, in which the Jews no longer had a great role to play, and had indeed sunk to the role of the enemies of God, would have filled Jesus with horror and dismay. He would not have understood the new meaning attached by Paul to the title 'Christ' or 'Messiah', by which it became a divine title instead of the time-honoured designation of

Jewish royalty.

Jesus, a Pharisee, would never have understood or accepted this new conception, which he would have regarded as blasphemous and idolatrous, and as contradicting the Jewish historical role as the opponents of god-kings and vicarious atonement by human sacrifice. Yet Paul, for whom Jesus was both a god-king and a human sacrifice, claimed to have been educated and trained as a Pharisee. We must now enter fully into the question of whether this claim was true or false.

The depiction of the Pharisees in the book of Acts shows the same contradictory pattern that we find in the Gospels, the only difference being that the contradictions have become even more blatant. On the one hand, the picture of persecuting Pharisees is continued through the character of Paul himself: just as the Pharisees are portrayed in the Gospels as persecuting Jesus, so Paul in his early days of alleged Pharisaism is shown persecuting the followers of Jesus. On the other hand, there are at the same time many indications in the text that the Pharisees were *not* opposed to the early Nazarenes, but, on the contrary, regarded them with sympathy. Indeed, Luke, the author of Acts, hardly bothers to continue the anti-Pharisee devices which he used in his Gospel and almost carelessly, as it seems, retains pro-Pharisee features in his narrative, relying on his portrayal of Paul to provide the anti-Pharisee note which is essential for his main drift.

A demonstration of the fundamental accord between the early followers of Jesus and the Pharisees will cast the gravest doubt on the contention of Acts that Paul was a Pharisee. A very important episode in this regard is that in which Gamaliel defends Peter and the other apostles. This has already been referred to several times, but now requires detailed analysis, as it is recounted in chapter 5 of Acts.

Peter has been warned by the High Priest not to preach about Jesus, but he and the other apostles continue their preaching. This moves the High Priest to action: 'Then the High Priest and his colleagues, the Sadducean party as it then was, were goaded into action by jealousy. They proceeded to arrest the apostles, and put them into official custody.' Unlike the Gospels, the book of Acts does not disguise the fact that the High Priest was a Sadducee and was thus opposed by the Pharisees; it is here stated quite explicitly that it was the Sadducee party which brought about the arrest of the apostles. The Apostles are brought before the Sanhedrin, described as 'the full senate of the Israelite nation', and accused of continuing to preach despite having been ordered to desist. Peter, on behalf of the apostles, replies, 'We must obey God rather than men.' The story continues:

51

This touched them on the raw, and they wanted to put them to death. But a member of the Council rose to his feet, a Pharisee called Gamaliel, a teacher of the law held in high regard by all the people. He moved that the men be put outside for a while. Then he said, 'Men of Israel, be cautious in deciding what to do with these men. Some time ago Theudas came forward, claiming to be somebody, and a number of men, about four hundred, joined him. But he was killed and his whole following was broken up and disappeared. After him came Judas the Galilean at the time of the census; he induced some people to revolt under his leadership, but he too perished and his whole following was scattered. And so now: keep clear of these men, I tell you; leave them alone. For if this idea of theirs or its execution is of human origin, it will collapse; but if it is from God, you will never be able to put them down, and you risk finding yourselves at war with God.' They took his advice. They sent for the apostles and had them flogged; then they ordered them to give up speaking in the name of Jesus, and discharged them. So the apostles went out from the Council rejoicing that they had been found worthy to suffer indignity for the sake of the Name.

The historical importance of this passage has not been adequately appreciated by scholars. It contradicts completely some of the leading assumptions of the Gospels and indeed of Acts. On the principle explained above, that passages which go against the grain of the narrative should be given particular attention, we should regard this passage as giving us a valuable glimpse into the real historical situation of the time.

The first point to notice is that Gamaliel does not in any way condemn the apostles as heretics or rebels against the Jewish religion. He regards them instead as members of a Messianic movement *directed against Rome*. The proof of this is the comparison he makes between them and other movements of the time. He mentions two such movements, that of Theudas and that of Judas of Galilee, and as it happens we have information about both these movements in the historical writings of Josephus, written about AD 90 and based on sources contemporary with the events (the date of the composition of the book of Acts is also about AD 90). Josephus confirms that both the movements mentioned were Messianic movements directed against Rome; neither of them was in any way directed against the Jewish religion. Theudas was a prophet figure who had no military organization but relied on a miracle from God to overthrow the Romans, in accordance with biblical prophecy.

Of course, there is no reason to suppose that the words in which the author of Acts reports Gamaliel's speech are exactly those which Gamaliel used before the Sanhedrin. But the substance of Gamaliel's remarks fits in so well with the actual historical conditions of the time that, unlike some of the other speeches given to various characters in the book of Acts, it has the ring of authenticity. This is not affected by the fact that some details are distorted; for example, the actual name 'Theudas' cannot be correct, for Theudas belonged to a period too late for this speech, since his insurrection took place in about AD 45. The author of Acts evidently substituted the name 'Theudas' for the original name in his source, which was that of some figure who had sunk into obscurity, but who was of the same Messianic type as Theudas, whose name would still be familiar to readers.

Judas of Galilee, on the other hand, belongs to the right period since his activities took place during the collection of taxes and the census of Quirinius in AD 6. As the founder of the great Zealot movement which remained in existence long after the death of Judas, his name was still familiar to the readers of Acts and so was allowed to stand unchanged. Judas, unlike Theudas, was a militarist who engaged in armed guerilla activity. He was in no way a rebel against Jewish religion, but on the contrary was a Pharisee rabbi.

Gamaliel put the Jesus movement into the same category as these two movements. The analogy between Theudas (or the proto-Theudas in the original source) and Jesus is closer than the analogy between Jesus and Judas of Galilee, for Jesus never engaged in organized military activity, but, like Theudas, relied on a miracle from God. When the climactic moment of Jesus' revolt took place, he asked his disciples whether they had swords and, when told that they had only two between them, he said, 'That will be enough' (Luke 22: 38). This incident, preserved by only one evangelist, shows that Jesus was no pacifist, but thought that a token show of fight on his part would be enough and God would do the rest. Here he followed the biblical example of Gideon. But this unmilitaristic stance of Jesus did not make him any less of an opponent to the Romans, who took Theudas seriously enough to kill him.[1]

If Jesus, as the Gospels represent, had actually been a rebel against the Jewish religion, declaring the Torah abrogated and himself able to cancel its provisions at will, why did Gamaliel the Pharisee, leader of a religious party whose loyalty to the Torah was renowned, have nothing to say about this when giving his opinion about what should be done to Jesus' immediate followers? If the Pharisees had really been Jesus' deadly enemies during his lifetime, why should their leader suddenly forget all about this shortly after Jesus' death and give his support to the very men with whom Jesus had consorted, including Peter, his right-hand man? If Jesus' apostles broke the sabbath and ignored other

Jewish laws, as conventional Christian belief requires them to have done in continuance of the attitudes of Jesus himself, why does Gamaliel the Pharisee say that their movement may be 'from God'? Finally, if this is the lenient attitude of the leader of the Pharisees (however inexplicable by conventional Christian theory), why does Paul, the alleged Pharisee, have an entirely different attitude, breathing fire and thunder against the followers of Jesus and hauling them off to the prison from which Gamaliel wanted them released?

Christian writers of the Church certainly found difficulty with these questions, and their answer was that Gamaliel was not a typical Pharisee, but was in fact a secret sympathizer with Christianity, i.e. with the Christianity of the Church, which they thought identical with that of the apostles. For anyone who knows the Pharisee records of Gamaliel, this solution is ridiculous, but it is somewhat anticipated by the failure of the narrative in Acts to make clear just how important a Pharisee Gamaliel was. It calls him 'a Pharisee called Gamaliel, a teacher of the law held in high regard by all the people', but it does not make clear that he was the Pharisee leader of his generation, a vital link in the chain of Jewish tradition, one of the veritable Fathers of Judaism. To say that he was a secret Christian, in the sense meant, is like saying that Saint Thomas Aquinas was a secret Hindu. Of course, Gamaliel undoubtedly was a sympathizer with the followers of Jesus, as the present passage shows, in the sense that he saw no harm in them and thought they might possibly turn out to be 'from God'; but he would not have had such sympathy if they had had the views ascribed to them and to Jesus by later Christian belief.

It is noteworthy, too, that Gamaliel is described as 'held in high regard by all the people'. This is a rare indication in the New Testament of the status of the Pharisees among the Jewish people. In the Gospels we are never allowed to understand this, but are shown the Pharisees as proud oppressors, laying grievous burdens on the people, making an ostentatious show of piety, but actually hypocrites. One would never guess from all this that the Pharisees were the party of the people, whose customs and traditions they guarded from Sadducee attack, and whom the people loved as their natural protectors from corrupt High Priests and Kings.

A more modern solution to the problems of the Gamaliel passage is to have recourse once more to the divisions among the Pharisees. According to this theory, Gamaliel belonged to the lenient Hillelite wing of the Pharisees, while Paul represented the more fanatical and rigorous Shammaiite wing.[2] This explains why two Pharisees could adopt such different attitudes to the followers of Jesus. This, however, explains nothing. It is true that Gamaliel was a Hillelite, for he was a descendant of Hillel himself. But there is no point of disagreement between the Hillelites and the Shammaiites that could make them adopt such different standpoints towards the early followers of Jesus. The whole argument is predicated on the view that the Nazarenes were in some way heretical in their doctrines or practices, but, in fact, they were not: they were orthodox Jews in their whole way of life, including the practice of circumcision and the observance of dietary laws, the sabbath and festivals, and of the Temple cult. The only thing that differentiated them from ordinary Pharisaic Jews was their belief in Jesus as Messiah, and since this did not include any belief in Jesus as a divine figure, this doctrine was well within the threshold of tolerance of other Jews, many of whom had similar Messianic beliefs about other figures such as Judas of Galilee or Theudas. There was thus no reason for any Pharisee, whether Hillelite or Shammaiite, to adopt an attitude of angry intolerance towards the followers of Jesus.

If anything, the Shammaiites would have had *more* sympathy with the early followers of Jesus than the Hillelites, for the Shammaiites were inclined to take a more activist line against the Roman occupation than the Hillelites. Thus any Messianic movement raising hopes of quick release from subjection to Rome would have received a warmer response from them than from the cautious Hillelites. Further, as already mentioned, there is some reason to believe that Jesus himself was a Shammaiite. This not to say that the Hillelites were resigned to collaboration with Rome and had lost all hope of Jewish independence in the foreseeable future. The speech of Gamaliel shows the contrary, for it is clear that this is an activist political speech, saying in effect, 'Nothing would please me better than the success of the hopes of the followers of Jesus, though in view of past failures of such groups, I must adopt a wait-and-see attitude.' This was indeed exactly the attitude of the moderate Pharisees, who continued to believe fervently in the coming of the Messiah and looked with hope, tempered by many previous disappointments, towards any Messianic claimant. Thus even the moderate Pharisees could switch from political passivity to activism quite easily, as happened during the Bar Kokhba revolt, and the Pharisee party was the continual centre of anti-Roman ferment. The political character of Gamaliel's speech contrasts strongly with the usual slant of New Testament accounts of relations between the Jesus movement and the Pharisees, which try to present the issues as religious only.

It may be asked why Luke, the author of Acts, preserved this revealing incident, which contradicts so much of the trend of presentation in the Gospels, including Luke's own. The answer seems to be that Luke had more of a historian's approach than the other Gospel-writers and often seems to be working from written sources of an archival character, which he likes to transmit with almost pedantic thoroughness. Thus, in his Gospel, he gives us the indictment of Jesus at the time when he was handed over to the Romans in a form that has the stamp of authenticity and was no doubt taken from some official source ('We found this man subverting our nation, opposing the payment of taxes to Caesar, and claiming to be Messiah, a king'). This tendency to quote his source *verbatim* sometimes lets in a breeze of political reality, which Luke then tries to counteract by various devices, not always very successfully. Thus, in the present passage, he attempts to divest the Apostles' trial before the Sanhedrin of political flavour by the speech he puts into Peter's mouth when he was questioned before the trial began: 'We must obey God rather than men. The God of our fathers raised up Jesus whom you had done to death by hanging him on a gibbet. He it is whom God has exalted with his own right hand as leader and saviour, to grant Israel repentance and forgiveness of sins. And we are witnesses to all this, and so is the Holy Spirit given by God to those who are obedient to him.' This speech is addressed to the High Priest, which makes the accusation 'whom you had done to death' not inappropriate; but the representation of Jesus as having a mission of forgiveness only, not as a liberator from Rome, makes the Jesus movement (or Nazarenes) into quite a different kind of party from that implied by Gamaliel in his subsequent speech. The term 'saviour' is indeed used, not in the Jewish sense of 'liberator', but in the later Christian sense of 'saviour from damnation'. Thus this speech is calculated to counteract the impression given in the subsequent Sanhedrin scene, though at the cost of consistency, for if the views of Peter and the Apostles had really been of this kind, Gamaliel would not have defended them at all. Luke made a much more plausible job of counteracting the indictment against Jesus which he quoted in his Gospel.

More effective, however, is another device which is used in the presentation of the Gamaliel episode: the depiction of Gamaliel as a lone voice and as unrepresentative of the Pharisees. This is done not only by hiding the fact that Gamaliel was the leader of the Pharisee party, but also by concealing the fact that the release of the apostles took place by a majority vote. Instead, it is simply said that Gamaliel managed to persuade the assembly to his point of view, which makes it appear that by a feat of eloquence he managed to induce the Sanhedrin to perform a unique act of clemency. This leaves Gamaliel as a solitary figure able to perform a near miracle of persuasion on one occasion, but by no means typical of the Pharisees in general, and this is how Christian writers have always understood the matter. Further, the clemency of the Sanhedrin is distorted by the assertion that the Apostles were flogged before being released, which hardly seems consistent with the advice of Gamaliel that the Council has accepted. In historical fact, Gamaliel, as leader of the Pharisees, would have carried with him all the Pharisee members of the Sanhedrin, but not the Sadducee members led by the High Priest. This was, therefore, a case of the Sadducees and the High Priest being outvoted by the Pharisees, evidence of important points that can be supported from other sources: that the High Priest frequently did not have his own way in the Sanhedrin, where the Pharisees had a majority, and that the views of the High Priest and those of the Pharisees should not be equated, as they still are by too many scholars.

Gamaliel, represented as a lone figure with an unusual attitude of friendliness towards the Nazarenes, thus takes his place alongside other figures of the same kind: Joseph of Arimathea and Nicodemus, who appear in the Gospels. Both of these men are described as Pharisees and members of the Sanhedrin; they took a sympathetic interest in Jesus' movement without joining it, and took pains to see that Jesus was given a decent burial after his crucifixion. While these figures are, in fact, strong evidence that there was no conflict between Jesus and the Pharisees, with whom he had personal links, the impression is given that they were uncharacteristic of the Pharisees, and so the hostile picture of the Pharisees in general is preserved. Yet if Jesus had in fact been a blasphemer, self-idolater and opponent of the Torah, no Pharisee at all would have been sympathetic to him or his followers. On the other hand, if he was not, there is no reason to suppose that the friendly attitude of Joseph of Arimathea, Nicodemus and Gamaliel was not shared by the Pharisees as a whole.

So, in the book of Acts, we have two figures – Gamaliel and Paul – both of whom are supposed to be Pharisees, but who are at opposite poles. In Gamaliel, we have the continuation of all the evidence to be found in the Gospels (though not on the surface) that Jesus was a Pharisee and his movement was regarded sympathetically by the Pharisees. In Paul (Saul) we have the representative of the main anti-Pharisee trend in the Gospels, so essential to the Gospels' explanation of Jesus' death; he is the raving, violent Pharisee who is outraged by Jesus' message and wishes to bring destruction to his movement. Gamaliel is an authentic, historical character, whose attitudes can be understood perfectly in the light of knowledge of the period: but Saul is a mere caricature, a bogeyman-Pharisee whose motivations cannot be understood at all. At least, they cannot be understood if Saul really was a Pharisee; but they can be understood very well if he was not one. And here we must examine Paul's relationship with the High Priest, for this is the best clue we have to the truth.

The High Priest, as we have seen (and as the New Testament bears witness), was the leader of the Sadducees and, as such, was in continual conflict with the Pharisees, not only on religious matters but also on the political question of how far to collaborate with the Roman occupation, where the main difference between them was that the Sadducees were willing to co-operate *actively* with the Romans, even if this meant handing over troublemakers to them for execution. As an appointee of the Romans, the High Priest was not just a ceremonial official with jurisdiction over the Temple; he was, in effect, a chief of police with his own armed force, his own police tribunal which was concerned with political offences[3], and his own penal system, including prisons and arrangements for flogging offenders. In the case of capital offences, however, such as serious insurrection against the power of Rome, he would hand over the offender to the occupying Roman power rather than attempt to impose sentence himself. The situation can best be understood by comparison with occupied France during the Second World War.

It is thus incredible that a prominent Pharisee, or indeed any Pharisee, would enter into close association with the High Priest, as Saul is reported to have done, for the purpose of dragging off to the High Priest's prisons persons who had offended in the High Priest's eyes. This was police work, for the High Priest was no grand inquisitor, concerned with pursuing heresy (indeed, as a Sadducee, he was regarded by the majority of the Jewish nation as a heretic himself, and would have been the first to suffer if there had been an Inquisition among the Jews). The only reason why the High Priest could use force at all is that he had been provided with the means by the Romans for their own purposes; and, though the High Priests were not above using the machinery for their own benefit (the sources attest that they used police officers to collect the priestly tithes by force, though they were supposed to be voluntary), their main concern was to produce results required by their Roman masters.

Thus, if Jesus' movement had been a heretical one, espousing theological doctrines that contradicted the traditional tenets of Judaism, the High Priest would have been entirely unconcerned, being no theologian. If the movement had been opposed to the Pharisees in matters of religion, the High Priest would even have been pleased, for that was his position also. (As a matter of fact, the Gospels, in their anxiety to put heretical doctrines into Jesus' mouth, occasionally give him things to say that are Sadducean in character[4], and have evidently been taken from Sadducean polemics against the Pharisees, on the principle that any stick is good enough to beat a dog with.) The only circumstances under which the High Priest would employ his police force to arrest and imprison people would be if they had shown themselves in some way to be a political threat to the Roman regime. If Saul was employed by the High Priest to arrest people and imprison them, it can only mean one thing: that Saul was a member of the High Priest's police force and his job was to arrest anyone who constituted a threat to the occupation. The last person who would be employed by the High Priest in such a capacity would be a Pharisee: *ergo*, Saul was not a Pharisee.

This conclusion is so inescapable that even scholars who never envisage the possibility that Paul was not a Pharisee make admissions that bring them very near to it. Thus, Johannes Munck in his book on the Acts of the Apostles[5] says that, in view of the evidence that the Pharisees were friendly to the Nazarenes, it must be concluded that Saul was the *only* Pharisee who joined forces with the High Priest to persecute the movement: 'The only Pharisee in the service of the chief priests was Paul, who had left Gamaliel and become an ardent persecutor of the Christians before an even more radical switch made him an apostle of Jesus.' The argument has here turned full circle. Instead of Gamaliel, as traditional Christian interpretation has it, being the only Pharisee to support Jesus' movement (despite one triumph of persuasion which was not repeated), now we have Paul as the isolated Pharisee – though in traditional Christian interpretation Saul was only following a typical Pharisee pattern when he persecuted the Nazarenes. To be forced to turn the story on its head like this just shows that there is something radically wrong with the story as it stands; and to substitute one improbability for another – a uniquely persecuting Saul for a uniquely tolerant Gamaliel – is no solution. The only solution that makes perfect sense is that Saul was not a Pharisee, but persecuted the Christians for exactly the same reason that the High Priest persecuted them – because they were opposed to Roman

59

domination of the Holy Land. Otherwise, what possible motive could a Pharisee have to persecute a group of people whom the entire body of Pharisees, headed by their revered leader, regarded as pious Jews, whose belief in Jesus as Messiah might possibly be vindicated by time?

What kind of Jew, then, might have taken up this political police work in the service of the High Priest? The police force of the High Priest was no doubt a motley crew, consisting partly of junior priests with an allegiance to the Sadducee party or belonging to those few families from whom the High Priest was traditionally selected, combined with foreign mercenaries of various kinds, including Jews or even non-Jews, who were relatively indifferent to Jewish patriotism and were prepared to endure the unpopularity which was the inevitable lot of those wielding power in the interests of a hated military occupation.

Here we may turn, not for the last time, to the account of Saul's origins which was given by the Ebionites, the community of Jewish Christians, who regarded him as the perverter of Jesus' message and as the founder of a new religion which Jesus himself would have rejected. According to the Ebionites, Saul was not a Pharisee and not even a Jew by birth. His parents in Tarsus were Gentiles, and he himself had become a convert and had thereupon journeyed to the Holy Land, where he found employment in the service of the High Priest. This is a very different story from that found in the New Testament, which has Saul as a prominent Pharisee, not so much entering the service of the High Priest as deigning to enter into an alliance with him. The account given by the Ebionites has always been rejected contemptuously both by Christian writers and by modern scholars as mere scurrilous polemics, intended to denigrate Paul, and based on nothing but spite and hostility. But the Ebionites deserve more consideration than this. As we shall see when we come to examine the character and history of the Ebionite movement, it could claim the possession of authoritative traditions (see chapter 15).

The arguments advanced in the present chapter should induce us to abandon the traditional contempt for the Ebionite account of Saul's origins and give it serious consideration. That Saul was a Pharisee is rendered most unlikely both by his persecution of the Nazarenes and by his association with the High Priest. But a person of foreign, non-Jewish extraction is just the kind of person that could be expected to enter the service of the High Priest and engage in police activities which a native-born Jew, resentful of Roman hegemony and of the Sadducean quisling regime, would regard with hostility and scorn. It would be natural for Paul, writing to communities for whom he was an inspired figure, to attribute to himself a more glamorous origin than was in fact the case and to explain his phase of serving in the High Priest's police force as actuated by religious zeal rather than by humdrum motives of earning a living by whatever unsavoury means were open to an immigrant. The communities to whom Paul was writing were unaware of the politico-religious situation in Judaea, and might well think that the Pharisees and the early followers of Jesus were at odds, and so not find it implausible that Paul's early opposition to the movement was actuated by Pharisaism. This explanation, first advanced by Paul himself in his letters (in which he did not even reveal that he was born in Tarsus, but carefully fostered the impression, without actually saying so, that he was a native-born Judaean) was afterwards incorporated by Luke in the Acts of the Apostles.

But how can we even consider such a theory, when so many scholars have found incontrovertible evidence, as they think, of Paul's training as a Pharisee in his own writings? The style of argument and thought in the Epistles of Paul, we have been repeatedly told, is rabbinical; Paul, though putting forward views and arguments which 'go far beyond' rabbinical thinking, uses rabbinical logic and methods of biblical exegesis in such a way that his education as a Pharisee is manifest. Beloved as this view is of scholars, it is entirely wrong, being based on ignorance or misunderstanding of rabbinical exegesis and logic. It will be necessary, therefore, to prove this point, before going on to deal with other objections to the view that the Ebionite account of Paul is nearer to the truth than the New Testament account.

CHAPTER 7

ALLEGED RABBINICAL STYLE IN PAUL'S EPISTLES

The leading ideas of Paul's Epistles are far removed from Pharisaic Judaism, as will be argued in detail later. Here it is only necessary to mention that Paul's elevation of Jesus to divine status was, for the Pharisees and for other Jews too, a reversion to paganism. Judaism had steadfastly refused to attribute divine status even to its greatest prophet, Moses, whose human failings are emphasized in scripture. Judaism had encountered a succession of human-divine figures throughout its history, from the deified Pharaohs of Egypt to the deified emperors of Greece and Rome, and had always found such worship to be associated with oppression and slavery. The Jews regarded their own anointed kings as mere human beings, whose actions were closely scrutinized and, if need be, criticized; so that the elevation of a Messiah ('anointed one') to divine status aroused in them not only their scorn of idolatry, but also deep political feelings of outrage at the usurpation of a position of power beyond the normal processes of criticism and constitutional opposition. While the Jews looked forward to the coming of the Messiah, they did not think that he would be a divine figure and thus beyond criticism; on the contrary, the Messiah would be accompanied by a prophet, who, like Elijah, would not hesitate to reprimand the anointed king if he failed in his duties or if he ignored the words of Deuteronomy 'that his heart be not lifted up above his brethren' (Deuteronomy 17: 20).

Paul's use of the term 'Christ' (the Greek term for the Hebrew 'Messiah') as a divine title has thus no precedent in Judaism, and would be felt by any Jew to be a complete departure from Jewish thinking about the Messiah. Further, the idea of 'being in Christ', which occurs frequently in Paul's letters, is entirely without parallel in Jewish literature, whether of the Pharisees or of any other sects. It means a kind of unity with, or sinking of the individuality into, the divine personality of Jesus, and a sharing of his experience of crucifixion and resurrection. Apart from the implied elevation of Jesus to divine status, this concept involves a relationship to the Divine that is alien to Judaism, in which the autonomy of the individual human personality is respected and guaranteed. The idea of 'being in Christ', however, can be paralleled without difficulty in the mystery cults.

Even more shocking to Jewish religious susceptibilities is Paul's use of the term 'Lord' (Greek, *kurios*) as a title of the deified Jesus. This is the term used in the Greek translation of the Hebrew Bible, the Septuagint, to translate the tetragrammaton or holy name of God Almighty, Creator of Heaven and Earth. To apply the name *kurios* or Lord in its divine sense[1] to a human being who had recently lived and died on Earth would have seemed to any Pharisee or other Jew sheer blasphemy. However, to the recipients of Paul's letters, the use of the term 'Lord' for Jesus would not have seemed shocking at all, for this was the regular term for the deities of the mystery cults, those salvation gods with whom the devotees united their souls in communal dying and resurrection.

The religious outlook of Paul's letters was thus shocking to Jews, but familiar to non-Jewish members of the Hellenistic culture. Paul, though, must have known that, in applying such ideas to a person who had lived in a Jewish context, he was doing something new and shocking – indeed he explicitly says that he is aware of this.[2] This has not prevented some scholars from trying to solve the problem of Paul's adoption of utterly unJewish ideas by seeking a continuity between Judaism and Paul's ideas. We shall be considering such attempts later in this book. Even those scholars, however, who have admitted an unbridgeable gulf between Paul's ideas and Judaism have insisted, nevertheless, that Paul began his religious life as a Pharisee. They are then faced with the problem of how Paul, a trained and convinced Pharisee, was able to make such an extraordinary transition to ideas so far removed from Pharisaism. The solution is found in the nature of Paul's conversion on the road to Damascus: this was no gradual development, but a shattering revelation in which all previous ideas and doctrines were swept away; consequently, there is no need to find continuity between Paul's christology and his previous religious standpoint, which stood at an opposite pole.

Yet even this approach has to acknowledge that Paul, after his conversion, was still the same person as he was before and was not able to obliterate all traces of his upbringing and education. It is accordingly regarded as axiomatic that Paul's writings will show strong traces of this education: that Paul, though thinking quite differently from when he was a Pharisee, would have continued to use techniques of expression and argument characteristic of Pharisaism, and could not have done otherwise, any more than a person can obliterate his own fingerprints. Paul's letters, then, it is asserted, show unPharisaic ideas expressed in a Pharisaic style, a confirmation of the New Testament account of Paul's early life.

Though many authors confidently assert that Paul's Epistles are full of Pharisaic expressions and arguments, few authors have made a serious attempt to substantiate this by giving examples. When they do (e.g. Schoeps or Klausner) it is quite startling to see how unconvincing they are. In fact, it may safely be said that if people had not already been convinced that Paul was a Pharisee (because of his own claim, and that made for him in Acts), no one would have thought of calling him a Pharisee or a person of 'rabbinic' cast of mind simply from a study of the Epistles. Instead, he would have been regarded as a Hellenistic writer, deeply imbued with the Greek translation of the Bible, like Philo, but not familiar with the characteristic approach of the Pharisee rabbis.[3]

If we free ourselves from the assumption that Paul was a Pharisee, then we are not compelled to identify the style of Paul's Epistles with that of Pharisaism, and can allot them their due place in Hellenistic literature. The attempts by scholars, both Christian and Jewish, to find Pharisaic fingerprints in the Epistles can be dismissed as one of the vagaries of scholarship, which will always make the attempt to find in a text what is believed, for extraneous reasons, to be there, whether the text itself gives support to the enterprise or not.

Let us then examine some of the examples usually given, by those who bother to give examples at all, to show how Pharisaic Paul's mind was. We may begin with an example of exegetical logic that is fundamental to Pharisaic thought.

One of the most important tools of Pharisaic reasoning was what was known as the *qal va-homer* argument. This is known in Western culture as the argument *a fortiori*, but it plays a far less important role in Western thinking, based on the logic of Aristotle, than it does in the thinking of the Pharisees and the Talmud. The *qal va-homer* (literally, 'light and heavy') goes like this: if something is known about one thing which has a certain quality in a relatively 'light' form, then it must be true 'all the more so' of some other thing that has the same quality in a relatively 'heavy' form. A typical example is found in the Bible: where the Lord says to Moses, after Miriam has offended by her criticisms and has been punished with leprosy, and Moses prays that she may be healed: 'If her father had but spit in her face, should she not be ashamed seven days? Let her be shut out from the camp seven days, and after that let her be received in again' (Numbers 12: 14). This example is actually cited in the rabbinical writings as a paradigm for a reason that will prove important in our argument about Paul. The argument may be paraphrased as follows: if offending a father (a relatively light thing) is punished with banishment for seven days, offending God (a relatively heavy thing) should all the more receive such a punishment (and therefore Miriam should not be forgiven immediately). To give a more easily comprehensible example from modern life: if a person should not drive a car after drinking a given quantity of beer, then all the more should he not drive after drinking the same quantity of whiskey.

Now Paul, in his Epistles, is quite fond of using the *a fortiori* argument, and this has been regarded as incontrovertible proof of his Pharisee training, which gave him a taste for arguing in this way even when he was arguing for a doctrine of which the Pharisees would have disapproved strongly. Examples of Paul's use of the *qal va-homer* are the following:

> For if, when we were God's enemies, we were reconciled to him through the death of his Son, much more, now that we are reconciled, shall we be saved by his life. (Romans 5: 10)
> For if by the wrongdoing of that one man death established its reign, through a single sinner, much more shall those who receive in far greater measure God's grace, and his gift of righteousness, live and reign through the one man, Jesus Christ. (Romans 5: 17)
> For if their rejection has meant the reconciliation of the world, what will their acceptance mean? Nothing less than life from the dead! (Romans 11: 15)
> For if you were cut from your native wild olive and against all nature grafted into the cultivated olive, how much more readily will they, the natural olive branches, be grafted into their native stock! (Romans 11: 24)

Out of these four *qal va-homer* arguments in Romans, three are invalid arguments by the canons of Pharisee logic, for it is a basic principle of that logic that in a *qal va-homer* argument, the conclusion cannot validly go beyond what is contained in the premise. (This is known as the

65

principle of *dayo*.[4]) To explain this principle, we may return to our first example, the biblical argument used about Miriam. It would be invalid, in Pharisee logic, to argue as follows: if offending a father deserves seven days' banishment, then offending God deserves fourteen days' banishment. Such an argument has no precision about it, for how do we know how much to add to the data given in the premise in order to arrive at the conclusion? The only precise form of the argument is this: if offending a father deserves seven days' banishment, then all the more so does offending God deserve seven days' banishment. This is the form of the argument actually found in the Bible, as the Pharisees pointed out to support their analysis.

In the four arguments quoted from Romans above, only the fourth one conforms to the correct pattern of a *qal va-homer* argument, the others going far beyond the conclusion warranted by their premise. One must conclude that Paul had no idea of the conditions of validity of this type of argument; one correct argument out of four shows only a random success.

The *qal va-homer* argument is a form of analogy, and in Greek logic the analogy was never regarded as capable of logical form or precision. Consequently, Greek logic confined itself to what would nowadays be called 'set theory' and thereby developed the formalization of the syllogism. This is useful in science, where the concern is with classification, but not in human relationships, where the form of reasoning usually employed is analogy. The Pharisees, with their keen concern for the network of human relationships known as 'law', felt the need for a logic of analogy, and thus developed a legal logic based on a formalization of the *a fortiori* argument. The principle of *dayo* is the basic means by which formal precision was achieved, but this enabled them to go further, and consider what types of formal objection might be offered to a *qal va-homer* argument, and how such objections might be answered. This powerful instrument of legal logic is only now being appreciated by legal theorists and logicians in the Western world.

Hellenistic writers, on the other hand, often used *a fortiori* reasoning, but only in a loose, rhetorical way, without regard for precision or formal validity. This is just the way that Paul uses such arguments, and this stamps him as someone who has never received a Pharisee's training. A trained Pharisee could never forget his education to such an extent as to produce woolly, imprecise reasoning in a field where the Pharisees prided themselves on their precision – any more than a Greek logician, however far he strayed from the academy, would be found perpetrating an invalid syllogism. Paul's use of *a fortiori* arguments has often been cited to show that he was a Pharisee by education, but in fact this attempted proof rebounds on itself. Nothing could display more clearly Paul's lack of Pharisee scholarship than his use of the *a fortiori* argument, which he employs in a rhetorical style that can be paralleled from the popular Stoic preachers of the Hellenistic world, but not from the rabbis.

Let us turn now to Paul's use of alleged *midrash* or biblical exegesis to reinforce his arguments. An example often cited to show Paul's rabbinical style is the following: 'Christ bought us freedom from the curse of the law by becoming for our sake an accursed thing; for Scripture says, "A curse is on everyone who is hanged on a gibbet"' (Galatians 3: 13). Here Paul adduces a verse from Deuteronomy in order to explain how great the sacrifice of Jesus was: he voluntarily took upon himself a curse by the manner of his death so that mankind would be freed from the curse of sin.

It has been assumed by most scholars that Paul's interpretation of the verse in Deuteronomy (i.e. that anyone hanged on a gibbet is under a curse) was part of contemporary Pharisee exegesis of that verse, and that consequently Paul took his basis for argument from the Pharisee stock, though he developed it in his own way. This, however, is an error. The idea that anyone hanged on a gibbet is under a curse was entirely alien to Pharisee thought, and the Pharisee teachers did not interpret the verse in Deuteronomy in this way. Many highly respected members of the Pharisee movement were crucified by the Romans, just like Jesus, and, far from being regarded as under a curse because of the manner of their death, they were regarded as martyrs. The idea that an innocent man would incur a curse from God just because he had been unfortunate enough to die an agonizing death on the cross was never part of Pharisee thinking, and only a deep contempt for the Judaism of the Pharisees has led so many scholars to assume that it was. The Pharisees never thought that God was either stupid or unjust, and he would have to be both to put a curse on an innocent victim.

Even if the hanged person was guilty of a capital crime, he was not regarded as being under a curse, but, on the contrary, as having expiated his crime by undergoing execution.[5] The verse in question (Deuteronomy 21: 23) was interpreted by the rabbis as follows: an executed criminal's corpse was to be suspended on a pole for a short period, but the corpse must then be taken down and not left to hang overnight, for *to do this* would incur a curse from God; in other words, the curse was placed not on the executed person, but on the people responsible for subjecting the corpse to indignity. One interpretation was: it is cursing God, or blasphemy, to allow the corpse of an executed criminal to hang, for the human body was made in the image of God.[6] The New English Bible translates the verse, 'When a man is convicted of a capital offence and is put to death, you shall hang him on a gibbet; but his body shall not remain on the gibbet overnight; you shall bury it on the same day, for a hanged man is offensive in the sight of God.' This is in accordance with the Pharisee interpretation of the passage, which was a correct reflection of the meaning of the original Hebrew.

Paul's interpretation was thus not taken from any Pharisee source, but was his own personal reaction to the rather ambiguous translation given in the Greek Septuagint. Far from providing an example of Pharisee *midrash*, Paul shows himself in this passage in Galatians to be far removed from the spirit of the *midrashic* interpretations. Vague concepts, such as being under a posthumous curse because of the baleful magical effect of the manner of one's death, belong to paganism, not to Judaism, much less Pharisaic Judaism, which regarded the manner of one's life as the decisive means of obtaining the favour or incurring the displeasure of God, not the manner of one's death, especially when the latter was not under one's control. As for the idea that Jesus removed a curse from other people by taking a curse upon himself, this too is alien to Jewish thinking, but this, of course, belongs to Paul's central theology, not to his style of argument, and will be discussed in a later chapter.

Some passages in Paul's Epistles have been thought to be typically Pharisaic simply because their argument has a legalistic air. When these passages are critically examined, however, the superficiality of the legal colouring soon appears, and it is apparent that the use of illustrations from law is merely a vague, rhetorical device, without any real legal precision, such as is found in the Pharisaic writings even when the legal style is used for homiletic biblical exegesis. An example from Romans is the following:

> You cannot be unaware, my friends – I am speaking to those who have some knowledge of law – that a person is subject to the law so long as he is alive, and no longer. For example, a married woman is by law bound to her husband while he lives; but if her husband dies, she is discharged from the obligations of the marriage-law. If, therefore, in her husband's lifetime she consorts with another man, she will incur the charge of adultery; but if her husband dies she is free of the law, and she does not commit adultery by consorting with another man. So you, my friends, have died to the law by becoming identified with the body of Christ, and accordingly you have found another husband in him who rose from the dead, so that we may bear

fruit for God. While we lived on the level of our lower nature, the sinful passions evoked by the law worked in our bodies, to bear fruit for death. But now, having died to that which held us bound, we are discharged from the law, to serve God in a new way, the way of the spirit, in contrast to the old way, the way of a written code. (Romans 7: 1–6)

The above passage is remarkably muddle-headed. Paul is trying to compare the abrogation of the Torah and the advent of the new covenant of Christianity with a second marriage contracted by a widow. But he is unable to keep clear in his mind who it is that corresponds to the wife and who to the husband – or even who is supposed to have died, the husband or the wife. It seems that the correspondence intended is the following: the wife is the Church; the former husband is the Torah, and the new husband is Christ. Paul tells us that a wife is released by the death of her husband to marry a new husband; this should read, therefore, in the comparison, that the Church was freed, by the death of the Torah, to marry Christ. Instead, it is the wife-Church that dies ('you, my friends, have died to the law by becoming identified with the body of Christ') and there is even some play with the idea that the new husband, Christ, has died. The only term in the comparison that is not mentioned as having died is the Torah; yet this is the only thing that would make the comparison valid.

On the other hand, there is also present in the passage an entirely different idea: that a person becomes free of legal obligations after his or her *own* death. This indeed seems to be the theme first announced: 'that a person is subject to the law so long as he is alive, and no longer.' The theme of the widow being free to marry after the death of her first husband is quite incompatible with this; yet Paul confuses the two themes throughout – so much so that at one point he even seems to be talking about a widow and a husband who are free to marry each other and have acceptable children because *both widow and new husband are dead*. Confusion cannot be worse confounded than this.

Thus what we have here is a case of someone trying to construct a legal analogy and failing miserably because of his inability to think in the logical manner one expects of a legal expert. The passage thus does not prove that Paul had Pharisee training – just the contrary. What we can say, however, is that Paul is here *trying* to sound like a trained Pharisee. He announces in a somewhat portentous way that what he is going to say will be understood only by those who 'have some knowledge of law', and he is clearly intending to display legal expertise. It is only natural that Paul, having claimed so often to have been trained as a Pharisee, should occasionally attempt to play the part, especially when speaking or writing for people who would not be able to detect any shortcomings in his performance. In the event, he has produced a ludicrous travesty of Pharisee thinking. In the whole of Pharisee literature, there is nothing to parallel such an exhibition of lame reasoning.[7]

What Paul is saying, in a general way, is that death dissolves legal ties. Therefore, the death of Jesus and the symbolic death of members of the Church by identifying themselves with Jesus' sacrifice all contribute to a loosening of ties with the old covenant. This general theme is clear enough; it is only when Paul tries to work out a kind of legal conceit or parable, based on the law of marriage and remarriage, that he ties himself in knots. Thus he loses cogency just where a Pharisee training, if he had ever had one, would have asserted itself; once more, he is shown to have the rhetorical style of the Hellenistic preachers of popular Stoicism, not the terse logic of the rabbis.[8]

This brings us back to the most obvious thing about Paul's writings, from a stylistic viewpoint, that they are written in Greek. Obvious as it is, this fact often seems to be ignored by those labouring to prove that Paul wrote and thought like a rabbi. Paul's Greek is that of one who is a native speaker of the language. It is not, of course, classical Greek or even literary Greek, but the living spoken language (known as *koine*) of the time, in both vocabulary and rhythm. He is so naturally at home in the Hellenistic world that he even quotes Menander[9] at one point and a contemporary tragic poet at another.[10] No such writing exists from the pen of any rabbi of the Pharisee movement, so if Paul was a Pharisee, he was unique in this regard.

The question arises whether Paul even had sufficient grasp of the Hebrew language to have engaged in studies at a Pharisee academy. We know that he could speak Aramaic (Acts 21: 40), but this did not require any study on his part, for that language was spoken as the common vernacular in his home city of Tarsus, where Greek was the language of commerce and government. But Hebrew is a different matter. This was the language of scholarship, both in its classical form as found in the Hebrew Bible and in its neo-Hebrew form as found in the Mishnah. The study of the Bible in the original Hebrew was the basis for all Pharisee studies. A knowledge of the Hebrew of the Bible was relatively rare in Paul's time, as is shown by the existence of the Targum, the translation of the Bible into Aramaic that was made for the benefit of the ordinary Jews who could not understand the Bible in Hebrew.

The indications from Paul's writings are that he knew very little

Hebrew. His quotations from the Bible (which number about 160) are from the Greek translation, the Septuagint, not from the original Hebrew. This is shown by the fact that wherever the text of the Hebrew Bible differs from that of the Greek, Paul always quotes the text found in the Greek, not that found in the Hebrew. For example, there is the famous quotation (1 Corinthians 15: 55), 'O death, where is thy victory? O death where is thy sting?' This comes from the Septuagint of Hosea 13: 14, but the Hebrew text has a different reading: 'Oh for your plagues, O death! Oh for your sting, O grave!' It is most unlikely that any Pharisee would adopt a policy of quoting from the Septuagint rather than from the Hebrew Bible, which was regarded as the only truly canonical version by the Pharisee movement.[11]

Thus there is nothing in Paul's writings to prove that he was a Pharisee, and much to prove that he was not. Great play has been made with certain references to legendary material in Paul's letters; it is claimed that this must have come from a Pharisaic source, but in fact this material was widely known throughout the Jewish world including the Greek-speaking Jewish areas of the Diaspora, and proves nothing. For example, Paul refers at one point to a legend about the miraculous well that followed the Israelites in their wanderings in the wilderness (1 Corinthians 10: 4). But this legend was by no means confined to the Pharisaic movement, being found in the compilation known as *Biblical Antiquities* (or Pseudo-Philo) which is extant now only in a Latin translation, but is known to have existed in a Greek version in the first century.[12] Paul could quite easily have come across this legend in a Greek book or even more probably from common conversation with the unlearned, just as a child today may be acquainted with one of Aesop's fables without having studied the Greek classics.

We must conclude, therefore, that the allegedly profound Pharisaic style and atmosphere of Paul's writings is itself a legend.

CHAPTER 8

PAUL AND STEPHEN

The New Testament's portrayal of Paul as having had a thorough Pharisaic training before his conversion to Jesus is central to the New Testament picture of how Christianity began, for two main reasons: the portrayal of Paul as a persecuting Pharisee reinforces the picture of persecuting Pharisees in the Gospels; and the authority of Paul as the great interpreter of Jesus' role is much strengthened by the belief that he was an expert in traditional Jewish religion, who was able to see the continuity between the new covenant and the old, and to guarantee, by his own bridging of the gap, that his interpretation of Jesus provides the true fulfilment of Old Testament religion. If it were proved that Paul was, in fact, never a Pharisee at all, a great mainstay of the traditional view of Christian origins would be knocked away. We would have to think of Paul much more in the role of an innovator, who created a myth about Jesus that had no roots either in Judaism or the actual historical circumstances of Jesus' life and teachings.

We have reason to believe that Paul was not in fact a Pharisee: that his persecuting role in relation to Jesus' followers contradicts evidence that the Pharisees did not persecute that movement at all; that the continuation of the picture of persecuting Pharisees from the Gospels is built on sand, for the evidence in the Gospels and from other sources is that Jesus was himself a Pharisee and was never persecuted by the Pharisees; and that the alleged evidence in Paul's writings that he had a Pharisee training is mere self-deception on the part of scholars who have persuaded themselves into finding what they were looking for. In addition, the historical evidence from the book of Acts that when Paul persecuted Jesus' followers he was acting on behalf of the High Priest, who was a Sadducee and an opponent of the Pharisees, shows once more that Paul was not a Pharisee.

We have also seen (though this has still to be proved in more detail in

72

later chapters) that Jesus' movement, as it was before the advent of Paul, did not hold any doctrine that would have brought upon itself any persecution from the guardians of Jewish religion, the Pharisees. For Jesus himself had merely claimed to be the Messiah, and this claim was not in any way blasphemous; and his followers, after his death, had merely continued to believe in his Messiahship in the same way (having come to believe that he had been brought back to life by a miracle), but without regarding him as a deity.

The only Christian doctrines that would have been regarded as blasphemous by the Pharisees were those introduced by Paul some time after his conversion. Before the conversion of Paul, therefore, there can have been no clash between the Nazarenes and the Pharisees on religious grounds; though there may well have been conflict between the Nazarenes and the High Priest on political grounds, since the High Priest, the quisling guardian of Roman interests, would certainly have regarded with suspicion a movement which still declared Jesus, a crucified rebel, as their leader.

There is one episode recorded in the book of Acts, however, that seems to challenge all the conclusions summarized above. This is the story of the death of Stephen, the first Christian martyr. For here we have the story of a member of Jesus' movement who was put to death on religious grounds, *before* the conversion of Paul. Moreover, Stephen is represented as putting forward views that were strongly opposed to those of the Pharisees and have much in common with the views held by Paul after his conversion. The case of Stephen has thus been strongly urged by all those concerned to argue that Paul was *not* the originator of Christianity as we know it; that the deification of Jesus and the abrogation of the Torah were doctrines held by the Jesus movement before Paul came on the scene, and, indeed, that the case of Stephen shows that, despite all contrary arguments, these heretical doctrines go back to Jesus himself, Stephen being the link that connects Jesus to Paul. Moreover, the personal involvement of Paul in the execution of Stephen allegedly proves that Paul's opposition to Jesus' followers was on religious grounds, and reinforces the traditional view of Paul as a persecuting Pharisee.

A careful examination of the Stephen episode, however, reveals many unhistorical features, and shows how it has been built up by the author of Acts precisely for the purpose of providing a link between Paul and Jesus.

The story given in Acts is that Stephen was denounced to the Sanhedrin by a group of Jews who had been arguing unsuccessfully with him. The charge against him was that he had made 'blasphemous statements against Moses and against God'. We·are then told: 'They produced false witnesses who said, "This man is for ever saying things against this holy place and against the Law. For we have heard him say that Jesus of Nazareth will destroy this place and alter the customs handed down to us by Moses." ' Stephen is then allowed a statement, and makes a long one which is a recapitulation of Jewish history. This speech seems mostly innocuous, giving an account with which all Jews would agree. (Even his remark that though Solomon built a house for God, 'the Most High does not live in houses made by men', is perfectly orthodox, since it is just what Solomon himself said at the inauguration of the Temple, 1 Kings 8: 27.) At the end of his speech, however, Stephen launches into a diatribe against the Jewish people and their history, going far beyond the kind of self-criticism which Jews were in the habit of making. This diatribe amounts to a repudiation of the Jews as incorrigible enemies of God: 'How stubborn you are, heathen still at heart and deaf to the truth! You always fight against the Holy Spirit. Like fathers, like sons. Was there ever a prophet whom your father did not persecute? They killed those who foretold the coming of the Righteous One; and now you have betrayed him and murdered him, you who received the Law as God's angels gave it to you, and yet have not kept it.'

This speech, the account proceeds, infuriated his hearers. It has little bearing, however, on the charges outlined before, that Stephen had spoken against Moses, against the Temple and against the law. Nor does the ensuing episode in which Stephen has a vision of Jesus, whom he calls 'the Son of Man', standing at the right hand of God. This, it is alleged, was regarded as blasphemy by Stephen's hearers, who immediately rushed him out to be stoned, oblivious of the fact that the 'blasphemy' of seeing Jesus as the Son of Man at the right hand of God was not what he had been brought to trial for. Yet the 'witnesses' who had testified ('falsely', it is said, though apparently the author of Acts thinks that Stephen would have been right in saying such things) that Stephen spoke against Moses, the Temple and the law, change their role with great versatility and act as chief participants in the stoning of Stephen for quite a different charge, that of regarding Jesus as the 'Son of Man'.

This extraordinarily muddled account cannot be regarded as providing us with a reliable historical record of the death of Stephen or of his views. The Sanhedrin was a dignified body that had rules of procedure, and did not act like a lynch mob. It would not suddenly switch the charges against a defendant, or drag him out for execution without even pronouncing sentence or formulating what he had been found guilty of.

There is, however, one way in which we can throw some light on the events leading to Stephen's death, and that is by noting the numerous similarities between the trial and execution of Stephen, as described in Acts, and the trial and execution of Jesus, as described in the Gospels. Such a comparison brings out numerous points of similarity between the two 'trials', even including similarities of illogicality and muddle. So great is the general similarity that we must conclude that the 'trial' of Stephen is simply a double or repetition of the 'trial' of Jesus, and its puzzling features can be explained by reference to the fuller accounts of the earlier 'trial'; the motives for the invention of fictitious aspects are the same in both.

1 Stephen is accused of speaking against the Temple: '. . . we have heard him say that Jesus of Nazareth will destroy this place. . . .' The same charge was made against Jesus: 'Some stood up and gave false evidence against him to this effect: "We heard him say, 'I will pull down this temple, made with human hands, and in three days I will build another, not made with hands' " ' (Mark 14: 59).

As argued earlier (page 48), to declare an intention to pull down the Temple and rebuild it was regarded as natural and in character for someone claiming to be the Messiah. There was no blasphemy in making such a Messianic claim, for, in Jewish eyes, the Messiah was not a divine figure, but simply a human king, a descendant of King David, who would one day drive out the foreign invaders and restore the political independence of the Jewish people; though some thought that this deliverance would coincide with the era of world peace prophesied by Isaiah and other prophets. The Messiah would naturally build a new Temple, for the present Temple, built by the wicked King Herod, was not expected to last into Messianic times. For the majority of Jews, therefore, Jesus' promise to build a new Temple brought not outrage or shock, but hope; perhaps this man was indeed the promised Messiah, since he dared to talk in this vein.[1] The people who would have been annoyed, however, at Jesus' declaration were the reigning Temple hierarchy, who were collaborators with Rome, owed their appointments to the Roman occupying forces, and had undertaken to help stamp out Messianic movements which might threaten the Roman occupation of Judaea. Jesus' declaration that he would pull down and rebuild the Temple was part of his challenge to Rome and to

75

its priestly henchmen. Only the High Priest and his entourage would feel threatened by it. (The rank-and-file priests, despite their daily participation in the Temple rites, would not feel threatened, because they would expect to continue their role in the rebuilt Temple.) So this charge against Jesus was not a religious but a *political* charge – one which would stir the High Priest into action, but would not concern the Pharisees or any religious Jews who were not committed to collaborate with Rome.

Stephen is represented as repeating this threat of Jesus: '. . . we have heard him say that Jesus of Nazareth will destroy this place. . . .' It is a mistake to think that Stephen is here prophesying the destruction of the Temple by the Romans in AD 70. Christians, indeed, have always regarded this destruction as a punishment for the alleged Jewish betrayal of Jesus, and Stephen's words here have been misread as confirmation of this. But if this were so, Stephen would not have said that *Jesus* would destroy the Temple, but that God would destroy it as a punishment for the death of Jesus. The parallel between Stephen's words and the actual threat uttered by Jesus during his lifetime is the clue to Stephen's meaning. Stephen believed that Jesus' absence from the scene was only temporary. Soon he would come back and resume his mission, which was to drive out the Romans and assume his position as God's anointed, on the throne of David and Solomon. Stephen, by repeating in his preaching the threat that had cost Jesus his life, was renewing Jesus' challenge to the Roman occupation and to its supporters, the High Priest and his entourage.

2 The strange switch by which the original charge is forgotten and a new *ad hoc* charge substituted is exactly similar in the trial of Jesus and in that of Stephen. In Jesus' trial, we have the following:

> Then the High Priest stood up in his place and questioned Jesus: 'Have you no answer to the charges that these witnesses bring against you?' But he kept silence: he made no reply. Again the High Priest questioned him: 'Are you the Messiah, the Son of the Blessed One?' Jesus said, 'I am; and you will see the Son of Man seated at the right hand of God and coming with the clouds of heaven.' Then the High Priest tore his robes and said, 'Need we call further witnesses? You have heard the blasphemy. What is your opinion?' Their judgment was unanimous: that he was guilty and should be put to death. (Mark 14: 60–64)

In Stephen's trial, after the initial charge and Stephen's long, irrelevant reply, we find this:

> But Stephen, filled with the Holy Spirit, and gazing intently up to heaven,

saw the glory of God, and Jesus standing at God's right hand. 'Look,' he said, 'there is a rift in the sky; I can see the Son of Man standing at God's right hand!' At this they gave a great shout and stopped their ears. Then they made one rush at him and, flinging him out of the city, set about stoning him.

The pattern of both trials, then, is that the defendant is charged with the offence of speaking against the Temple, but this charge is forgotten when the defendant bursts out during the trial with what is regarded as a blasphemous statement. Formal procedures are then thrown to the winds and the defendant is found guilty of an alleged crime committed *during the trial itself*, and different from the crime for which he was brought to trial in the first instance. This travesty of legal procedure in a body like the Sanhedrin, famous for the dignity and formality of its legal procedures, is clearly fictional. This conclusion is reinforced by the consideration that the alleged blasphemy is not blasphemy in Jewish law at all. To claim to be the Messiah was simply to claim the throne of David, and involved no claim to be God. The title 'Son of God' also involved no blasphemy, as every Jew claimed to be a son of God when he prayed daily to God as 'Father'. The Davidic King, however, had a particular claim to this title, since God had made a special promise to regard Solomon and his successors as his 'sons' (II Samuel 7: 14): 'I will be his father, and he shall be my son. If he commit iniquity, I will chasten him with the rod of men, and with the stripes of the children of men.' Note that, so far from the title 'Son of God' bringing with it divine status, it made the Jewish king especially liable to divine punishment if he sinned. To claim to be 'the Son of Man' was also not blasphemy, since this was also a title of the Messiah (derived from Daniel 7: 13) and did not imply divinity. Neither 'coming with the clouds of heaven' nor 'sitting at the right hand of God' constituted blasphemy, since both these epithets were applied to the Messiah by Jewish tradition without entailing any doctrine of the Messiah's divinity (the *midrash* says that the Messiah will sit on God's right hand and Abraham on His left).

Moreover, the accounts of the trials of Jesus and Stephen before the Sanhedrin are quite inconsistent with the account given of the trial of Peter before the Sanhedrin (Acts 5), in which Peter was defended by Gamaliel, and an attitude of tolerance was shown towards the Messianic claims of Jesus and other Messianic claimants. Gamaliel was by no means an untypical Pharisee, being their chief represent-ative. Where, then, was Gamaliel at the alleged trials of Jesus and Stephen? Why should those 'trials' have been so different from the trial of Peter that unanimous hostility and intolerance was shown towards Jesus' Messianic claims, and Stephen's trial degenerated into a lynching? The trial of Peter is perfectly credible in the light of what we know of the Pharisees and of their thinking on the subject of Messianic movements, while the 'trials' of Jesus and of Stephen are incredible, because they depend on a definition of the terms 'Messiah', 'Son of God' and 'Son of Man' that did not exist in the Jewish religion of the time, but *did* exist in the later doctrines of the Christian Church, when all three expressions had been given a connotation of divinity.

We must conclude, therefore, that the trials of Jesus and of Stephen have been falsified in exactly the same way: namely, an originally *political* charge has been worked over in order to represent it as a religious charge of blasphemy. The facts in the case of Stephen appear to be that he roused the anger of the High Priest's entourage by outspoken declarations of the approaching fall of the Temple and its establishment, on the return of Jesus and his defeat of the Romans and their hangers-on. Since Stephen represented a threat to the quisling power of the High Priest, he was assassinated without a trial by henchmen of the High Priest; unlike Jesus, he was not handed over to the Romans for punishment. Stephen was thus the first martyr of the 'Church' in Jerusalem; but when the Pauline Christian Church took over the leading role, its Gentile leaders faced the same difficulties with Stephen as those which had led them to depoliticize the condemnation of Jesus and to remodel it as a trial for heresy and blasphemy. They could not demote Stephen from his honoured role as first martyr, but they changed the reasons for his martyrdom in order to disguise his anti-Roman motivation and make him into a victim of Jewish religious intolerance instead.

Stephen, therefore, cannot be regarded as a precursor of Paul in regarding Jesus as a divine figure with the authority to abolish the Torah. The Gospels and the book of Acts are concerned to argue that Paul was preceded in his doctrines by Stephen and indeed by Jesus himself; but close scrutiny shows that this is an illusion, and that Paul's doctrines were a new departure, radically different from the claims and teachings of Jesus and the 'Jerusalem Church'. We can now return to the consideration of Paul, with a full consciousness of the startling originality of his interpretation of the life and death of Jesus.

In the light of the above interpretation of the standpoint of Stephen, we may discern the probable meaning of the puzzling beginning of Acts 8, following immediately on the death of Stephen: 'This was the beginning of a time of violent persecution for the church in Jerusalem;

and all except the apostles were scattered over the country districts of Judaea and Samaria.' It is, of course, extremely puzzling that the body of Jesus' followers were persecuted and ejected from Jerusalem, yet their leaders were allowed to remain. One would have thought that the leaders, in such a persecution, would have been the first to be ejected. This verse, therefore, has been taken to provide evidence that the 'Jerusalem Church', at this time, contained two factions, the 'Judaizers' and the 'Hellenists'.[2] The 'Judaizers', on this theory, were led by James and Peter, who had turned away from the radical, heretical views of Jesus and had returned to allegiance to the Torah and traditional Judaism. The 'Hellenists', on the other hand, continued to hold the anti-Torah views which had brought Jesus to his death, and their leader was Stephen, who had thus incurred the wrath of strict adherents to Judaism. After Stephen's death, his followers of the 'Hellenistic' party suffered a persecution which forced them out of Jerusalem, but the 'Judaizers' who followed James and Peter were unaffected by this persecution.

The existence of such a party of 'Hellenists' depends entirely on this one verse, taken together with the earlier verses describing the complaint of the 'Hellenists' about the distribution to widows. The word 'Hellenists', however, does not connote any kind of unJewish religious faction, but refers only to the *language* primarily spoken by the members of the group. Jews who spoke Greek were not necessarily any less loyal to the Torah than Jews who spoke Hebrew or Aramaic, as the same chapter in Acts testifies, when it singles out the members of Greek-speaking synagogues as allegedly adopting a bigoted attitude towards Stephen. There is no real reason to suppose, therefore, that there was any 'Hellenistic' free-thinking group among the 'Jerusalem Church', beloved as this fiction is to commentators.

The real explanation of the immunity of the Apostles (and, presumably, their closest followers) from the persecution is probably this. Stephen was the leader of the activist section of the 'Jerusalem Church', which believed in continuing anti-Roman propaganda and Messianic activity even in the absence of Jesus. The Apostles, however, took a more quietist view: Jesus, they believed, was on the point of returning, but in the meantime they would wait quietly in hope and refrain from any political activity until they could engage in it by his personal direction. Consequently, when the activist members were ejected by the pro-Roman High Priest's party after the assassination of Stephen, the quietist section of the Nazarenes was left alone. It should be noted that belief in Jesus could actually lead to the *cessation* of

Messianic activity; for example, the Jewish Christians withheld their support from the Messianic revolt of Bar Kokhba[3], not because they were pacifists, but because Bar Kokhba was not Jesus and was, therefore, in their eyes the wrong Messiah.

We may now turn to consideration of the part played by Paul personally in the persecution of Stephen. We are told:

> The witnesses laid their coats at the feet of a young man named Saul. So they stoned Stephen, and as they did so, he called out, 'Lord Jesus, receive my spirit.' Then he fell on his knees and cried aloud, 'Lord, do not hold this sin against them,' and with that he died. And Saul was among those who approved of his murder. (Acts 7: 59–60)

Some scholars have thought that this passage smacks too much of literary artifice to be regarded as historically true. It introduces the character of Saul, later to prove the hero of the whole book of Acts, in a dramatic way, underlining the contrast between his personality before his conversion and after it. Though Paul, in his Epistles, expresses contrition for his earlier role as a persecutor of Jesus' movement, he never mentions that he had anything to do with the death of Stephen; in fact, he never mentions Stephen at all. It may be argued that the author of Acts, having given the death of Stephen such a prominent place as the first Christian martyr, could not resist the theatrical touch of introducing Saul into the scenario at this point. For if indeed Saul played a subordinate role in the Stephen affair in the manner described and if Paul himself never referred to the matter, it would be hard to see how the author of Acts could have obtained information about Saul's participation, and it would seem more likely that he invented it as a graphic addition to the story.

On the other hand, there is an aspect of the matter that has been overlooked. This is that Saul is in some ways excused for his role in the Stephen affair. It is said that he was only a 'youth' at the time (the Greek word *neanias* means an adolescent youth, and is somewhat inadequately rendered by the New English Bible translation 'young man'). This means that his responsibility is lessened; and this impression is reinforced by the way in which he is given no active role in the execution of Stephen. He does not throw any stones, but only looks after the coats of those who do. His participation is confined to 'approving' the killing of Stephen. It seems that the author of Acts cannot bear the idea that Saul might have had active responsibility for bloodshed and thus makes him more a passive spectator than a wholehearted participant.

This suggests that the somewhat unreal air of the story of Saul's participation arises from a watering down process, rather than from pure invention by the author of Acts. By turning Saul into a 'youth' and by making him the person at whose feet the witnesses laid their cloaks, the narrator has made the presence of Saul seem peripheral and almost accidental – a kind of symbolic coincidence, fraught with ironic meaning in view of Saul's future. But according to the Ebionite account, Paul did not come to Judaea from Tarsus until he was a grown man. This is also partly confirmed by the narrative of Acts, which, without any apparent interval, presents us with Saul 'harrying the church' and 'seizing men and women, and sending them to prison', hardly the activities of a tender youth. So the likelihood is that Saul, being already a full member of the High Priest's police force, played a prominent part in the Stephen affair, not the peripheral role given him by the author of Acts. The death of Stephen, as argued above, was not a judicial sentence, but an assassination carried out by the henchmen of the High Priest, a police force consisting of heterogeneous elements and not characterized by any elevated ideology or nice scruples. It is not surprising that, later in his life, Paul, having transformed his persecution of the Nazarenes into an ideological affair motivated by Pharisaic zeal, suppressed the worst aspect of this phase of his career, his prominent role in the elimination of Stephen as a dangerous anti-Roman agitator.

It is worthy of note too that the persecutors of Stephen are never called Pharisees in the narrative of Acts; nor is Saul himself at this stage of the story identified as a Pharisee. It is only in the light of the later identification of Saul as a Pharisee that generations of readers have assumed that Saul's participation in the murder of Stephen and his harrying of the Nazarenes arose from Pharisaic zeal. The author of Acts is evidently working, in the early chapters of his story, from sources that have not yet identified Saul as a Pharisee; though Paul's own assertions to this effect in his letters have coloured the later chapters of Acts.

We have arrived, then, at a picture of Saul that is quite different from the fire-breathing Pharisee fanatic of tradition. How, then, did Saul, the police mercenary in the service of the Sadducean High Priest, a man of doubtful antecedents and few ideals, come to be converted to Jesus' movement, engage in controversy with its leading figures, and eventually transform it into a new religion which Jesus himself would have regarded with consternation?

PART II

PAUL

CHAPTER 9

THE ROAD TO DAMASCUS

We are now in a position to consider the meaning of the great event which was the beginning of the Christian religion: the conversion of Paul on the road to Damascus. It was through this event that Jesus' movement changed from being a variety of Judaism into a new religion with a theology and myth distinct from those of Judaism. This outcome was not immediate, even in the mind of Paul himself. But it was the Damascus event that provided the germ of all the later developments.

Paul (at this stage, still called Saul) was on his way to Damascus on a mission described as follows: 'He went to the High Priest and applied for letters to the synagogues at Damascus authorizing him to arrest anyone he found, men or women, who followed the new way, and bring them to Jerusalem' (Acts 9: 2). This account presents several problems. The High Priest had no authority over synagogues as such, for his jurisdiction in Jewish law extended only over the Temple in Jerusalem. The synagogues, which were set up for prayer and study wherever there was a population of Jews, both inside and outside the Holy Land, did not form part of the Temple organization, but were under lay supervision and authority, as they are to this day. The priests or *kohanim* (the descendants of Aaron) were given certain honours in the synagogue service, such as being called up first to the reading of the law and pronouncing the priest's blessing on festival days, but they had no role of leadership in the synagogue community. The lay administrators of the synagogue were elected by its members, and the spiritual guidance of the community was in the hands of a rabbi, at this time not a paid office. The High Priest, therefore, had no right to send his officers into the synagogues to arrest people whose activities he disapproved of.

Nevertheless, within Judaea the High Priest was able to do this, not

85

by religious right, but simply by virtue of the power assigned to him by the Roman occupying forces. It was as chief of police, not as a figure of religious standing, that the High Priest was able to send officers such as Saul into synagogues to arrest members of Jesus' movement and haul them off to prison. As we have seen, he did this, not because he disapproved of their theology, but because he regarded them as a menace to the Roman occupation.

Outside Judaea, however, the High Priest had no such police authority, and it is therefore difficult to understand how any 'letters' he might give to Saul 'authorizing him to arrest' followers of Jesus would have any validity. The difficulty is all the greater in that Damascus at this time was not even under Roman rule, having been ceded by Caligula (AD 37). It belonged to the independent Arab kingdom of Nabataea, under the rule of King Aretas IV (9 BC–AD 40). This King, who was jealous of his independence, would hardly take kindly to the entry into his territory of an emissary of the Roman-ruled area of Judaea for the purpose of arresting and dragging away citizens or even aliens who were under his protection.

It seems, then, that the details of Saul's allotted task in Damascus need to be amended. It cannot be that he had letters from the High Priest authorizing him to arrest indiscriminately members of Jesus' movement in Damascus. On the contrary, it was precisely in order to escape from the jurisdiction of the High Priest and of the Romans that Jesus' followers had left Judaea and gone to Damascus. Saul must have been on a clandestine mission to kidnap certain leading Nazarenes and bring them back to Judaea for imprisonment or for handing over to the Roman authorities. As we have seen, one wing of Jesus' movement, of which Stephen had been a leader, was adopting an activist line against the Roman occupation, and had been forced into exile (while the quietist wing, which was waiting for the triumphant return of Jesus himself, was allowed to remain unmolested). No doubt some activists still remained in Judaea underground, and were receiving help and advice from their comrades in Damascus, who were proving a thorn in the flesh of the High Priest. Saul, the trusted police officer of the High Priest, was therefore sent with a band of mercenaries to put an end to this menace by illegally entering Damascus and carrying off the ringleaders of subversion.

An echo of this has survived in later Christian literature. In the pseudo-Clementine *Recognitions* (i. 70 ff.), a work known to contain some material taken from Jewish Christian literature, we are told that when Saul travelled to Damascus it was with the intention of arresting no other than Peter, who had fled there after a persecution involving the near-murder of James. While this account cannot be reconciled with the statement of Acts that the leading apostles were not being molested at this time, it may well be a garbled version of genuine historical fact, which was that leading members of Stephen's faction were in Damascus, and Saul was in pursuit of them.

An interesting confirmation of this version of events can be found in Paul's own writings. In II Corinthians 11: 32–3, he writes: 'When I was in Damascus, the commissioner of King Aretas kept the city under observation so as to have me arrested; and I was let down in a basket, through a window in the wall, and so escaped his clutches.' This refers to the period after Paul had entered Damascus, having been struck blind by his vision of Jesus, cured by Ananias and become a public advocate of Jesus. But the account of the same event in Acts presents a surprising contrast:

> But Saul grew more and more forceful, and silenced the Jews of Damascus with his cogent proofs that Jesus was the Messiah. As the days mounted up, the Jews hatched a plot against his life; but their plans became known to Saul. They kept watch on the city gates day and night so that they might murder him; but his converts took him one night and let him down by the wall, lowering him in a basket. (Acts 9: 22–5)

Paul's version is, of course, much closer to the actual events (Paul was writing his letters from about AD 55 to about AD 60, while Acts was not written until about AD 90). And Paul tells us that the reason why he had to steal secretly away from Damascus was that the police chief of King Aretas was seeking to arrest him. In Acts, however, it is said that Paul's life was threatened by the Jewish residents of Damascus, who objected to Paul's advocacy of the Messiahship of Jesus. This is a most instructive contrast. It is a perfect example of how the shift, found throughout the Gospels and Acts, from a political to a religious account of events results in vilification of the Jews as the villains of the story.

If it was the 'commissioner of King Aretas' who was seeking to arrest Paul, and not the Jews, Paul must have been thought guilty of some political offence. Some scholars have tried to argue that the commissioner was acting on behalf of the Jews; but there was no reason for the Nabataean chief of police to concern himself with religious disputes among the Jewish residents of Damascus. Much more likely is that he had discovered that Paul was himself a police agent of the High Priest of Jerusalem and that he was in Damascus on a mission that constituted an infringement of Nabataean sovereignty. The situation must have been quite a common one in Damascus, which was a refuge for political dissidents fleeing areas under Roman authority. The fact that Paul had given up the mission on which he had been sent would not have been believed by the commissioner, who would regard Paul's conversion merely as a front for an undercover agent. The commissioner would therefore have acted promptly on information received about Paul's status, and Paul had to beat a hasty retreat from Damascus to avoid arrest.

The Jews of Damascus would not have had anything against Paul just because he had been converted to the belief that Jesus was the Messiah. Paul, at this early period of his conversion, had not yet formulated his new and heretical views about the divine status of Jesus and the abrogation of the Torah, so he would be regarded as simply another follower of Jesus; and the Nazarenes in Damascus would be regarded with sympathy by all Jews as a patriotic party working for the liberation of the Jewish homeland. There would be no Jews in Damascus who would sympathize with the collaborationist views of the High Priest, for there would be no pro-Roman party among Jews living in a city that had been removed from Roman rule.

The book of Acts, however, having transformed Saul from a police agent into a fanatical Pharisee, has to represent his mission to Damascus as religious, not political, and consequently, when Saul becomes converted to Jesus' movement, the Jews of Damascus become the cruel, intolerant Pharisees who oppose him, just as in the Gospels the Pharisees are set up as the opponents of Jesus. The clear evidence of tampering with the facts, shown by the changing of the story from Paul's account of what happened to that given in Acts, should alert us to a similar process wherever the Jews are portrayed as persecutors.

We may now return to the experience of Paul near Damascus that changed his life and that of the Western world. There are three accounts of this event in the book of Acts (in chapters 9, 22 and 26), and there are some curious inconsistencies between the three accounts; also there is a fourth account in the first chapter of Galatians, written by Paul himself, that raises problems of its own. We may begin with the first account (Acts 9: 1–31):

> While he was still on the road and nearing Damascus, suddenly a light flashed from the sky all around him. He fell to the ground and heard a voice saying, 'Saul, Saul, why do you persecute me?' 'Tell me, Lord,' he said, 'who you are.' The voice answered, 'I am Jesus, whom you are persecuting. But get up and go into the city, and you will be told what you have to do.' Meanwhile the men who were travelling with him stood speechless; they

heard the voice and could see no one. Saul got up from the ground, but when he opened his eyes he could not see; so they led him by the hand and brought him into Damascus. He was blind for three days, and took no food or drink.

According to this account, Saul's vision is characterized by (a) its suddenness; (b) the presence of a great light; (c) the hearing of a voice declaring itself to be that of Jesus; (d) an instruction to go into the city for further information; and (e) the onset of temporary blindness. Several of the details are contradicted in the other accounts: thus, in chapter 22, we are told that the men with Saul did *not* hear the voice, though they saw the light; and in chapter 26, we are told that Jesus made a much longer speech, telling Saul that he was appointing him on a mission to the Gentiles.

According to the account quoted above, Jesus gave no details of the mission he had in mind for Saul, but told him that he would be further informed in Damascus, where he was indeed visited by Ananias, who cured his blindness, converted him to Jesus' movement by baptism and also (presumably, though this is not said explicitly) informed him of his mission to the Gentiles. Ananias in chapter 9 is a Christian, but in chapter 22 he is a pious Jewish observer of the law, and it is not explained why as such and being 'well spoken of by all the Jews of that place' he then urges Saul to be baptized. (If Ananias can combine being a follower of Jesus with Jewish piety and friendliness with all the other Jews, why does Saul's conversion to Christianity bring upon him the enmity of the Jews of Damascus?)

Despite the above inconsistencies in the narrative, which are somewhat surprising in the course of a single book by a single author, it is possible to piece together an intelligible account of Saul's experience. He had a sudden overwhelming attack, in which he saw a flashing light and fell to the ground and heard a voice which convinced him of the presence of Jesus. He did not, apparently, see the face and form of Jesus, but only the bright light. When the experience was over, he got up from the ground and found that he was blind. The content of the experience was vague: he did not yet know how it was to affect his future life, but only that the Jesus whose followers he had been persecuting had appeared to him in supernatural guise and reproached him, and that this meant that he, Saul, had been chosen for a great role.

Some commentators have tried to assign a physical cause to Saul's experience, such as epilepsy. Such explanations really explain nothing. Much more to the point is to investigate the psychological conditions for such a sudden conversion experience, and here the work of William James and other investigators is of value. They have shown that the background to such an experience is the 'divided self'. It is when a sensitive person is struggling, against great difficulties, to achieve psychical unity that there may occur a unification experience of startling suddenness, after which the individual is able to embark on a new life with purpose and energy.

Paul's own statement of his spiritual dilemma is one of the classic portrayals of psychological conflict:

> We know that the law is spiritual; but I am not: I am unspiritual, the purchased slave of sin. I do not even acknowledge my own actions as mine, for what I do is not what I want to do, but what I detest. But if what I do is against my will, it means that I agree with the law and hold it to be admirable. But as things are, it is no longer I who perform the action, but sin that lodges in me. For I know that nothing good lodges in me – in my unspiritual nature, I mean – for though the will to do good is there, the deed is not. The good which I want to do, I fail to do; but what I do is the wrong which is against my will; and if what I do is against my will, clearly it is no longer I who am the agent, but sin that has its lodging in me.
>
> I discover this principle, then: that when I want to do the right, only the wrong is within my reach. In my inmost self I delight in the law of God, but I perceive that there is in my bodily members a different law, fighting against the law that my reason approves and making me a prisoner under the law that is in my members, the law of sin. Miserable creature that I am, who is there to rescue me out of this body doomed to death? God alone, through Jesus Christ our Lord! Thanks be to God! In a word, then, I myself, subject to God's law as a rational being, am yet, in my unspiritual nature, a slave to the law of sin.
>
> The conclusion of the matter is this: there is no condemnation for those who are united with Christ Jesus, because in Christ Jesus the life-giving law of the Spirit has set you free from the law of sin and death. What the law could never do, because our lower nature robbed it of all potency, God has done: by sending his own Son. . . . (Romans 7: 14–8: 1)

Many Christian commentators, especially of the German school, have asserted that the religious dilemma outlined here by Paul is typical of Pharisaism, and thus reveals him as the archetypal Pharisee before his conversion. For, according to these commentators, the Pharisees were guilt-ridden, under the burden of the Torah, with its many complicated laws and were obsessed with the fear that they might have failed to observe the law in its entirety. Paul thus (according to this theory) saw Jesus as the solution to his anxiety-ridden state as a Pharisee: instead of having to strive with nagging consciousness of failure to fulfil a law which human nature was too degraded to obey, he could now rely, not on his own puny efforts, but on the initiative of God, who had sent His Son to take away the moral burden from mankind. Actually (though some of the writers of this school have failed to recognize this), there is no criticism of the Torah itself, or even of the rabbinical additions to it, in this passage: Paul is saying that the demands of the Torah are just, but that human nature is unable to comply with those demands because of the weakness of the flesh; and therefore, the Torah is no help to mankind in its moral dilemma, since it only serves to make clear its moral inadequacy, for which only the grace of God can compensate.

More recent scholarship, however, has completely refuted the view of a gloomy, guilt-ridden Pharisaism, constantly in fear of damnation for having omitted the observance of some petty law. For there is no such sense of inevitable human failure to live up to the demands of the law; and on the other hand, in Pharisaism, there is the constant possibility of repentance and forgiveness, if any sin or error is committed. The emphasis, in Pharisaism, is just the opposite of that found in the above passage of Paul: that the demands of the law are reasonable and not beyond the power of human nature to fulfil; and this is merely the continuation of the emphasis of the Hebrew Bible itself, which says:

> For this commandment which I command thee this day, it is not too hard for thee, neither is it far off. It is not in heaven, that thou shouldest say: 'Who shall go up for us to heaven, and bring it unto us, and make us to hear it, that we may do it?' . . . But the word is very nigh unto thee, in thy mouth, and in thy heart, that thou mayest do it. (Deuteronomy 30: 11–14)

If, however, human nature being admittedly frail, temptation is too strong and a sin is committed, Pharisaism stresses the availability of God's forgiveness through repentance and reparation; so that there is no sense of unbearable strain because *every* commandment has to be perfectly obeyed, as appears to be the case with Paul, both here and (more explicitly) in Galatians 3: 10–12. On the contrary, Pharisaism everywhere stresses the concept that the Torah may be fulfilled on various levels, according to the state of spiritual advancement of the individual: thus there are the minimum requirements for ordinary people, but also the 'measure of saintliness' (*middat hasidim*) for those who wish to acquire supererogatory virtue, though no one is blamed for not proceeding to such a level – and may even be blamed for seeking it prematurely.

Further, the psychological dualism found in Paul's statement is most uncharacteristic of Pharisaism. The dichotomy, in Paul's thinking,

91

between the flesh and the spirit, in which evils proceed from the flesh, which can be redeemed only by an inpouring of spirit from above, reflects a view of human nature that issued in the Christian doctrine of original sin. This doctrine is radically opposed to the Pharisaic concept of the essential unity of human nature. In Pharisaic thinking, there is indeed a conflict in the human psyche between two formations or inclinations, the 'good inclination' (*yetzer ha-tov*) and the 'evil inclination' (*yetzer ha-r'a*); but neither of these inclinations is identified with the flesh or body and both of them are regarded as equally human. In this struggle between good and evil tendencies, the human being is regarded as having the initiative in his own hands, and not to require supernatural help. The instruction to be found in the Torah, however, is regarded as the greatest aid towards the victory of the good inclination; but, again, this instruction can be gained only by initiative on the part of the human being, who has to set himself to the task of studying the Torah and applying it to his life. The very effort involved in this essential process of education and study is regarded as efficacious against the power of the evil inclination. Thus, the application of energy and effort to the moral life is of the essence of Pharisaism, and nothing could be more alien to it than a moral despair which declares that human effort is useless and the only remedy lies in the grace exercised by God. Yet this moral despair is precisely the attitude powerfully described in Paul's account of his own dilemma.

Furthermore, in Pharisaic thinking, the moral struggle is directed not so much to the obliteration of the evil inclination as to its sublimation and redirection. It is recognized that the selfish energies of the evil inclination are essential to the vitality of the psyche and of the community, so that we find such expressions as the following (Midrash Rabbah on Ecclesiastes 3: 11):

> Nehemiah, the son of Rabbi Samuel ben Nahman, said: 'And behold, it was very good' (Genesis 1: 31) – this alludes to the creation of man and the Good Inclination, but the addition of the word 'very' alludes to the Evil Inclination. Is, then, the Evil Inclination 'very good'? It is in truth to teach you that were it not for the Evil Inclination, nobody would build a house, marry and beget children, and thus Solomon says, 'That it is a man's rivalry with his neighbour' (Ecclesiastes 4: 4).

In other words, the impulse of aggression and rivalry provides the psychic energy for all action, and though the good inclination is engaged in building up a spirit of co-operation, it cannot do so by suppressing the selfish instincts but only by making use of them.

Thus the Pharisaic psychology of morality by no means sinks into an easy optimism about human nature, but declares morality to be a continual struggle; yet its theory not only unifies the psyche by giving it power over all its own processes, but also declares that the psyche becomes more and more unified as it progresses in the moral struggle.

At the opposite pole to this is Paul's picture of the moral struggle, in which he portrays the psyche as hopelessly divided and unable to progress without direct supernatural intervention. There is thus no confirmation to be found in this passage of Paul's alleged Pharisaism; on the contrary, he seems, on this evidence, to have been in a spiritual situation entirely different from that of Pharisaism before his conversion to Jesus. If Paul was a Pharisee, he was a unique one. This is a result which we have reached in other contexts too – for example, in the context of Paul's alliance with the High Priest. When Paul repeatedly comes to appear so untypical as to be unique, it seems a more plausible hypothesis that he was not a Pharisee at all.

But if we look for a parallel to Paul's analysis of the human condition among the philosophies and creeds of the ancient world, it is not hard to find. In style, terminology and content, Paul's declaration can be paralleled in the writings of the Gnostics. This will be shown more fully in a later chapter, but at present it is relevant to point out that Paul's psychological dualism, here expressed, is clearly grounded in a metaphysical dualism. Paul is saying that there are two laws in the world: the law of the spirit (*pneuma*) and the law of the flesh (*sarx*). If there are two independent and conflicting laws (or systems of organization) in the universe, it is clearly implied that there are two opposing forces, that of the spirit and that of the flesh. This is the doctrine characteristic of Gnosticism. It is also a doctrine to which the Pharisaic rabbis were utterly opposed, as the form of idolatry (or denial of the unity of God) that was endemic in their era. Thus Paul's espousal of this philosophy shows him to be not only unPharisaic, but unJewish, for not only Pharisaism but every variety of Judaism opposed it.

Some recent writers[1] have proposed a different interpretation of the passage under discussion. Aware of the fact that a knowledge of Pharisaism does not bear out the German interpretation of the passage (as a diagnosis of the spiritual dilemma of the typical Pharisee), they argue that Paul is here not discussing his *own* spiritual situation (before conversion to Jesus) at all. Being a Pharisee (as they assume) he could not possibly be starting from such a dilemma, since Pharisees were too confident in the efficacy of their covenant with God, and grateful for the instruction given to them in the Torah, to find themselves in such an *impasse*. Moreover, as a Pharisee, Paul would surely be aware of the availability of God's forgiveness for any sins committed, through repentance and reparation; yet Paul makes no reference to this as a factor in the situation. Therefore, these writers urge (Stendhal, Gager, Gaston), what Paul is writing about here is the spiritual situation of a *Gentile*, who is aware of the saving grace of the Torah, but feels himself excluded from it. As Apostle to the Gentiles, Paul had special sympathy for Gentiles who had been awakened to a sense of guilt by acquaintance with the Jewish Torah, but had no means of appeasing this guilt; it was for them, and not for the Jews, that Jesus Christ had come to Earth and suffered, and it was through him that Gentiles could attain the same state of grace that, for Jews, could be attained through the Torah. Thus, according to this interpretation, Paul was not abrogating the Torah at all, but simply providing an alternative mode of salvation for Gentiles; the idea that salvation through Jesus Christ implied the abrogation of the Torah even for Jews was a later unfortunate aberration, caused by a misreading of Paul's writings.

The writers of this school all seem entirely unaware that Judaism already provided a way of salvation for Gentiles, and that therefore no Pharisee (as Paul is assumed to be in this argument) would feel pity for the exclusion of the Gentiles from salvation. There were two methods of salvation for Gentiles in Pharisee thinking: either by full conversion to Judaism, in which case the convert would become a full Jew and participate in the covenant with Israel; or by adherence to the Noahide Laws (see page 142) which constituted a covenant and a Torah for Gentiles as revealed by God to Noah, the patriarch of the Gentiles.[2]

In any case, this whole interpretation is a most unnatural reading of the passage in question, which has always been held, with great literary and psychological justification, to be a moving expression of Paul's own personal dilemma. The idea that when Paul says 'I' in this passage he is merely putting himself sympathetically into the place of the Gentiles is most unconvincing to anyone who reads with an ear for the resonances of the passage. It is true that Paul is not referring *only* to himself; he is universalizing his own situation, and giving a representation of the universal human plight, as he sees it, but with the special depth of feeling of one who has felt this plight in his own soul and for whom the normal distractions of life have proved ineffectual.

But the new reading of the passage has at least the merit that it directs our attention to the undoubted fact that it is an expression of the plight of the Gentiles in the face of a Torah which they despair of mastering. This indeed is a most valuable insight; but it needs to be supplemented by the further insight that Paul identifies himself so completely with the situation he describes that he cannot be regarded as a Pharisee empathizing with the Gentiles, but instead must be recognized as a Gentile himself, i.e. as a Gentile convert to Judaism who has failed in his quest and has entered into a state of despair from which only some psychological revolution can rescue him. The passage mirrors so perfectly the spiritual situation of one who has tried and failed to become a Jew that it can only be regarded as evidence (taken together with the other evidence presented in this book) that this was indeed Paul's situation. This throws light on those passages in Paul's letters in which Paul actually speaks of himself as a Gentile by the use of 'we' to comprehend both himself and the Gentiles. These passages have proved somewhat puzzling to commentators, who, however, have found the ready explanation that Paul's sympathy with the Gentiles has made him regard himself as one of them, despite his Pharisaic upbringing. (An example is Galatians 3: 14: '. . . that in Christ the blessing of Abraham might come upon the Gentiles, that we might receive the promise of the Spirit through faith.') A better explanation, in the light of the evidence presented in this book, is that Paul here, in the heat of his emotion, has forgotten his *persona* as Pharisee, and has lapsed into his real identity and motivation.

We may now turn back to Paul's revelation outside Damascus. The psychological conditions for such an experience are extreme turmoil of mind, induced by a sense of spiritual failure or disaster. Such a condition is likely to arise in a person who is torn between two different cultures, to one of which he is emotionally tied, while his ambitions and highest aspirations are centred on the other. This is the situation of a convert; and Paul's Damascus experience becomes psychologically and sociologically understandable as soon as we think of him as a recent convert to Judaism, instead of as a Pharisee. There is thus the strongest similarity between Paul's mental condition and that of his greatest follower in the later Church, Saint Augustine, who also struggled painfully against a pagan background and found his rest, after a mental explosion, in the same kind of synthesis, and in a sense of deep affinity with the ideas of Paul.

If we follow, then, the Ebionite account of Paul as a convert to Judaism, we may trace the biographical events that led to the road to Damascus.

On becoming converted to Judaism, he adopted the Hebrew name Saul, which was the name of the ill-fated King of Israel who came from the tribe of Benjamin. It was probably for this reason that Paul later invented for himself a genealogical descent from the tribe of Benjamin (Romans 11: 1; Philippians 3: 5). As it happens, it was impossible for any Jew at this time to describe himself truthfully as of the tribe of Benjamin. While it is true that part of the tribe of Benjamin survived in Palestine after the deportation of the Ten Tribes by Shalmaneser of Assyria, the Benjaminites later intermarried with the tribe of Judah to such an extent that they lost their separate identity and all became Judahites or Jews. Only the Levites, the priestly tribe, and that section of the Levites called the *kohanim* or priests (the descendants of Aaron) retained their identity because they needed to do so for cultic reasons. All other Jews were simply known as Israelites for cultic purposes (e.g. for entry into the various areas of the Temple, consumption or non-consumption of the *terumah* or priestly food) and no distinction was made for any religious purpose between Judahites or Benjaminites, so that there was no motive for preserving the distinction. Consequently, when Paul described himself as 'of the tribe of Benjamin', this was sheer bluff, though the recipients of his letters, being Gentile converts to Christianity, were in no position to know this.[3]

What was Saul's name before he became converted to Judaism? It was probably some Greek name, such as Solon, that sounded something like Saul, or at least had the same initial letter. His original Gentile name was certainly not Paul, for this name was adopted by him for the first time later in his career as a Christian.[4]

According to the Ebionites, Saul's parents were Gentiles who had not been converted to Judaism; Saul himself, then, was the first of his family to be converted. Nevertheless, it is quite possible that Saul's parents were semi-converts of the type known as 'God-fearers'; i.e Gentiles who were attracted to Judaism and believed in its main tenets, but did not wish to take the drastic step of full conversion to Judaism, which involved circumcision, in the case of males, and adoption of Jewish nationality. 'God-fearers' were given a respected status in Pharisaic theory, and were regarded as having attained salvation even without conversion to full Judaism, since such full conversion was regarded as more a matter of vocation than of necessity. But it was quite a common pattern for the child of 'God-fearing' parents to proceed to full conversion, and it may well be that Saul was conforming to this pattern. Even as the son of 'God-fearing' parents, however, Saul would have been exposed in his early childhood to pagan influences far more than a fully Jewish boy. In Tarsus, his education would have been with pagan children, and his imagination would have been impressed by the beautiful pagan ceremonies of mourning and joy associated with the death and resurrection of certain pagan gods worshipped in Tarsus.

In Acts 23, we find mention of Paul's 'sister's son' who lived in Jerusalem and acted as Paul's messenger to the Roman commandant. This has been taken to be confirmation of Paul's claim in his letters that his family were native-born inhabitants of Jerusalem, and we thus often find in the writings of scholars references to 'Paul's married sister, who lived in Jerusalem'. However, the fact that Paul had a nephew in Jerusalem does not prove that his sister and her husband lived there too. It is more likely that Paul's nephew, following his example, had left Tarsus and had come to Jerusalem, either as a convert or as a 'God-fearer'. As a matter of fact, if Paul did have a whole constellation of relatives in Jerusalem, it is surprising that none of them is mentioned, apart from his nephew, as taking any interest, positive or negative, in his career.

What was the status of Paul's parents? It is often thought that they must have been wealthy, but this is not necessarily the case. Paul was an artisan by trade, and this is hardly consistent with being the son of wealthy parents. Paul's trade has been traditionally identified as that of a tent-maker; but more accurate scholarship has shown that the Greek word involved really means 'leather-worker'.[5] It has been asserted that Paul's engagement in this rather humble trade is not inconsistent with wealthy parenthood, since it was the practice of Pharisee rabbis to engage in such trades in order to preserve their independence and avoid making their living out of their knowledge of the Torah. Since Paul, on the argument of this book, was not at any time a Pharisee rabbi, the point is irrelevant; and, in any case, those Pharisee rabbis who had large independent incomes did not engage in such trades. The rabbinical injunction sometimes adduced that a father should 'teach his son a trade' is also not relevant, since this again applied only to those who could not provide their sons with an independent income.

On the other hand, there is evidence, taken to be incontrovertible, that Paul's father was a wealthy man: this is that he was both a Roman citizen and a citizen of Tarsus. Undoubtedly, Paul is represented as claiming that not only he, but his father too, were Roman citizens (Acts 22: 28). But we shall find reason later to show that this was not the case; the mistake is probably that of Luke, the author of Acts. Paul acquired his Roman citizenship, not by birth, but by special circumstances when he was an adult (see page 161). As for Paul's claim to be a citizen of Tarsus, this is not very definite. He says at one point, 'I am a Jew, a Tarsian from Cilicia, a citizen of no mean city.' At another point, he merely calls himself 'a native of Tarsus in Cilicia'. It may be that he was speaking loosely (or represented as speaking loosely) when he called himself a 'citizen of no mean city', meaning by 'citizen' merely 'city-dweller' rather than in the technical sense of one who was formally a citizen. If, in fact, Paul was a full citizen of Tarsus, this would certainly mean that his father was one before him; and this would argue a certain degree of wealth, since full citizenship was granted only to people of some wealth and prominence. It would also, incidentally, make it unlikely that Paul's father was a Jew, since membership in the citizen body of a Greek *polis* involved membership of a native *phyla* or tribe and participation in pagan worship.

We conclude then that Paul's father was possibly a Tarsian citizen, though not a Roman citizen, and that, even if moderately well off, he was not wealthy enough to provide his son with an independent income. The young Saul, therefore, knew that he had to make his way by his own skill and wits.

Even though Saul, after his conversion to Judaism and emigration from Tarsus to Judaea, never actually became a Pharisee rabbi, the mere fact that he felt a strong urge in later life to represent himself as having been one must be significant. It means that at some point in his life this had been his dream. If his parents were indeed 'God-fearers', they must have told him in his youth about the famous Pharisees of Judaea, who occupied the apex of Jewish religious learning and piety, and were almost legendary figures to the Jews and 'God-fearers' of the Diaspora. The young Saul would have heard the names of the greatest Pharisee leaders, Hillel, Shammai and Gamaliel. Perhaps even in Tarsus, he may have seen one or two of the noted Pharisee figures of his day, for many of the sages were travellers, who briefly visited Jewish communities in both the Roman and Parthian Empires, in order to preach and deliver messages from the central authorities of Pharisaism in Jerusalem. The young Saul, planning to be a full convert, would be impelled by his naturally ambitious nature to see himself as no ordinary convert, but as progressing so well in his studies and piety as to become a great Pharisee leader himself. This was not unheard of, for some converts to Judaism had indeed reached such eminence: there was, for example, Onkelos the Proselyte, whose translation of the Pentateuch into Aramaic became a standard work in the Pharisaic movement. It was even taught among the Pharisees that one of the biblical prophets, Obadiah, was a proselyte, for which reason the name Obadiah was often adopted by proselytes to replace their pagan names.

Unfortunately, young Saul's dream was doomed to disappointment. The fact that we find him, some time after his arrival in Judaea, employed as a police official in the pay of the Sadducean High Priest shows that his plans had gone awry. We may surmise that he made an abortive attempt to rise in the Pharisee movement; that he enrolled with some Pharisee teacher for a while (though not with Rabban Gamaliel, who accepted only advanced students), but proved a failure. His Epistles show him to be eloquent and imaginative, but lacking in logical ability; and this would have been an insurmountable obstacle in a Pharisee academy. Moreover, his educational base was too feeble; he had too much to learn to be able to shine and, being a person of soaring ambition (as his subsequent career shows), he would not be able to endure mediocrity. He broke off his studies and in desperation took whatever job he could obtain. Instead of his dream of respected status as a rabbi, the reality was ignominy as a member of the High Priest's band of armed thugs.

CHAPTER 10

DAMASCUS AND AFTER

We have seen, then, in Saul's background and present circumstances all the ingredients for extreme mental turmoil and near breakdown. Not only is his mind torn between the pagan background of Tarsus and the Judaic religious outlook, but his personal ambitions have been cruelly frustrated and he is suffering from a shock to his self-esteem. In his vivid imagination, the sacred history of the Hebrew Bible (in its Greek translation, the Septuagint) with its heroes and prophets jostles with memories of the sacred processions of the mystery god Baal-Taraz, the dying and resurrected deity who gave Tarsus its name. The prestige of Pharisaic Judaism, which excited his aspirations, has proved so elusive and disappointing that his mind searches for some way of escape from the demands of Judaism; and the consolations of the mystery religion of his youthful environment with its colourful and moving ceremonies of mourning and rejoicing beckon to him with a promise of relief from his misery, but, at the same time, arouse in him the fear of apostasy, regression and the abandonment of his hopes.

In such circumstances of conflict and disappointment, many individuals would have suffered mental collapse. Some individuals, however, of great gifts and psychical resources can meet the situation by a sudden psychological leap, an overwhelming synthesis or multiple insight that unites all the disparate elements of conflict into a single solution. Such a solution is apt to take the form of a vision, welling from the unconscious mind without apparent ratiocination or conscious effort, and so having for the person involved a supernatural quality.

Saul's vision on the road to Damascus, shattering and painful as it was, solved all his conflicts and raised him from the abyss of self-hatred and failure. By it, he was able to reconcile all the conflicting needs of his complex nature. The panorama of Jewish sacred history was combined with the individual salvation and consolation of pagan mystery religion; the divide in his own soul was answered by a divide in the universe, similar to that found in the dualism of Gnosticism; and, finally, from the personal point of view, his desire for a surpassing role for himself was satisfied in a way far beyond his previous ambitions.

Saul had just been taking part in the sordid persecution of Jesus' followers by the politically motivated High Priest. He had now been give a task of surreptitious violence; to kidnap certain persons from Damascus and convey them to the High Priest's custody for condemnation as plotters of sedition against the Roman occupation of Judaea. The fact that he had been entrusted with this mission, and made the leader of the band of kidnappers, shows that Saul was regarded with some favour by the High Priest. Yet Saul must have regarded his promotion in the secret police with a mixture of feelings: how different from the kind of promotion he had pictured for himself when he came to Judaea as a hopeful convert.

This conflict of feelings was exacerbated by the nature of the movement which he had been deputed to investigate and persecute. For at the centre of the beliefs of this movement was a figure who had died and had been resurrected. When Saul, in the course of his duties of arrest and interrogation, probed into the belief of Jesus' followers in the resurrection of Jesus, he must have felt a shock of recognition from his pagan background. Here again, where he least expected it, was the figure who had moved him as a child, despite the warnings of his 'God-fearing' parents: the dying and resurrected deity, who was always the same under all his names and guises, whether Attis, Adonis, Osiris or Baal-Taraz. Bound up with the worship of this ubiquitous deity was a deeply emotional experience: that of dying and being reborn together with the deity, as his *agon* was enacted in dramatic and ecstatic ceremonies.

Because of his pagan background, Saul would have read into the story of the death and resurrection of Jesus meanings which were in fact absent from the minds of the Nazarenes themselves, for these followers of Jesus were people of Pharisee background on the whole and indeed still regarded themselves as Pharisees, and, therefore, as utterly opposed to pagan schemes of salvation based on dying and resurrected deities. Their belief in the resurrection of Jesus was conceived within the patterns of Jewish thought; that is to say, they thought of it as a miracle wrought by God, but did not think of Jesus himself as anything other than human. No doubt they read some sacrificial meanings into the event, for the idea of vicarious suffering by saints on behalf of a sinful community was not alien to Judaism, being found in the Bible in

101

the story of Moses, for example, or in the figure of the suffering servant of Isaiah. But the idea of the sacrifice of a *deity* was utterly alien to every variety of Judaism. Jesus, to his early followers, was not a deity, but a Messiah: i.e. a human king of the House of David, whose mission was to liberate Israel from foreign rule and the world from the sway of military empires. That instead of succeeding in this he had met with crucifixion was interpreted by them to mean that the sins of Israel had not been sufficiently expiated by the campaign of repentance which Jesus had conducted among 'the lost sheep of the house of Israel', and that therefore Jesus himself had had to fill up the measure of expiation by undergoing a cruel death, preparatory to his miraculous resurrection as a triumphant conqueror. But his return to Earth as a resurrected figure would not change his status as a human king, any more than the resurrection of Lazarus raised the latter above human status.

To Saul, however, the idea of Jesus as a sacrificial figure would have had resonances that were quite different. The personal and individual significance of the death of the god in the mystery cults would have been aroused in him, especially in his highly individualized plight; whereas, for the Nazarenes in general, the significance of the death and resurrection of Jesus was more of communal than individual or personal significance, presaging the coming of the restoration of the Jewish commonwealth and the universal Messianic age on Earth. The mystery cults had arisen in a Greco-Roman environment in which national loyalties had been crushed by the vast machine of a bureaucratic empire; consequently, detribalized individuals had sought individual salvation in them, hoping for an individual immortality by dying and rising with the deity. Among the Jews, this disintegration of community feeling had not occurred; to them, salvation still meant the salvation of the community and of all mankind in an earthly kingdom of God, not an escape into an otherworldly disembodied state.

While persecuting Jesus' followers, Saul would have become aware of Jesus as a figure that seemed strangely familiar to him, answering a need in his soul suppressed since his childhood by the rationality and conscious verities of Judaism. In particular, his strong imagination would have been captured by the picture of Jesus dying on the cross. For this picture would have reminded him irresistibly of the ikons he had seen in Cilicia of the god Attis in his various guises – the hanged god, whose dripping, flayed body fertilized the fields and whose mysteries renewed the souls of his frenzied devotees. It is significant that, in later times, the imagination of Paul played round the Deuteronomic passage discussed above about the curse (as Paul understood it) adhering to the body of the hanged one.

At this time, however, these thoughts had not yet broken into full consciousness. Saul was attempting to live an unspiritual life, that of a secular police officer, his hopes of attaining spiritual stature in the Pharisaic movement having been disappointed. But the disquiet of his soul could not be stilled; and when his distress erupted into a psychological seizure on the road to Damascus, the centre of the disturbance was occupied by the figure which had been forming in his unconscious mind – that of the Hanged God, the focus of both guilt and hope. By identifying this figure with Jesus, whose followers he had been persecuting, Saul made sense out of the meaninglessness into which his life had degenerated. For instead of being merely a hireling of the quisling High Priest, harrying people for pay, he now saw himself as a historically significant person – he who had persecuted the dying and resurrected god and who, by his very guilt, could switch to the antithetical role of the god's chief acolyte. This sudden change from utter sinfulness to utter release and sinlessness became the motif of the new religion which he began to develop from the vision which had marked him out from all mankind.

We may now turn to an examination of the account which Paul himself gives of the crisis of his life, his vision of Jesus and the mission resulting from it:

> You have heard what my manner of life was when I was still a practising Jew: how savagely I persecuted the church of God, and tried to destroy it; and how in the practice of our national religion I was outstripping many of my Jewish contemporaries in my boundless devotion to the traditions of my ancestors. But then in his good pleasure God, who had set me apart from birth and called me through his grace, chose to reveal his Son to me and through me, in order that I might proclaim him among the Gentiles. When that happened, without consulting any human being, without going up to Jerusalem to see those who were apostles before me, I went off at once to Arabia, and afterwards returned to Damascus. (Galatians 1: 10–17)

Paul introduces this account in the following way: 'I must make it clear to you, my friends, that the gospel you heard me preach is no human invention. I did not take it over from any man; no man taught it me; I received it through a revelation of Jesus Christ.' It is clear from this that it is wrong to talk about the experience of Paul on the road to Damascus as a 'conversion', as is usually done. The use of this term presupposes something that ought not to be presupposed: that Christianity already existed before Paul had this experience, and that therefore all that was required was that Paul should be 'converted' to this already existing religion. The correct designation of Paul's experience is the word he uses himself: 'revelation'. In fact, Christianity, as a religion separate from Judaism, stems from this event. Paul's vision of Jesus was the epiphany or divine appearance which initiated Christianity, just as the appearance of God in the burning bush initiated Judaism. Just as Moses was marked out by the revelation of the burning bush as the founding prophet of Judaism, so Paul by his Damascus vision became the founding prophet of Christianity.

Paul, throughout his Epistles, insists on referring to 'my gospel' or, as here, 'the gospel announced by me' (translated above, in the New English Bible translation as 'the gospel you heard me preach', which is inexact and misleading, in that it makes Paul sound more modest than he was). Paul is thus claiming a direct line to Jesus – not only because of his Damascus revelation, but also because of other revelations subsequent to it. Paul is claiming a much higher authority than that of the Jerusalem apostles, Peter, James and John; for their claim derived from acquaintance with the earthly Jesus, while Paul's claim derived from acquaintance with the heavenly Jesus, now divorced from all weakness of the flesh and assuming the omniscience of a transcendent deity.

The leaders of the 'Jerusalem Church' (as will be argued in full in a later chapter) did not regard themselves as the founders of a new religion. They regarded themselves as Jews, who were differentiated from their fellow Jews only by their belief in Jesus as Messiah. They confidently believed that when the resurrected Jesus returned to Earth, which they expected to happen very soon, God would perform through his agency such astounding miracles – the defeat of the Romans by supernatural means and their expulsion from the Holy Land – that all Jews would accept him as the Messiah, and would be united under his royal rule in a theocracy governed by the prescriptions of the Torah of Moses, as interpreted by the Oral Law, administered by the Pharisee masters. They did not envisage any split between Jesus' movement and the main body of Jewish believers. They themselves observed the Jewish laws and prayed in the same words as their fellow Jews, with the addition of certain prayers (such as the Lord's Prayer) which were added to the normal services in the way that special groups among the Jews (for example, the Hasidim) have always done without any sense of schism. The Jerusalem Jesus movement did *not* observe the special service known as the Eucharist, Communion or Mass that marked off Christianity as a separate religion eventually (see next chapter).

Paul was the very first to envisage Christianity as a new religion, different from Judaism. In order to do this, he asserted his own claim to special authority through his series of visions of the heavenly Jesus Christ (as he called him, for the first time using 'Christ' as a divine title), beginning with his Damascus vision. In the passage quoted above, it will be seen how he insists on his independence of the Jerusalem authorities. He says that, after his Damascus revelation, 'without consulting any human being, without going up to Jerusalem to see those who were apostles before me, I went off at once to Arabia, and afterwards returned to Damascus.' By this statement Paul is rejecting the idea that he was a convert to Christianity. A convert is a person who humbly approaches the authorities of the religion which he wishes to join and submits himself for instruction. Paul denies such a description of his entry altogether: he does not seek instruction either in Damascus or in Jerusalem; instead he goes off 'to Arabia'. The impression conveyed by the latter information is to reinforce the analogy between Paul and Moses. Just as Moses, on receiving the tablets of the law, stayed in the Arabian wilderness for forty days and forty nights (Exodus 34: 28), so Paul retired to the desert to assimilate and meditate on the new revelation before returning to impart it to mankind.

Of course, the story told in the Acts of the Apostles is very different. Here we are told that Paul did indeed seek instruction, first in Damascus and then in Jerusalem. In Damascus he is cured of his blindness (which Paul himself, in Galatians, does not mention) by Ananias, who then instructs him in his mission; and then Paul, after escaping from Damascus, goes immediately to Jerusalem, where he is introduced by Barnabas to the Apostles, and where he adopts an active but subordinate role in Jesus' movement. The picture given in Acts is thus indeed that of a convert, not of the founder of a new religion, but we have to consider the purpose and standpoint of the book of Acts, in order to understand the startling difference between its account and that of Paul himself in Galatians. The book of Acts, we must remind ourselves, was written about forty years *after* Paul's letter to the Galatians, and a great deal had happened to Jesus' movement in that time. It had turned into the Christian Church, which had adopted the ideas of Paul, but was concerned to derive these ideas from Jesus himself and therefore to deny Paul originality. Moreover, the Christian Church had adopted an account of the early Nazarenes in which there had been no rift between Paul and the Jerusalem Apostles: the myth now was that *all* the Apostles, including Peter and James, had believed, like Paul, in the divine Jesus and in his role as a divine sacrifice for the sins of mankind – in other words, in the mystery religion doctrine for which, in historical fact, Paul alone had been responsible. In order to preserve the doctrine of the essential unity of the early Church (and thus its unbroken continuity with Jesus himself, which would have been seriously jeopardized by any acknowledgement of Paul's originality and his break with the Jerusalem Apostles, who provided the real link with the historical Jesus), Paul had to be represented as just one of the Apostles, indeed the latest and least authoritative of them, who had learnt his Christianity from James and Peter, even though he was given a special role as 'apostle to the Gentiles'. The book of Acts and indeed the Gospels themselves were composed (or rather edited from previous materials) in order to consolidate this myth of the unity of the early Church and to derive from Jesus himself the ideas of the later Church, which in fact were based on those of Paul. The utter originality of Paul and his status as the founder of Christianity have thus been obscured; even though Paul is the hero and central character of the book of Acts, his real status and role in the foundation of Christianity are played down and transformed in that work. The rift between Paul and the Jerusalem Apostles is indeed not entirely absent from Acts: it has been edited and disguised, but it is still there, as we shall see later. But the main aim is to achieve an appearance of continuity.

If, however, we read Paul's own account of his revelation at Damascus without any presuppositions in our minds derived from the much later account in Acts, we can begin to appreciate what enormous claims Paul was making. We have already seen one instance in which the New English Bible translation has played down Paul's claims, but in another phrase, this translation plays them down even more. For where the New English Bible has 'God . . . chose to reveal his Son to me and through me' (Galatians 1: 16), what the Greek actually says is '. . . to reveal his Son in me', as the Revised Version says. Paul is saying, quite straightforwardly, that he is himself the incarnation of the Son of God. He is thus claiming to have even higher status in his new religion than was claimed for Moses in Judaism. It may be replied that Paul is here only claiming for himself what, in his view, is possible for every Christian: an identification and merging with the personality of Jesus as divine saviour; Christ, it may be said, is 'in' every Christian, just as every Christian is 'in' Christ. Even so, Paul is claiming to be the first person in whom this miraculous merging has taken place. His 'revelation' is thus more even than a revelation: it is a transformation and a deification of Paul himself as the supreme manifestation of the phenomenon of impregnation by God. Other Christians may be able to partake of this state, having been shown the way by Paul, just as other

Buddhists may find Nirvana, having been shown the way by the Buddha; but Paul, like Buddha, remains pre-eminent and quasi-divine.

Further confirmation of Paul's sense of his own uniqueness can be found in his letters. Thus, he claims that he has supreme mystical experience, quite apart from his Damascus revelation: that he was 'caught up into the third heaven', and that he was 'caught up into paradise and heard words so secret that human lips may not repeat them' (II Corinthians 12: 2–3). Even more important for an understanding of Paul's view of his own status is his claim to have special marks or stigmata on his body, showing the depth of his self-identification with the sufferings of Jesus on the cross (see Galatians 6: 17). This phenomenon became common among ecstatic Christians in the Middle Ages, starting with Saint Francis, and has been much studied by psychologists. In the early Church, however, only Paul is known to have experienced such a physical manifestation. There are remarkable parallels, however, in other forms of ancient mystery religion. The devotees of Attis, for example, at the height of their ecstasy, castrated themselves in order to experience the same *agon* as their god, and so sink their individuality in his and become 'in' him. Thus the stigmata of Paul, whether self-inflicted or psychosomatically produced, made him, in his own eyes and those of his followers, the supreme embodiment of the power of the mystery god, the Lord Jesus Christ.

Here we must note the parallel between Paul and other mystagogues of the period, who also sought to found a new religion, based on their own embodiment of a divine power. Simon Magus is a good example. He is mentioned in Acts as having started a movement among the Samaritans, claiming to be 'that power of God which is called "The Great Power" '. That Paul and Simon Magus were regarded widely as similar figures is shown by the fact that in certain anti-Pauline documents, Paul is referred to under the code-name 'Simon Magus'. This brings home to us that the picture of Paul found in the book of Acts as merely one of the Apostles, with no claim to a special doctrine of his own or to outstanding pre-eminence as the possessor of divine, mystical power, is untrue to the way in which Paul, as a historical fact, presented himself.

Yet we must not forget the aspect that differentiated Paul from all the other mystagogues of the time and ensured that his religion, unlike theirs, was not forgotten. This was Paul's determination to connect his new religion to Judaism and thus give it an historical basis going back in time to the beginning of the world – rather than basing it solely on his own personality. This was the feature that gave Paul's religion substance and impressiveness in the eyes of the Greco-Roman world, so that his followers felt themselves to be carried along in the sweep of cosmic history – though again, Paul was not unique in this harnessing of the Jewish Bible to his purposes, for this had been done by some of the Gnostic sects, particularly the Sethians, as we shall see.

Paul's feeling for the Jewish Bible, which he had absorbed in its Greek translation and had studied avidly during his phase of ambition of Pharisaic eminence, can be seen even in the account quoted above of his Damascus revelation. Not only does he refer obliquely to Moses, as we have seen, but there is also a plain identification of himself with the prophet Jeremiah. He says, '. . . God, who had set me apart from birth and called me through his grace, chose to reveal his Son to me and through me. . . . ' Once more, the New English Bible has blurred the matter by its search for modern English idioms, rather than literal representation of the original. The literal translation, as in the Revised Version, is '. . . God, who separated me from my mother's womb . . .', and this immediately recalls the summons to prophecy of Jeremiah: 'Before I formed thee in the belly I knew thee; and before thou camest forth out of the womb I sanctified thee, and I ordained thee a prophet unto the nations' (Jeremiah 1: 5). Paul, too, declared himself to have a mission to the nations, but he wished this mission to have biblical sanction, and he therefore described himself in terms derived from the biblical prophet Jeremiah. In so far as Paul likens himself to Moses, he is thinking of himself as the founder of a new religion; but in so far as he likens himself to Jeremiah, he sees himself as the continuator of Judaism, even though his message is not for the Jews but for the whole world.

Thus Paul's Damascus revelation not only resolved the conflicts of a convert struggling to find his feet in the Jewish world by reinstating the pagan romanticism of his childhood; it also gave satisfaction to the yearnings of one who had regarded the Jewish tradition with awe and envy, and had sought to master it, only to meet with failure and rebuff. Paul fantasized a career as a successful Pharisee, which he had voluntarily renounced; this consoled him for his actual failure. But he also wove for himself a far greater fantasy: that his status was far above the Pharisees (none of whom claimed prophetic status), for in him the biblical gift of prophecy had been renewed; and that the whole panorama of biblical prophecy had existed merely to culminate in him, a greater prophet than Moses, and the initiator of the culminating phase of history, for which a new type of religion, transcending but containing that of the Bible, was required.

CHAPTER 11

PAUL AND THE
EUCHARIST

It may be urged, in accordance with received Christian doctrine, that the Eucharist was instituted by Jesus himself, and therefore constitutes evidence that Paul was not the originator of the mystery cult interpretation of the death of Jesus, but that this interpretation originated with Jesus.

The Eucharist signifies the mystical incorporation of the initiate into the godhead by eating the body and drinking the blood of Christ. Such a ceremony implies the deification of Jesus and is quite impossible to reconcile with a view of Jesus as merely a Messiah in the Jewish sense. Moreover, the Eucharist, as well as implying a doctrine of participation in the godhead, implies a doctrine of the sacrifice of Jesus as an atonement for mankind; the worshipper partakes of the body of the sacrificed Jesus much as the Jewish worshippers used to eat the Paschal lamb (to which Jesus is likened in 1 Corinthians 5: 7). Such a concept of the death of Jesus cannot be reconciled with any variety of Judaism, for it amounts to the reinstatement of human sacrifice, which for Judaism was anathema – indeed a large part of the Hebrew Bible constitutes a campaign against human sacrifice. The institution of animal sacrifice was understood to entail the complete supersession of human sacrifice; and the story of the *akedah* or Binding of Isaac in which God finally renounces human sacrifice in favour of animal sacrifice is the validating myth of this advance.

While it is true that the idea of vicarious atonement is not wholly alien to Judaism, as pointed out earlier, it is peripheral and forms no part of the main pattern of salvation. The story may be told in the *midrash* that Rabbi Judah's sufferings ensured good harvests (Genesis Rabbah 33), but this does not mean that the average Jew was encouraged to lay his burden of sin upon Rabbi Judah or other such figures and abandon his own individual struggle against the evil inclination by the guidance of the Torah. Even the story in the Bible about Moses's offer to sacrifice himself for the Israelites is a peripheral narrative device, heightening the character of Moses as a lover of Israel, rather than pointing a way to salvation. In any case, Moses's offer is immediately refused by God in terms that reinforce the usual pattern of individual responsibility: 'And the Lord said unto Moses, "Whosoever hath sinned against me, him will I blot out of my book" ' (Exodus 32: 33). The implication of the Eucharist that salvation is to be obtained through Jesus' death and the shedding of his blood is thus a radical departure from Judaism and a return to pagan concepts of atonement. If the Eucharist, then, was indeed instituted by Jesus, we would have to say that Jesus, not Paul, was the founder of Christianity.

Equally relevant is the fact that the Eucharist, as the basic sacrament of Christianity, marks it off from Judaism as a separate religion. If Jesus instituted the Eucharist, then he was founding a new religion thereby, if only in the institutional sense of providing a central ceremony not contained in Judaism and taking the place of the Jewish sacraments of the Temple or (in the absence of the Temple) of the Shema, the affirmation of the unity of God, which forms the central act of Jewish worship. The institution of the Lord's Prayer by Jesus, as pointed out before, did not constitute any such radical departure from Jewish practice, for it was quite usual for rabbis of the Pharisaic movement to compose some personal prayer, for the use of themselves and their immediate disciples, which would be used in addition to the normal prayers.[1] A number of such prayers have been preserved in the Talmud, and some of them have actually been incorporated into the Jewish Prayer Book and are used by all Jews today. It was only when the Lord's Prayer, after the death of Jesus, was made into a central feature of the daily service, instead of being added to the normal Jewish prayers, that it became a specifically Christian observance; for in itself, it contains nothing contrary to Judaism, and is indeed a characteristically Jewish prayer.

In the Gospels, certain familiar texts portray Jesus as founding the Eucharist. The earliest of these is in Mark: 'And as they did eat, Jesus took bread, and blessed, and brake it, and gave it to them, and said, "Take, eat: this is my body." And he took a cup, and when he had given thanks, he gave it to them: and they all drank of it. And he said unto them, "This is my blood of the new testament, which is shed for many" ' (Mark 14: 22–4). Matthew and Luke give the same account,

111

with some small variations. This account forms part of the story of the Last Supper. John, however, strangely enough, does not mention this incident in his account of the Last Supper, but instead attaches the Eucharistic idea to a quite different phase of Jesus' life, his preaching in Galilee in the Capernaum synagogue:

> Verily, verily, I say unto you, Except ye eat the flesh of the Son of man, and drink his blood, ye have no life in you. Whoso eateth my flesh, and drinketh my blood, hath eternal life; and I will raise him up at the last day. For my flesh is meat indeed, and my blood is drink indeed. He that eateth my flesh and drinketh my blood dwelleth in me, and I in him. As the living Father hath sent me, and I live by the Father: so he that eateth me, even he shall live by me. This is that bread which came down from heaven: not as your fathers did eat manna, and are dead: he that eateth of this bread shall live for ever. (John 6: 53–8)

In the Synoptic Gospels (Mark, Matthew and Luke), Jesus is represented as performing a ceremony (distributing bread and wine to his disciples), but not as instituting a rite to be observed by his followers in perpetuity. It is left to the reader to surmise that this story provides a historical or aetiological origin for the rite of the Eucharist as practised in the Christian Church. In John, on the other hand, Jesus does not even perform a ceremony: he merely expresses some ideas, dark and cryptic even to his disciples, some of whom are alienated by them (John 6: 66). Where, then, do we find the first expression of the notion that Jesus actually instituted the Eucharistic rite as a regular sacrament in the Christian Church?

The earliest assertion of this is to be found in Paul's Epistles, and this is indeed the earliest reference to the Eucharistic idea too, i.e. to the idea that there is salvific power in the body and blood of Jesus:

> For I have received of the Lord that which also I delivered unto you, that the Lord Jesus the same night in which he was betrayed took bread; and when he had given thanks, he brake it, and said, Take, eat: this is my body, which is broken for you: this do in remembrance of me. After the same manner also he took the cup, when he had supped, saying, This cup is the new testament in my blood: this do ye, as oft as ye drink it, in remembrance of me. For as often as ye eat this bread, and drink this cup, ye do shew the Lord's death till he come. Wherefore whosoever shall eat this bread, and drink this cup of the Lord, unworthily, shall be guilty of the body and blood of the Lord. But let a man examine himself, and so let him eat of that bread, and drink of that cup. For he that eateth and drinketh unworthily, eateth and drinketh damnation to himself, not discerning the Lord's body. For this cause many are weak and sickly among you, and many sleep. (1 Corinthians 11: 23–30)

From this passage, it is abundantly clear that *Paul himself was the inventor and creator of the Eucharist*, both as an idea and as a Church institution. For Paul says quite plainly that the Eucharist was founded on a revelation which he himself received: 'For I have received of the Lord that which also I delivered unto you.'

The fact that Paul says here that he received directly 'from the Lord' (i.e. by direct revelation from Jesus himself, in one of the many appearances which Paul claims occurred to him) the details of how Jesus instituted the Eucharist (or what Paul calls 'the Lord's Supper', verse 20), has been glossed over by scholars in a manner that might be considered extraordinary; but it is really quite understandable, for there is a great deal at stake here. To admit that Paul was the creator of the Eucharist would be to admit that Paul, not Jesus, was the founder of Christianity. It means that the central sacrament and mystery of Christianity, which marks it off as a separate religion from Judaism, was not instituted by Jesus. Nor are the ideas underlying this sacrament – the incorporation of the worshippers in the body of the divine Christ by a process of eating the god – part of Jesus' religious outlook: indeed, he would have found such ideas repugnant, though not unfamiliar, for they were a well-known aspect of paganism, especially in its mystery religion manifestations.

Even Christian scholars, however, have not been able to hide from themselves completely that Paul is here claiming to have received by revelation from Jesus personally how, at the Last Supper, Jesus gave instructions about the institution of the Eucharist. A typical comment is the following: 'Perhaps St Paul means that he received this information by revelation, though the preposition *apo* (from) rather suggests his having received it from the Lord through the elder apostles or other intermediaries' (Evans, *Corinthians*, Clarendon Bible, 1930). While allowing that it is possible that Paul is here claiming a revelation (though without admitting how momentous such an interpretation would be, or why it has to be fended off so desperately), this scholar takes refuge in a grammatical comment of little weight.[2]

We must accept, then, that Paul is saying here that he knows about Jesus' words at the Last Supper by direct revelation, not by any information received from the Jerusalem Apostles, some of whom were actually at the Last Supper. It would obviously be absurd for Paul to ascribe to an exclusive revelation of his own an institution already well known in the Church since the days of Jesus himself. This explains the otherwise inexplicable fact that, as we shall see, the Eucharist was not observed by the 'Jerusalem Church' at all, but only by those

113

churches that had come under the influence of Paul. For if Jesus himself had instituted the Eucharist, one would expect it to be observed, above all, by those who were actually present at the Last Supper – unless they had unaccountably forgotten Jesus' words, and needed to be reminded of them through a special revelation given to Paul.

The Gospels, of course, do assert that the Eucharist was instituted by Jesus – or, at least, that as an institution it was based on something that Jesus did and said at the Last Supper. But we must remind ourselves, once more, that the Gospels were all written after Paul's Epistles, and were all influenced by Paul's ideas. Of course, there is much in the Gospels that is not derived from Paul, especially in relation to Jesus' earthly life, in which Paul did not take much interest. But here is one alleged incident in Jesus' life about which, for once, there is a close correspondence between something in Paul's Epistles and the account of the Gospels. It is significant that this one incident concerns an institution so central for the Christian Church, which had a strong motive to ascribe its institution to Jesus, since otherwise it would have to admit that Jesus had no intention of founding a new religion at all. We are forced to the conclusion that the source from which the Gospels derive their account of the Last Supper, in its Eucharistic aspects, is, in fact, Paul's account of his revelation on the matter in Corinthians.

The Gospels, in general, have other sources for their accounts of Jesus' last days. But the Gospel-writers, being members of a Church in which the Eucharist was already centrally important, and having no other source for the institution of the Eucharist than Paul's account, had to turn away from their usual sources and draw on Paul directly in order to write into the story something corresponding to what Paul alleged to have seen in his vision of the Last Supper. This explains the numerous verbal correspondences between the accounts given in the Synoptic Gospels and Paul's words in Corinthians. These cannot be a coincidence, but must mean that the Gospel authors had Paul's words before them as they wrote (they cannot be from a common source, since Paul says explicitly that he did not have them from any source but by personal revelation).

Though the Synoptic Gospels follow the outline of Paul's account closely, they do not go as far as Paul in ascribing to Jesus the actual institution of the Eucharistic rite; instead they portray Jesus as performing a ceremony which was afterwards made the basis of the Eucharistic rite. The absence of the whole incident in their other sources must have embarrassed the Synoptic writers to the extent that they inserted only a pared down version of Paul's visionary incident.

The author of John, on the other hand, omitted the incident altogether from his account of the Last Supper. This was certainly not because he was indifferent to the Eucharist, for, in another context, he gives a much longer and more impassioned version of its theory than is found in any of the Synoptic Gospels, making it essential to the attainment of eternal life, and evidently regarding it as a mystery of incorporation with the divine just as in the mystery cults. His omission of the topic from the Last Supper must mean that he was unacquainted with the Epistle of Paul in which the topic was attached to the Last Supper for the first time. Nevertheless, as a member of a Church in which the practice of the Eucharist was regarded as essential for salvation (though unaware that this doctrine came from Paul), he included a long defence of the institution as part of Jesus' preaching. Thus all the Gospels provide some kind of basis in Jesus' life for the Eucharistic rite of which Jesus, in historical fact, knew nothing.

John shows himself well aware of the shocking character of the Eucharistic idea in Jewish eyes when he portrays even the disciples as offended by it, and some of them as so alienated that 'they walked no more with him'. What John is describing here is not the shock felt by Jewish hearers of Jesus (for Jesus never expressed any Eucharistic ideas) but the shock felt by hearers of Paul when he grafted on to the practice of Christianity a rite so redolent of paganism, involving a notion of incorporation of the godhead by a procedure with strong overtones of cannibalism.

This is not to say, of course, that Jesus did not distribute bread and wine to his disciples at the Last Supper. This was quite normal at a Jewish meal, whether at festival time or not. The leading person at the table would make a blessing (blessing is the original meaning of the word 'eucharist') and then break the loaf of bread and pass a piece to everyone at the table. Then at the end of the meal, grace would be said over a cup of wine, which would be handed round at the end of grace. (This cup of wine of grace seems to be what is referred to in the Synoptic accounts and in 1 Corinthians, rather than the *kiddush* wine of sabbath and festivals, which *preceded* the bread.) This procedure, which is still practised today at Jewish tables, has no mystical significance; the only meaning of it is to thank God for the meal He has provided. The addition of mystery religion trappings (i.e. the bread as the body of the god, and the wine as his blood) was the work of Paul, by which he turned an ordinary Jewish meal into a pagan sacrament. Since the blood even of an animal was forbidden at a Jewish meal by biblical law (Leviticus 7: 26), the idea of regarding the wine as blood would be

115

found disgusting by Jews. Here again, Paul seems to be deliberately removing himself from the Jewish ethos and canons of taste, and aligning himself with the world of paganism.

It is worthy of note that the term Paul uses for the Eucharist is 'the Lord's Supper' (Greek *kuriakon deipnon*). This same expression was used in the mystery religions for the sacred meals dedicated to the saviour-god. There is evidence that in the early Church, this ceremony was indeed regarded as a mystery, for an atmosphere of secrecy surrounded it, and non-Christians and even catechumens (those being inducted into Christianity) were not allowed to witness it. Paul's expression 'the Lord's Supper' was so redolent of mystery religion that the early Fathers of the Church became embarrassed by it, and they substituted for it the name 'Eucharist', which had Jewish, rather than pagan, associations. Thus the Fathers sought to align the Christian ceremony with the non-mystical, non-magical *kiddush* of the Jews, in which the wine and the bread were 'blessed' (or, more accurately, God was blessed for providing them). Despite this change of name, however, the Eucharist continued to have magical associations, since it was believed that a miracle occurred every time it was celebrated: the bread and wine turned into the body and blood of Christ. This magical significance existed from the first institution of the rite by Paul, as can be seen from his expressions concerning the magical effect of the proper performance of it: 'For he that eateth and drinketh unworthily, eateth and drinketh damnation to himself, not discerning the Lord's body. For this cause many are weak and sickly among you, and many sleep.'

Nevertheless, even Paul had no wish to cut off his new religion, with its new rite of communion, from Judaism entirely. Even though he gave authority to the new rite by a vision, it was not his own authority that he cited, but that of Jesus. He would thus have approved of the effort later put into the Gospels and Acts to derive Paul's doctrines, including the Eucharist, from Jesus, and thus to play down the role of Paul himself. Paul had no wish to be acclaimed as the founder of a new religion; on the contrary, he wished his doctrines to be accepted as the logical continuation of Judaism, and therefore to have the backing of the whole panoply of history contained in the Jewish scriptures. Consequently, even in his institution of the Eucharist, he seeks to stress biblical antecedents. Thus he relates the sacrifice of the Eucharist and the eating of the body and blood of Christ to the sacrifices of the Temple (1 Corinthians 10: 18), and the imbibing of Christ's blood to the imbibing of miraculous water by the Israelites in the wilderness (1 Corinthians 10: 4). By surrounding what was, in fact, an audaciously pagan ceremony with a web of scriptural allusions, Paul hoped to attach his cult of Jesus as a saviour-god to the Jewish background which he still cherished as a convert and in which he had aspired to reach great heights. In this way he could think of himself as a prophet, like Jeremiah. He had not broken from the Pharisees whom he had hoped to conquer through his gifts; instead, he had transcended them, and so conquered them in a different way. His abject failure had been turned into triumph. The Gamaliels and Hillels on whom his youthful admiration had been bestowed were now small fry: mere epigones of the prophets, among whom Paul took his place. If the Pharisees now wished to achieve any eminence, they could do so only by attaching themselves to *him*, and seeking salvation by the route which only he could show.

It remains to demonstrate that the Eucharist ceremony was not practised by Jesus' followers in Jerusalem, who were led by the disciples of Jesus himself, who would surely have known whether Jesus had given them this new foundation rite.

As the celebrated scholar Hans Lietzmann indicated long ago, the evidence of the book of Acts points to the conclusion that the Eucharist was not practised by the Jerusalem Nazarenes. Instead, a sense of community was instilled simply by having communal meals, as in the case of other Jewish fellowships. Thus, we find the following: 'They met constantly to hear the apostles teach, and to share the common life, to break bread, and to pray. . . . With one mind they kept up their daily attendance at the temple, and, breaking bread in private houses, shared their meals with unaffected joy, as they praised God and enjoyed the favour of the whole people' (Acts 2: 42–6). The expression 'to break bread' (Hebrew *betzo'a*) simply means to initiate a meal in a ceremonious way; the host or some prominent guest makes a blessing over a loaf of bread and then breaks the loaf, giving a piece to each person present. This was done (and still is done) by Jews at all communal or celebratory meals, whether on a week day or a festival day, and nothing is said to suggest that the bread has any symbolic or mystical significance.

If these communal meals of Jesus' followers in Jerusalem had had a Eucharistic character (i.e. if they were sacraments with a mystical significance of eating the body and drinking the blood of Jesus), something would surely have been included to indicate this: at the very least, the wine would have been mentioned, which it is not. It may be asked why Luke, who did not scruple to include in his Gospel a Eucharistic element in his account of the Last Supper, did not venture to give a Eucharistic colouring to his account of the communal meals in Acts. Luke himself must have been familiar with Eucharistic practice, since at the time of the writing of Acts (about AD 90), the Eucharist was an established rite of the Church. Yet he did not think of inserting into his account of the practices of the 'Jerusalem Church' that they performed the Eucharist. This is merely an example of how difficult it is to rewrite history without leaving tell-tale traces of the original story. One alteration always implies others; but the redactor does not always think of the repercussions of an alteration he has inserted, and so leaves other parts of his work unaltered and inconsistent with his pattern of adaptation of the original.[3]

A survey of the evidence thus confirms that Paul and no one else was the creator of the Eucharist. He gave authority to this new institution, which he actually derived from mystery religion, by adducing a vision in which he had seen Jesus at the Last Supper, giving instructions to his disciples about performing the Eucharistic rite. This vision of Paul's was later incorporated as historical fact into the Gospels, in the accounts given there of the Last Supper, and thus has been accepted as historical fact by the vast majority of New Testament scholars. The followers of Jesus in Jerusalem, who were pious Jews and would have regarded the idea of eating Jesus' body and drinking his blood as repugnant, never practised this rite, but simply took communal meals prefaced by the breaking of bread, in the manner sanctioned by Jewish tradition for fellowships within the general community of Judaism.

CHAPTER 12

THE 'JERUSALEM CHURCH'

The book of Acts does not disguise the fact that the Nazarenes of Jerusalem, in the days immediately following the death of Jesus, consisted of observant Jews, for whom the Torah was still in force. For example, we are told that 'they kept up their daily attendance at the Temple' (Acts 2: 46). Evidently, then, Jesus' followers regarded the service of the Temple as still valid, with its meat and vegetable offerings, its Holy of Holies, its golden table for the shewbread, and its *menorah* or candelabra with its seven branches symbolizing the seven planets. All these were venerated by the followers of Jesus, who made no effort to set up a central place of worship of their own in rivalry to the Temple. Also, their acceptance of Temple worship implied an acceptance of the Aaronic priesthood who administered the Temple. Though Jesus' movement had a system of leadership of its own, this was not a rival priesthood. Every Jewish movement, including the Pharisees, had its internal system of leadership (e.g. the rabbis), but this was in addition to the priesthood of the Temple, not instead of them. It was not until the Christian Church proper was set up, under the influence of Pauline ideas, that a rival priesthood was instituted, with priestly vestments patterned partly on Jewish and partly on pagan models, and with sacraments, particularly the Eucharist, intended to supersede the sacraments of the Jewish Temple. Indeed, the Christian Church produced a proliferation of temples, for, while in Judaism only one sacramental centre was allowed, i.e. the Jerusalem Temple, in Christianity every church was a centre for sacramental rites, while the vast cathedrals reached an ornateness undreamt of even in the Jewish Temple, much less in the simple conventicles or synagogues in which ordinary prayer and study took place. Moreover, the new priesthood

119

instituted in the Pauline Christian Church was accorded an awesome authority which the Jewish priesthood never enjoyed, since the latter were regarded as mere functionaries with no authority to pronounce on matters of religious practice or ethics, or to perform absolutions or excommunications.

At the time of the Jerusalem Apostles, who were the companions of Jesus himself and continued his work, no such developments were in sight. The Apostles showed by their attendance at the Temple that they did not claim priestly status for themselves. Also, they and their followers attended the synagogues for normal Jewish daily worship. This is shown by the easy access of the preachers of Jesus' movement, including Paul, to synagogues at all times; even the alleged prophecy included in John that 'they shall put you out of the synagogues' (John 16: 2) shows that Jesus' followers, in the early days, were accepted as attenders at the synagogue and also that they were themselves quite willing to attend the synagogues. Of course, this does not mean that they had no meeting places of their own; but these meeting places were themselves synagogues, and did not differ in kind from the various synagogues which catered for specialized groups of Jews, e.g. for Jews who came from the same area of the Diaspora (see, for example, Acts 6: 9: 'the Synagogue of Freedmen, comprising Cyrenians and Alexandrians and people from Cilicia and Asia. . . .'). This type of synagogue for Jews of similar interests or background exists today, even in Israel. The followers of Jesus thus formed a separate group, but by no means a Church; religiously, it was an integral part of Jewry. The expression 'the Jerusalem Church' is thus, at this stage, a misnomer.

Now this immediately constitutes a difficulty for the conventional Christian believer, for the Gospels say quite distinctly that Jesus founded a Church. Why, then, did the Apostles of Jerusalem act as if no Church had been founded, and they were still members of the Jewish religious community? This leads to the further puzzling question: if Jesus, as the Gospels say, chose Peter as the leader of the Church, why were the Nazarenes, after Jesus' death, led not by Peter, but by James, the brother of Jesus, a person who is not even mentioned in the Gospels as a follower of Jesus in his lifetime? This is the kind of contradiction that, if logically considered, can lead us to the true picture of the history of Jesus' movement in Jerusalem, as opposed to the picture which the later Church wished to propagate. We shall also be able to understand much better the nature of the conflict which broke out between the Jerusalem 'church' and Paul.

In Matthew, we find the following account of Peter's election:

'And you,' he asked, 'who do you say I am?' Simon Peter answered: 'You are the Messiah, the Son of the living God.' Then Jesus said: 'Simon, son of Jonah, you are favoured indeed! You did not learn that from mortal man; it was revealed to you by my heavenly Father. And I say this to you: You are Peter, the Rock; and on this rock I will build my church, and the forces of death shall never overpower it. I will give you the keys of the kingdom of heaven; what you forbid on earth shall be forbidden in heaven, and what you allow on earth shall be allowed in heaven.' (Matthew 16: 15–19)

This account, which appears only in the Gospel of Matthew, was combined with a second-century legend locating Peter's death in Rome to provide support for the claim of the Roman Catholic Church to supremacy over Christendom. Peter was conceived to have been the first Bishop of Rome or Pope and, since Peter had been declared by Jesus to be the rock on which the Church was to be built, this made Rome the centre of Christendom, and the papal succession the true hierarchy founded by Jesus himself. This is, of course, mere power politics and not to be taken seriously as historical fact. To Jesus, a Jew, the idea that his teaching would have its administrative centre at Rome, the capital of the military power against which his whole life was directed, would have seemed astonishing and dismaying.

But to return to historical realities, what was the relationship between Peter, evidently the leader of the Apostles during Jesus' lifetime, and James, the brother of Jesus? Why was it that Peter did not become the unchallenged leader of the movement after the death of Jesus?

To understand this, we must remind ourselves of what Jesus really was. He was not the founder of a Church, but a claimant to a throne. When Peter, as recorded in the passage cited above, hailed Jesus as 'Messiah', he was using this word in its Jewish sense, not in the sense it acquired later in the Christian Church. In other words, Peter was hailing Jesus as King of Israel. Jesus' response was to give Peter his title of 'Rock' and to tell him that he would have 'the keys of the kingdom of Heaven'. The meaning of this phrase, in its Jewish context, is quite different from what later Christian mythology made of it, when it pictured Saint Peter standing at the gate of Heaven, holding the keys, and deciding which souls might enter. The 'kingdom of Heaven' is the same as the 'kingdom of God' (since 'Heaven' was used in Hebrew as a title of God), and the reference is not to some paradise in the great beyond, but to the Messianic kingdom on Earth, of which Jesus had just allowed himself to be proclaimed King – i.e. the Jewish kingdom, of which the Davidic monarch was constitutional ruler, while God was

121

the only real King.

By giving Peter the 'keys of the kingdom', Jesus was appointing him to be his chief minister. King Hezekiah's chief minister was called Shebna; and when the prophet Isaiah predicted that this official would be dismissed in favour of Eliakim, he did so in the following terms:

> And I will drive thee from thy station, and from thy state shall he pull thee down. And it shall come to pass in that day, that I will call my servant Eliakim the son of Hilkiah: and I will clothe him with thy robe, and strengthen him with thy girdle, and I will commit thy government into his hand: and he shall be a father to the inhabitants of Jerusalem, and to the house of Judah. And the key of the house of David will I lay upon his shoulder; so he shall open, and none shall shut; and he shall shut, and none shall open. And I will fasten him as a nail in a sure place. (Isaiah 22: 19–23)

The similarities between this and Jesus' charge to Peter are striking. Where Eliakim is given the key of the house of David, Peter is given the keys of the Messianic kingdom; where Eliakim is told that 'he shall open, and none shall shut; and he shall shut, and none shall open,' Peter is told, in effect, that he shall bind and none shall loose, and he shall loose and none shall bind. (The New English Bible destroys the immediacy of the original by its concern for idiomatic English, turning the 'bind' and 'loose' of the Authorized Version and Revised Version into 'forbid' and 'allow'.) The terms to 'bind' and to 'loose' are used in the rabbinical literature as the powers of the Sanhedrin and other rabbinical courts, so that Jesus by giving Peter these powers is appointing him not only chief minister at his royal court but also head of the Sanhedrin; this is the only difference between the appointment of Eliakim and that of Peter. This is perhaps the reason why Jesus gives Peter the 'keys' in the plural.

Peter, then, is appointed chief minister of King Jesus. This explains fully the relationship between Peter and James, the brother of Jesus, in the movement, and why James suddenly rises to prominence at this point. When Jesus became King, his family became the royal family, at least for those who believed in Jesus' claim to the Messiahship. Thus, after Jesus' death, his brother James, as his nearest relative, became his successor; not in the sense that he became King James, for Jesus was believed to be alive, having been resurrected by a miracle of God, and to be waiting in the wings for the correct moment to return to the stage as Messianic King. James was thus a Prince Regent, occupying the throne temporarily in the absence of Jesus.

Further proof that this was the situation can be derived from what is known about other members of Jesus' family. After James, Jesus' brother, was executed by the High Priest, the Sadducee Ananus, in AD 62, he was succeeded by another member of Jesus' family, Simeon, son of Cleophas, who was Jesus' cousin. This again shows that the structure of the 'Jerusalem Church' was monarchical, rather than ecclesiastical. Moreover, there is evidence that the Romans saw the matter in this light, for they issued decrees against all descendants of the house of David, ordering them to be arrested; and Simeon, son of Cleophas, was eventually executed by the Romans as a pretender to the throne of David.

The position of Peter, then, after the death of Jesus, is thus easily understood. He could not become the leader of the Jesus movement, because he was not of the royal blood. But he could and did retain his position as chief adviser and minister of the royal court, the holder of the 'keys of the kingdom'. Often such a minister is the real ruler, and Peter, carrying the authority of having been an apostle and disciple from the beginning, dominated the early scene. James, however, seems to have had a strong character too, and eventually he used his position as Prince Regent to become the effective ruler of the movement. But on the usual interpretation of the 'Jerusalem Church' as a purely religious, non-political movement, it is a complete mystery why James, who was not one of Jesus' twelve chief disciples, should have been made the official leader of the movement after Jesus' death, over the heads of all the main figures including Peter.

Nevertheless, the New Testament contains certain features which obscure the situation outlined above, and create the impression that the early movement was primarily a religious one, and indeed a new religion intended to replace Judaism. One of these features we have already considered: the ascription of the Eucharistic rite to Jesus, as the foundation rite of a new communion incompatible with adherence to the communion or covenant of Judaism. The author of the book of Acts does not take advantage of this feature, and does not portray the early 'Church' as practising the Eucharist. Instead, he apparently stresses a different alleged foundation event, that of the First Pentecost. This, then, requires some consideration.

The second chapter of Acts, having described in the first chapter the appearance of the resurrected Jesus to the Apostles, gives an account of a miraculous event which took place on the day of the Jewish feast of Pentecost. The Twelve Apostles received inspiration and began to 'talk in other tongues'. This phenomenon was accompanied by others: the sound of a rushing wind was heard and tongues of fire were seen resting on each of the Apostles. A crowd then gathered, attracted by these phenomena, and Peter addressed them, explaining the significance of the occasion. He tells them: 'These men are not drunk, as you imagine; for it is only nine in the morning. No, this is what the prophet spoke of: "God says, 'This will happen in the last days: I will pour out upon everyone a portion of my spirit; and your sons and daughters shall prophesy; your young men shall see visions, and your old men shall dream dreams.' " ' Peter then announces that Jesus has been resurrected:

> Men of Israel, listen to me: I speak of Jesus of Nazareth, a man singled out by God and made known to you through miracles, portents and signs, which God worked among you through him, as you well know. When he had been given up to you, through the deliberate will and plan of God, you used heathen men to crucify and kill him. But God raised him to life again, setting him free from the pangs of death, because it could not be that death should keep him in its grip.

He then goes on to say that the psalmist David had prophesied that one of his descendants, who would 'sit on this throne', would be resurrected from the dead and would be 'Lord and Messiah'.

The account then says that many Jews were convinced by Peter's address and asked him what to do, upon which he said, 'Repent and be baptized.' Three thousand were then baptized and 'were added to their number'.

Throughout the centuries, this occasion has been regarded by Christians as the inauguration of the Christian religion. Scholars have pointed out that the feast of Pentecost or of Weeks (*Shavuot*) was regarded in the rabbinical movement as the foundation date of the Jewish religion, since it was held that the giving of the Torah on Mount Sinai took place on that date. Moreover, the reference to baptism is held to show that this rite now became the entry rite to the new Christian religion, taking the place occupied by circumcision in the Jewish religion.

No doubt the author of Acts did see the matter in this light; yet it is remarkable how little support is given to this interpretation by the actual account which he gives, evidently based on early records of the Jerusalem Nazarenes. For nothing is said here about the founding of a new religion. The doctrines characteristic of Christianity as it later developed under the influence of Paul are not present. Thus Jesus is not described as a divine figure, but as 'a man singled out by God'. His resurrection is described as a miracle from God, not as evidence of Jesus' own divinity; and Jesus is not even described as the son of God.

124

Everything said, in fact, is consistent with the attitudes of a Jewish Messianic movement, basing itself entirely on the fulfilment of the Jewish scriptures, and claiming no abrogation or alteration of the Torah.

The belief that Jesus had been resurrected was indeed the mark of the movement after Jesus' death. Without this belief, the movement would simply have ceased to exist, like other Messianic movements. But this belief did not imply any abandonment of Judaism, as long as it did not involve a deification of Jesus or the abrogation of the Torah as the means to salvation. It simply meant that, unlike other Messianic movements whose leaders had been killed by the Romans or their quisling henchmen, the Jesus movement intended to continue, with exactly the same objective as before, i.e. the restoration of the Jewish monarchy, the re-establishment of Jewish independence, and the end of military empires throughout the world. Jesus was still alive and would soon return to continue his mission; meanwhile like other figures of Jewish folk legend (Enoch, Eliezer, Methuselah, Hiram of Tyre, Eved-Melekh, Bithiah, Serach, the three sons of Korah, Elijah and Rabbi Joshua ben Levi) he had entered Paradise while alive and was waiting for the moment to return to Earth.[1]

The belief that the Apostles had spoken in tongues and had experienced a rushing wind and tongues of flame does not imply the founding of a new religion, but merely the importance of the new conviction, reviving the Messianic hopes of the movement (hitherto in despair at the death of Jesus) that Jesus was still alive. Such phenomena occur frequently in the rabbinical literature to mark some moment of great mystic illumination, and certainly do not imply any abandonment of Judaism.[2] It is interesting that the homely touch is preserved that the bystanders thought the Apostles were drunk. This shows that the rushing wind and tongues of fire were observed by the Apostles alone, and are psychological phenomena of a kind familiar to investigators of religious possession. (Of course, the recognition by bystanders of their own languages being spoken is inconsistent with their thinking the Apostles drunk, and is a later addition, though still part of the authentic tradition of the Jerusalem Nazarenes.)

The call by Peter to baptism also cannot be regarded as a call to conversion to a new religion, except by reading into the practice of baptism a meaning that it acquired later in the Pauline Christian Church. Jesus himself had called people to baptism, and the same thing had been done before him by John the Baptist. This was always associated, as it is here in the case of Peter, with repentance. Baptism

125

was an ancient Jewish ceremony that could have many meanings: it was used for the removal of ritual impurity (in order to prepare someone for eating holy food or entering holy precincts), but it was also part of the process of induction of a proselyte into Judaism, in addition to circumcision (or instead of circumcision, in the case of women). It could also be used symbolically, as a sign of repentance and regeneration, and, in this sense, it was especially associated with Messianic movements, which generally began with a campaign of repentance (i.e. return to the observance of the moral and ritual requirements of the Torah).[3] Thus Peter's use of baptism was simply a continuation of the practice of Jesus and John the Baptist: not an induction into a new religion, but symbolic of a return to God in preparation for the great event of the Messianic kingdom – in this case to be inaugurated by the reappearance of Jesus, expected in the near future.

In view of the lack of evidence in what they said and did that they were conscious of starting a new religion, the mere dating of the event at Pentecost cannot be accorded the weight put upon it by scholars. There may be some idea in the mind of the author of Acts that this date is significant in view of its importance in Judaism as the time of the birth of the Jewish religion; but even this is doubtful, since nothing is said explicitly to this effect. Certainly there is no need to suppose that the people who actually took part in the event – Peter and the other Apostles – interpreted its timing in this way. Nor does the reception of the Holy Spirit point to the beginning of a new religion; it merely means, as Peter points out, that the gift of prophecy has been renewed. This was expected to happen in the Messianic age, and the belief that this expectation had been fulfilled was in no way a contravention of Judaism.

Thus everything points to the conclusion that the leaders and members of the so-called 'Jerusalem Church' were not Christians in any sense that would be intelligible to Christians of a later date. They were Jews, who subscribed to every item of the Jewish faith. For example, so far from regarding baptism as ousting the Jewish rite of circumcision as an entry requirement into the religious communion, they continued to circumcise their male children, thus inducting them into the Jewish covenant. The first ten 'bishops' of the 'Jerusalem Church' (as Gibbon pointed out, basing his statement on the information provided by Eusebius) were all circumcised Jews. They kept the Jewish dietary laws, the Jewish sabbaths and festivals, including the Day of Atonement (thus showing that they did not regard the death of Jesus as atoning for their sins), the Jewish purity laws (when they had to enter the Temple, which they did frequently), and they used the Jewish liturgy for their daily prayers.

The book of Acts provides plentiful evidence that the above was the case. For example, the first follower of Jesus with whom Paul had friendly contact, Ananias of Damascus, is described as 'a devout observer of the Law and well spoken of by all the Jews of that place' (Acts 22: 12). This shows that not only the Jerusalem movement but also those of them who had had to flee abroad because of political persecution were loyal to the Torah. Further evidence is the following passage:

> Next day Paul paid a visit to James; we were with him, and all the elders attended. He greeted them, and then described in detail all that God had done among the Gentiles through his ministry. When they heard this, they gave praise to God. Then they said to Paul: 'You see, brother, how many thousands of converts we have among the Jews, all of them staunch upholders of the Law. Now they have been given certain information about you: it is said that you teach all the Jews in the gentile world to turn their backs on Moses, telling them to give up circumcising their children and following our way of life. (Acts 21: 18–21)

It is abundantly clear from this that James and his followers in the Jerusalem movement saw no contradiction between being a member of their movement and being a fully observant Jew; on the contrary, they expected their members to be especially observant and to set an example in this respect. The corollary of this is that they did not regard themselves as belonging to a new religion, but as being Jews in every respect; their belief that the Messiah had come did not in any way lessen their respect for Judaism or lessen their fellowship with other Jews, even those who did not share their Messianic belief.

Nineteenth-century New Testament scholarship, on the whole, recognized these facts and gave them due weight. It has been left to twentieth-century scholarship, concerned for the devastating effect of this recognition on conventional Christian belief, to obfuscate the matter. Thus the editor of the prestigious Anchor Bible *Acts of the Apostles*, Johannes Munck, states roundly that nineteenth-century research on this subject was 'not correct'. He states further that 'the Jewish element in Jewish Christianity had been devalued to nothing more than popular customs without any reference to salvation'. This is given no solid backing and flies in the face of the evidence adduced above.

It is not at all surprising, however, that such attempts to turn back

127

the clock should be made. For the beliefs of the Jerusalem movement throw valuable light on the views of Jesus himself. If James, Jesus' own brother, and the apostles who had lived and worked with Jesus had apparently never heard of the doctrines of later Christianity – the abrogation of the Torah and the deification of Jesus – or of its central rites of the Eucharist and baptism (in its Christian sense), the natural inference is that Jesus himself had never heard of them either. In that case, we cannot regard Jesus as the founder of Christianity, and must look elsewhere for someone to fill this role. But Christian belief depends on the idea that Jesus himself founded Christianity. Attempts have been made (particularly by Rudolf Bultmann[4]) to argue that this is not necessarily so: that Christianity is based on the 'post-Resurrection Jesus' (i.e. on the mythical Jesus invented by Paul), not on the historical Jesus, who may well have been a purely Jewish figure with no inkling of the Christian myth. The attitude is a little too sophisticated for the average Christian, or even the average Christian scholar, who likes to feel that Christian reverence for Jesus is directed towards the real Jesus, not towards a figment, however mythologically acceptable.

Another line of approach, which attempts to preserve the idea of Jesus as a rebel against Judaism and the founder of a new religion, is to say that what we find in the Jerusalem movement is an instance of 're-Judaization'. Later movements in Christianity, such as the Ebionites, are regarded as re-Judaizing sects, which lapsed back into Judaism, unable to bear the newness of Christianity. Re-Judaizing tendencies are seen in certain passages of the Gospels, especially that of Matthew, where Jesus is portrayed as a Jewish rabbi: this, the argument goes, is not because he was one, but because the author of the Gospel or the section of the Church to which he belonged was affected by a re-Judaizing tendency, and therefore rabbinized Jesus and tempered the extent of his rebellion against Judaism. All the evidence of the Jewishness of Jesus in the Gospels, on this view, is due to late tampering with the text, which originally portrayed Jesus as rejecting Judaism.

This is a line that was fashionable at one time and is still to be found in many textbooks. Its implausibility, however, has become increasingly apparent.[5] The Gospel of Matthew, for example, takes a hostile stance, in general, towards the Jews and Judaism (see, for example, chapter 23), so that it is incredible that its author is a re-Judaizer. On the contrary, the evidence in this Gospel of the Jewishness of Jesus goes against the grain of the narrative, and must be regarded as an outcrop of an older stratum.

The implausibility of the 're-Judaization' approach cannot be better illustrated than when it is applied to the Jerusalem movement led by

128

James and the Apostles. This would mean that Jesus' new insights had been lost so quickly that his closest associates acted as if they had never been. Of course, it may be said that Jesus' closest associates never did understand him and, in support of this, various passages in the Gospels may be adduced, e.g. Peter's altercation with Jesus, upbraiding him for announcing the necessity of his sacrificial death, after which Jesus was so angry with Peter that he said, 'Away with you, Satan; you think as men think, not as God thinks' (Mark 8: 33). But here the following question is appropriate: which is more likely, that Jesus' closest disciples failed to understand his most important message, or that Pauline Christians, writing Gospels about fifty years after Jesus' death, and faced with the unpalatable fact that the 'Jerusalem Church' was unaware of Pauline doctrines, had to insert into their Gospels denigratory material about the Apostles in order to counteract the influence of the 'Jerusalem Church'? Mark's story about Peter, so far from proving that Peter misunderstood Jesus, is evidence of the dilemma of Pauline Christianity, which was putting forward a view of Jesus that was denied by the most authoritative people of all, the leaders of the Jerusalem movement, the companions of Jesus. It is a late addition, and tells us nothing about the true relationship between Jesus and Peter.[6]

Those who hold to the 're-Judaization' theory of the 'Jerusalem Church' then have to explain how the allegedly revolutionary ideas of Jesus did not become lost altogether. The episode of Stephen is seized upon as providing a link between Jesus and Pauline Christianity. We have already seen that the Stephen episode cannot be understood in this way, though it was intended by the author of Acts to provide such a link. Nor can the incident of the 'Hellenists' be used to hypothesize the existence of a reforming party among the adherents of the 'Jerusalem Church'; this is a scholarly fantasy conjured out of the text.

Another incident in Acts, however, also functions as an attempted link between a reforming Jesus and the Pauline Church: this is the curious incident of Peter's dream.

The story, in chapter 10 of Acts, concerns the reception into Jesus' movement of a Gentile, the Roman centurion Cornelius, at Caesarea. He is described as follows: 'He was a religious man, and he and his whole family joined in the worship of God' (verse 2). In a vision, he sees an angel, who tells him to summon Peter, who is at Joppa. Meanwhile, Peter too has a vision, in which he sees 'creatures of every kind, whatever walks or crawls or flies. Then there was a voice which said to him, "Up, Peter, kill and eat." But Peter said, "No, Lord, no: I have never eaten anything profane or unclean." The voice came again a

second time: "It is not for you to call profane what God counts clean." '
Messengers from Cornelius arrive, and escort Peter to Joppa, where he
enters Cornelius' house, where the centurion and his family and friends
are gathered. Peter says to them: 'I need not tell you that a Jew is
forbidden by his religion to visit or associate with a man of another race;
yet God has shown me clearly that I must not call any man profane or
unclean. That is why I came here without demur when you sent for me.'
Peter instructs the assembly in the doctrine of Jesus' resurrection, and
says that he (Jesus) 'is the one who has been designated by God as
judge of the living and the dead. It is to him that all the prophets testify,
declaring that everyone who trusts in him receives forgiveness of sins
through his name.'

The Holy Spirit now comes upon all present, and Peter and his
disciples are astonished to see that even Gentiles have received the gift
of the Holy Spirit. Peter then orders them to be baptized 'in the name of
Jesus Christ'. In the following chapter, Peter, on his return to
Jerusalem, faces criticism from 'those who were of Jewish birth', who
say, 'You have been visiting men who are uncircumcised, and sitting at
table with them!' Peter then repeats at great length his dream at Joppa,
and the doubts are silenced. 'They gave praise to God and said, "This
means that God has granted life-giving repentance to the Gentiles
also." '

This story contains a mass of confusions and contradictions, and it
will be useful to tease these out, for we shall then be able to discern the
method of the author of Acts in his attempt to disguise the gulf that
existed between the Petrine Jesus movement and the Pauline Christian
Church, and to represent Peter as moving towards a Pauline position.

The story implies the asking of three questions, which are in fact
distinct, though the story does not keep them distinct. They are:

1 Should Gentiles be admitted to membership of the Jesus movement, even without prior conversion to Judaism?

2 Should Jewish followers of Jesus enter into social relations with
Gentiles, by visiting their homes and sitting at table with them?

3 Should Jesus' followers adhere to the Jewish dietary laws, or
should they eat all foods indiscriminately?

The passage as a whole is evidently about the question of whether
Gentiles should be admitted to Jesus' movement without prior
conversion to Judaism, the matter being decided by the fact that the
Holy Spirit fell upon Gentiles in an unconverted state. So far, the
conclusion would be: Gentiles can be members of Jesus' movement
without observing the special provisions of the Torah (e.g. abstaining

from forbidden foods), but Jews who are members of Jesus' movement should continue to observe the Torah. Peter's dream, on the face of it, does not have the message, 'The distinction between clean and unclean foods is hereby abolished for Jews,' for, as Peter later interprets the dream, it was only *symbolically* about clean and unclean foods, and was really about clean and unclean people, signifying that *this* was the distinction that was to be abolished. Yet the message of the story is not as clear as this. There is a confused intention in the story that Peter's dream is to be understood on *both* a symbolic level and a literal level, though this is not stated explicitly. For the picture of Peter, in the dream, refusing in horror to kill and eat unclean animals, but being told by a heavenly voice to do so, for 'it is not for you to call profane what God counts clean', reaches beyond the symbolic level at which it is interpreted, '. . . God has shown me clearly that I must not call any man profane or unclean' (verse 28). It is an attack on the deep-seated Jewish concept of holiness; even though this is a dream, Peter's Jewish sanctities are being threatened, and the thought is being planted that, 'even though the dream refers symbolically to clean and unclean people, can the literal distinction between clean and unclean foods survive either?'

Thus the method of the story is to say explicitly that Peter was forced to the conclusion that Gentiles should be admitted to the Jesus movement, but to hint at something much more radical: that the whole distinction between Jews and Gentiles was to be broken down, for the special provisions of the Torah, marking out the Jews as a 'kingdom of priests' with a distinctive code of holiness to observe, were to be abolished. Peter has not yet reached this stage of understanding, except perhaps unconsciously. He continues to observe the holiness code of clean and unclean foods, even after his dream, which he understands to refer only to the question of the admission of Gentiles. Yet his adherence to the holiness code is now shaken, for has he not heard a voice from heaven saying, 'It is not for you to call profane what God counts clean', in reference to 'creatures of every kind, whatever walks or crawls or flies'? The story thus represents a half-way stage: Peter is pictured as coming part of the way towards the Pauline position about the Gentiles, but is still only obscurely understanding the full Pauline position, that the distinction between Jews and Gentiles no longer exists, and that there is no longer any obligation even on Jews to observe the Torah. This situation is conveyed by the story in a manner which may be regarded as employing ambiguity artistically though the element of *non sequitur* somewhat detracts from the artistic effect.

Peter's half-way position, as portrayed in this story in Acts, is thus rather similar to his equivocal stance in an earlier story found in Paul's letter to the Galatians:

> But when Cephas [i.e. Peter] came to Antioch, I opposed him to his face, because he was clearly in the wrong. For until certain persons came from James he was taking his meals with gentile Christians; but when they came he drew back and began to hold aloof, because he was afraid of the advocates of circumcision. The other Jewish Christians showed the same lack of principle; even Barnabas was carried away and played false like the rest. But when I saw that their conduct did not square with the truth of the Gospel, I said to Cephas, before the whole congregation, 'If you, a Jew born and bred, live like a Gentile, and not like a Jew, how can you insist that Gentiles must live like Jews?' (Galatians 2: 11–14)

Paul's story about Peter (here given his Aramaic name of 'Cephas', which, like the Greek name 'Peter', means 'Rock', being the title given to Simon by Jesus) is, however, much more hostile to Peter than the story in Acts. Paul describes Peter as vacillating in his attitude to Gentile Christians, at first consenting to eat with them, but later, when emissaries from James arrived in Antioch, withdrawing from these contacts out of fear of Jewish Christian reactions. In Acts, however, Peter is not described as vacillating, nor is he criticized in any way: though he is reluctant and doubtful at first, his dream convinces him that he should have social relations with Gentiles, and also that they should be admitted to Christianity without prior conversion to Judaism. He maintains this view despite questioning and criticism from the Apostles and members of the Jerusalem movement.

It seems, indeed, that the story of Peter's dream in Acts is simply a reworked version of Paul's story in Galatians. Though the scene has been shifted from Antioch to Caesarea, the same themes are present: admission of Gentiles to Christianity without prior conversion to Judaism, entering into social and eating relationships with Gentiles, facing criticism from members of the 'Jerusalem Church'. No doubt, there was also available to the author of Acts some story about the conversion to Christianity of a Roman centurion called Cornelius; but on to this story he has grafted the subject-matter of the passage in Paul's letter, thus removing Paul himself from the scene of the story. The function of this rearrangement is to remove the sharp conflict between Paul and the 'Jerusalem Church' that appears so plainly in Paul's own account. Instead of a 'Jerusalem Church' at one extreme and Paul at another, with Peter uneasily shifting between the two, we have a picture of the whole 'Jerusalem Church', guided by Peter (himself under divine guidance), moving steadily in the direction of a Pauline standpoint. Thus the general aim of the book of Acts, which is to give a picture of essential unity in the early Church, and hide the fact that there was deep conflict between Paul and the 'Jerusalem Church' under the leadership of James and Peter, is achieved. By the time that the confrontation occurs in Jerusalem (to be discussed in the next chapter), the sting of opposition to Paul by the Jerusalem leaders has already been drawn, and they can be portrayed as having no great or irreconcilable points of conflict with him.

Of course, the question remains: why was it necessary for Peter to have a special vision to tell him something that, according to the Gospels, he had already been taught by Jesus? Why does Peter say, with such unthinking conviction that he even contradicts a voice from God in saying it, 'No, Lord, no: I have never eaten anything profane and unclean,' thus proclaiming his adherence to the Torah, when Jesus is supposed to have abrogated the Torah? Peter, apparently, has never heard of the abrogation of the Torah, so that now, several years after the death of Jesus, he has to be slowly and painfully educated into abandoning his unquestioning loyalty to it. The answer given in the Gospels is that Peter and the other Apostles were thick-witted, and this solution is continued in the story in Acts now under discussion. To be quite so thick-witted, however, is incredible; and the solution, on the level of history, rather than pro-Pauline propaganda, is that Jesus never did abrogate the Torah. The adherence of the leaders of the so-called 'Jerusalem Church' to Judaism proves that Jesus was never a rebel against Judaism. The Pauline Church, however, was not content to base its rejection of the Torah on Paul alone, for this would have meant the abandonment of the authority associated with the prestigious 'Jerusalem Church', and would have left a suspicious gap between Jesus and Paul. This would have made it clear that the abrogation of the Torah derived solely from Paul's contacts with the post-Resurrection Jesus, not from any tradition derived from the historical Jesus. A gradual process of enlightenment is therefore ascribed to the leaders of the 'Jerusalem Church', James and Peter, by which their obtuseness is slowly dispelled, and they reach at last the realization that Jesus, during his lifetime, was telling them something that they quite failed to comprehend at the time.

We may now ask the question, so far postponed: what, actually, was the teaching of Judaism about social relationships with Gentiles and about eating with them? This will lead to the further question, were there any special difficulties, as regards relationships with Gentiles, in the position of a Messianic movement such as that of Jesus' movement?

As far as eating with Gentiles was concerned, there were three separate areas of difficulty for observant Jews:

1 Certain foods (more precisely, certain forms of meat and fish) were forbidden to Jews by the Bible (which, however, does not forbid these foods to non-Jews).

2 It was forbidden to Jews to eat any food from which an offering or libation had been made to an idol; at pagan meals, such offerings were usually made.

3 *At certain times*, it was necessary for an observant Jew to be in a state of ritual purity, and this was possible only if he shared his meal with others observing ritual purity.

We note that, in the case of Cornelius, point two is irrelevant, since he was not a pagan (i.e. a worshipper of the Roman gods), but a 'God-fearer' (Acts 10: 2). This means that he was a monotheist, who acknowledged the One God worshipped by the Jews, but had decided not to become a full Jew by circumcision and commitment to the Torah. Such 'God-fearers' are mentioned frequently in the New Testament,[7] which gives valuable testimony to the existence of this class, which would otherwise be known only from later rabbinical literature, though it is most probable that the 'God-fearers' mentioned in the biblical book of Psalms are people of this category. The 'God-fearers' (who will be important in the argument of the next chapter) were regarded with respect by the Jews, as is shown by the passage in Acts which says that Cornelius was acknowledged as a good and God-fearing man by the whole Jewish nation (Acts 10: 22). There would certainly be no difficulty about sharing a meal with such a person on grounds of idolatrous offerings made from his food, since the 'God-fearers' were not regarded as idolaters, but as having a pure and valid form of religion which was acceptable to God. The 'God-fearers' were regarded, too, as having their own covenant with God, just as valid in its way as the Torah: namely, the covenant made with Noah (Genesis 9), which, in Pharisee exegesis, comprised a kind of Torah for the Gentiles, and was called the Seven Laws of the Sons of Noah (Noah being regarded as the patriarchal ancestor of the Gentiles, just as Abraham was the patriarchal ancestor of the Jews).

Nor would there be any necessary difficulty about sharing a meal with Cornelius on the grounds stated in point three, that of ritual purity, for this was not required of Jews except in special circumstances, i.e. when about to eat holy food (e.g. the Passover sacrifice), or when about to enter the Temple precincts. Even if ritual impurity were incurred, this posed no great difficulty, since it could be removed by a simple ablution in the ritual bath. It is important to realize firstly that ritual impurity was not required of even the most observant Jew *at all times*; and secondly that there was no sinfulness in being ritually unclean – this was just a state that everyone was in most of the time; the only sinfulness lay in entering holy areas or eating holy food before washing off the ritual impurity. The capacity of Cornelius, a Gentile, to impart ritual impurity was no greater than that of any ordinary Jew in the normal state of impurity which Jews were usually in. (Remember, too, that it was sometimes a *duty* for a Jew to enter a state of ritual impurity, e.g. when attending a funeral.) There were some Jews (known as *haverim*) who dedicated themselves to a higher state of ritual purity than was normally required (probably in order to help with the separation of the *terumah* or holy tithe on behalf of the priests[8]), but even these Jews did not have to be in a state of ritual purity at all times (which was impossible).[9] The *haverim* did, however, have meals together in ritual purity throughout the duration of their vows, and only if Peter was a *haver* would he have had to be concerned about ritual purity at mealtimes. Thus the statement attributed to Peter that 'a Jew is forbidden by his religion to visit or associate with a man of another race' is not historically correct. How, indeed, could the 'whole Jewish nation' have expressed their respect to Cornelius, or responded to the fact that 'he gave generously to help the Jewish people' (verse 2), if they all treated him like a leper? In historical fact, there was great social intercourse between Jews and non-Jews, as is shown by the fact of widespread proselytization, commented on by many ancient authors and attested in the Gospels. The insertion of this speech into Peter's mouth is thus a piece of Pauline Christian propaganda, intended to emphasize the contrast between the universality of Pauline Christianity and the alleged particularism of the Jews.

The only possible impediment to Peter's sharing a meal with Cornelius would have been on the grounds stated in point one, the question of forbidden foods, such as pork or certain kinds of fish, which Cornelius might have had on his table, and Peter would have been forbidden by the Torah to eat. But Cornelius, being a 'God-fearer', would have been well aware of this, and would have had the courtesy not to have had such foods on his table if he had a Jewish guest. The forbidden foods all belonged to the categories of meat and fish; a vegetarian meal would therefore have been unobjectionable to Peter or any other observant Jew. The biblical book of Daniel (written during the Hellenistic period) shows that this solution to social intercourse between Jew and Gentile was regularly applied (see Daniel chapter 1). On the other hand, if the Jew was the host and the Gentile the guest, there were no difficulties at all.

We now turn to the question of whether there were any special difficulties in the position of a Messianic movement, such as the Jesus movement, in relation to Gentiles.

On the one hand, the Messiah, in the pre-Pauline Jesus movement, was the King of the Jews and therefore not directly relevant to Gentiles. The Messiah was the human descendant of King David, who would restore the Jewish monarchy and Jewish national independence. He would not reign over the whole world, for each nation would retain its own independence, with its own king or ruling senate, or whatever system of government it preferred. Jewish Messianism was not the hope of a Jewish world empire.

On the other hand, indirectly, the Messiah *was* relevant to Gentiles, for the coming of the Messiah would mean the end of military empires all over the world and particularly of the Roman Empire. Though the Messiah would not be a world emperor, he would be the leader of a priest nation, which, in the Messianic age, would come into its own as the spiritual guide of the whole world: the doctrines of monotheism, peace and love of neighbour which it had pioneered would be accepted by all nations, and it would be given special honour as the nation which had fought through the centuries for these ideals.

Many Gentiles had been attracted to Judaism just because of its everyday doctrines, without reference to its Messianic aspect, and had therefore become attached to Judaism, either by becoming full Jews or by becoming 'God-fearers'. But a special Jewish movement with a strong Messianic aspect, promising the near approach of the Messianic age – an age of peace when the swords would be beaten into ploughshares – would have a particular missionary appeal to Gentiles weary of the politics of the sword.

The question now arose whether it was possible for a Gentile to share in devotion to the awaited resurrected Messiah without becoming a full Jew. This was a puzzling question for the Jerusalem Jesus movement because the problem was new. Other Messiah figures had made no appeal beyond the Jewish confines, because their movements had fizzled out together with their political failure; once the Messiah figure had been crushed by the Romans, the hopes of his followers had died with him. The Jesus movement was unique because of its doctrine of resurrection, by which its hopes were kept alive even after the crucifixion of Jesus. The Nazarene movement, continuing in existence, began to attract the attention of Gentiles, who were specially disposed to become converted to Judaism just because Judaism now offered a Messiah near at hand.

At first, it seemed obvious that any Gentile particularly attracted by Jesus would have to become a full Jew, i.e. become circumcised, commit himself to the Torah, and join the Jewish nation, for if not, when Jesus returned to Earth as King of the Jews, no Gentile would belong to his nation or be his subject. Even those Gentiles who had become 'God-fearers' would not belong to the nation of the Messiah, but still belong to their own nation, revering the Messiah from a distance. Moreover, it was thought, there was some urgency in the matter; for it was a Pharisaic doctrine that full converts to Judaism would not be accepted any more after the advent of the Messiah (since it would then be to everybody's advantage to become a Jew, and sincere conversion would be impossible).[10] Consequently, any Gentile who wished to be part of the inner Messianic circle after the advent of the Messiah should become a full Jew, and not be content with the status of a 'God-fearer'.

However, this produced the anomalous situation that, whereas the average Pharisaic synagogue contained its nucleus of full Jews and its outer circle of 'God-fearers', the Nazarene synagogues of Jesus' followers contained only full Jews, whether born or converted. There was thus some pressure towards accepting 'God-fearers' as members of the Jesus movement, so that the pattern of Nazarene missionary activity should come in line with that of Judaism in general, even though the logic of Messianism seemed to demand the acceptance of full converts only into the Nazarene movement, since the King of the Jews could not be a king over other nations too. As members of a Messianic movement, the Nazarenes were interested in adding to the subjects of King Jesus; but as Jews, they were interested, like other Jews, in adding to the subjects of God, whether in the form of Torah-observing Jews or Gentile 'God-fearers'.

The 'God-fearers' thus constituted a problem for the Nazarenes, and the story of Cornelius shows that the 'Jerusalem Church' was divided on the question. Peter was criticized by Paul for his alleged vacillation in this matter, but, of course, Paul had quite a different starting-point from Peter in weighing the question, for Paul was convinced, by this time, that the Torah had been abolished by the divine Jesus, and that therefore the distinction between Jews and Gentiles had been abolished. Peter had quite different considerations in mind: he was concerned that it might not be doing a kindness to Gentile 'God-fearers' to admit them to the Nazarene movement, when on the advent of King Jesus they would have to be treated as foreigners and sent back to their own kingdoms, or, at best, be regarded as resident aliens.[11] Surely it would be better to encourage them to become full Jews and so have a full share in the Messianic kingdom? Yet, on the other hand, the right of a Gentile to seek his salvation under the Noahide dispensation had to be respected.

The above discussion shows that the Nazarene movement had special problems not because it was a new religion, which it was not, but because it was a monarchical, Messianic, political movement *within* Judaism. This does not mean that it was a political party in the modern sense, for its aims were always primarily religious; but its religious aims were couched in political terms, in a way characteristic of Judaism generally. Just as political liberation had been the theme of Judaism from its inception in the exodus from Egypt, so the Nazarene movement made the religious future of the Jews and of the world depend on liberation from the Roman Empire.

Pauline Christianity, as expressed in the New Testament, in depoliticizing Jesus, also depoliticized the 'Jerusalem Church', representing it as an other-worldly religious sect, looking forward to a saviour of souls, not of bodies or of polities. An incidental result was that the various political persecutions suffered by the Nazarenes were turned into religious martyrdoms. Thus the killing of James, the son of Zebedee, by King Herod Agrippa[12] and the killing of his namesake, James, the brother of Jesus,[13] by the High Priest Ananus in AD 62, are represented as martyrdoms for the transcendent Pauline Christ, when they were in fact casualties in the resistance against Roman occupation and its minions, the Jewish quislings. Just as Jesus himself was falsely represented as a victim of Judaism through the depoliticization of his life work, so the tragedies among his followers in the Nazarene movement were removed from the account of Roman oppression and laid at the door of Judaism, in a myth of Jewish persecution of the Nazarenes, who were in fact not at odds with their co-religionists but were loyal both to the Torah and to the Jewish nation.

CHAPTER 13

THE SPLIT

We have seen that Christianity, as a new religion distinct from Judaism, with a doctrine of salvation through the divine sacrifice of Jesus Christ and with new sacraments of baptism and Eucharist, did not arise through the 'Jerusalem Church', which indeed was not a 'Church' at all, but a monarchical movement within Judaism, with a belief in the miraculous resurrection of a human Jesus. The founder of Christianity as a separate religion was Paul, who first deified Jesus and claimed revelations from this new deity as the basis of the doctrines of his new religion. We must now enquire about the steps by which the split took place between Paul and the Jerusalem Nazarenes to whom, for a period, he was uneasily attached.

As we have seen, the purposes of the book of Acts is to minimize the conflict between Paul and the leaders of the 'Jerusalem Church', James and Peter. Peter and Paul, in later Christian tradition, became twin saints, brothers in faith, and the idea that they were historically bitter opponents standing for irreconcilable religious standpoints would have been repudiated with horror. The work of the author of Acts was well done; he rescued Christianity from the imputation of being the individual creation of Paul, and instead gave it a respectable pedigree, as a doctrine with the authority of the so-called 'Jerusalem Church', conceived as continuous in spirit with the Pauline Gentile Church of Rome. Yet, for all his efforts, the truth of the matter is not hard to recover, if we examine the New Testament evidence with an eye to tell-tale inconsistencies and confusions, rather than with the determination to gloss over and harmonize all difficulties in the interests of an orthodox interpretation.

The first hint of dissension in Acts is at the beginning of chapter 15:

Now certain persons who had come down from Judaea began to teach the brotherhood that those who were not circumcised in accordance with

139

Mosaic practice could not be saved. That brought them into fierce dissension and controversy with Paul and Barnabas. And so it was arranged that these two and some others from Antioch should go up to Jerusalem to see the apostles and elders about this question.

Paul and Barnabas then travel to Jerusalem, where they are welcomed by 'the church and the apostles and elders'. But again, there is criticism: 'Then some of the Pharisaic party who had become believers came forward and said, "They [i.e. the Gentile converts] must be circumcised and told to keep the Law of Moses." ' Then follows an account of the meeting held to discuss this matter: whether Gentile converts to Jesus' movement should become full converts to Judaism. A long debate takes place, but finally Peter makes a speech, urging his own experience (with Cornelius), and arguing that conversion to Judaism is not necessary: 'He [God] made no difference between them and us: for he purified their hearts by faith. Then why do you now provoke God by laying on the shoulders of these converts a yoke which neither we nor our fathers were able to bear? No, we believe that it is by the grace of the Lord Jesus that we are saved, and so are they.'

The final word is given by James, as leader of the Nazarene movement:

My judgment therefore is that we should impose no irksome restrictions on those of the Gentiles who are turning to God, but instruct them by letter to abstain from things polluted by contact with idols, from fornication, from anything that has been strangled, and from blood. Moses, after all, has never lacked spokesmen in every town for generations past; he is read in the synagogues sabbath by sabbath.

The above account contains many confusions, and has been coloured by later Pauline Christian interpretation, but it is quite possible to work out from it what actually happened at this important conference.

The main clue is the list of commandments drawn up by James as the basis of conduct for Gentile adherents to the Jesus movement. For this list bears a strong resemblance to the list of Laws of the Sons of Noah drawn up by the Pharisee rabbis as the basis of conduct for Gentiles who wished to attach themselves to Judaism without becoming full Jews. With a little exegesis, the two lists can be shown to be even more similar than they appear at first sight.

To abstain from things polluted by idols. This does not refer to ritual purity, for this was never regarded as a concern of non-Jews. The term 'pollution' here is thus not meant in any technical sense, but only in its general metaphorical sense, as referring to the abomination of idol-worship. The meaning is thus that the Gentile worshippers were to refrain from eating anything that had been involved in the worship of idols. This does not mean merely food brought as offerings in pagan temples, for, as pointed out earlier, libations and offerings of food were made to the gods even at ordinary meals, thus rendering the whole meal a service to the gods. Thus, this commandment prevents the Gentile worshippers from sharing meals with idol-worshippers, and is therefore more far-reaching than it appears at first sight. The effect of this commandment, then, is to prohibit for Gentile 'God-fearers' everything that is forbidden to full Jews under the heading of 'partaking in idolatry'.

To abstain from fornication. This refers to the grave sexual offences: adultery, incest, sodomy and bestiality. Intercourse of unmarried partners was not regarded as a grave offence against biblical law, though frowned on as inconsistent with a serious life.

To abstain from anything that has been strangled. This means that meat is forbidden unless the animal is killed in the Jewish way (*shehitah*), by which the blood is drained away. The meat must be, as far as possible, bloodless. This commandment has an obvious connection with the command given to Noah (and therefore to all Gentiles), '. . . you must not eat flesh with life, that is to say blood, in it' (Genesis 9: 4). This does not mean, however, that the other Jewish dietary laws are to apply to Gentile 'God-fearers'. They may eat the meat of all animals, since these were permitted to the descendants of Noah ('. . . every living and crawling thing shall provide food for you' Genesis 9: 3), but must abstain from the blood of all animals.

To abstain from blood. This appears to be a repetition of the third commandment, but a glance at the commandments given to Noah will provide the true meaning. Immediately following the prohibition of animals' blood comes a prohibition of the bloodshed of one's fellow man: 'He who sheds man's blood shall have his blood shed by man' (Genesis 9: 6). The meaning here, then, contrary to the commentary usually given, is a prohibition of *bloodshed* or murder.

The four commandments given to the 'God-fearers' are thus basic moral imperatives. Many commentators have tried to explain them differently, as mere dietary laws, intended to facilitate social intercourse and the sharing of meals between Jewish and Gentile adherents to Christianity. This interpretation cannot explain the second commandment at all, since no ingenuity can turn this into a dietary law, and it also depends on inadequate understanding of the other three commandments. In any case, these commandments do *not* facilitate the

141

sharing of meals by Jewish and Gentile Christians, for they still permit the eating of pork and other 'unclean' meats by the Gentiles, which could not be shared by the Jews. We must therefore conclude that the Jerusalem Council here laid down a basic moral code for Gentiles, and we must consider what this implies about the intentions of the Council.

It is important to be clear that the drawing up of a basic moral code for Gentiles was one of the preoccupations of the Pharisaic rabbis, and the Jerusalem Council was by no means making a pioneering effort in this regard. To draw up such a code did not in any way throw doubt on the validity of the Torah as a code for Jews. It was a familiar concept in the Pharisaic movement that the Torah was never intended for more than a small minority of mankind: for those who were born Jews (who were under an obligation to keep it from birth), and for those Gentiles who elected to become full Jews and thus join the 'kingdom of priests' (who thus undertook full observance of the Torah for themselves and their descendants). The majority of mankind, i.e. the 'sons of Noah', were obliged to keep only the commandments which were given to Noah after the Flood by God. There were differences of opinion among the rabbis (as on so many other topics) about the exact details of these Noahide laws, and about how to derive them by exegesis from the relevant verses in Genesis; but they were agreed that these laws were few in number, but that by keeping them Gentiles were accounted righteous and were eligible to have 'a share in the World to Come'.

The list of the Seven Laws of the Sons of Noah, as found in the rabbinical sources, is as follows: prohibitions against idolatry, blasphemy, fornication, murder, robbery and eating limbs cut off from a live animal; and, finally, an injunction to set up courts of law to administer justice. Three of these are identical to laws included in the list drawn up by the Jerusalem Council: idolatry, fornication and murder. The one dietary law differs, however: the Jerusalem Council forbids 'anything that has been strangled', while the rabbis substitute the prohibition of 'a limb from a live animal'. This difference clearly arises from differing interpretations of the verse, 'You must not eat flesh with life, that is to say, blood, in it' (Genesis 9: 4). This difference of interpretation is well within the limits of rabbinical disagreement, and, though the rabbinical writings which have come down to us do not preserve a record of the interpretation given to the verse by James and the Jerusalem Council, this is an opinion that may well have been held by a minority of the rabbis.[1] The difference does not militate against the general explanation given here that we have to do with a version of the Noahide laws, but, on the contrary, confirms this explanation, since the difference is evidently an outcome of exegesis of the same biblical verse, which forms part of the biblical passage which (together with God's injunctions to Adam) is the basis of the Noahide laws.

This leaves three of the Seven Laws unmentioned in our passage of Acts: the prohibitions against blasphemy and robbery, and the injunction to set up courts of law. Actually, the manuscripts show considerable divergence at this point: some omit 'from fornication', some omit 'from anything that has been strangled', and some even add '. . . and to refrain from doing to others what they would not like done to themselves' (an interesting negative version of the Golden Rule, taking the form used by Hillel, not the positive form ascribed to Jesus in the Gospels). It is clear that there were different traditions about the list of commandments and this is not surprising, since there are divergencies in the various Talmudic lists too, and there was no unanimous agreement about how to list the Noahide laws. The omission of the injunction to set up courts of law is understandable, as this was intended to apply to whole nations who became converted to monotheism, not to individual 'God-fearers' who attached themselves to the synagogues. The omission of 'blasphemy' may be because it was felt to be implied by the prohibition of idolatry; and similarly the prohibition of 'robbery' may have been regarded as implied by the prohibition against bloodshed; but, again, these may both have been included in the original list and have dropped out through the reluctance of Christian editors to admit that the list is, in fact, a version of the Noahide laws. Indeed, we find throughout chapter 15 a strong reluctance to interpret the commandments listed by James as Noahide commandments, for to do so would be to admit that, when James issued these commandments, he was in no way going beyond accepted Jewish thought.

Thus, the speech ascribed to Peter in the above account of the debate in Jerusalem goes far beyond the question of whether Gentile converts should be required to adopt the whole of the Torah: it slips over into the assertion that the Torah is not necessary for Jews either: 'He made no difference between them and us: for he purified their hearts by faith. Then why do you now provoke God by laying on the shoulders of these converts a yoke which neither we nor our fathers were able to bear? No, we believe that it is by the grace of the Lord Jesus that we are saved, and so are they.'

This speech is full of Pauline concepts which were quite alien to the Jerusalem community of Jesus' followers, who, as Acts testifies elsewhere, did not regard the Torah as a yoke too burdensome to bear,

143

but on the contrary as a gift from God for which they were grateful. Peter here has been given his usual role in Acts, in keeping with his dream: he is represented as being the stepping-stone between the old dispensation and the new.

James, on the other hand, is not given this treatment. Nowhere in Acts is he represented as anything other than a loyal follower of the Torah. In this passage under discussion, he does not respond to Peter's suggestions that the Torah should be regarded as altogether abrogated, even for Jews. James's final judgment assumes just the contrary; that the Torah remains valid, but that Gentile converts to the community of Jesus should not be required to become full converts to Judaism, but only to the Noahide laws. His final remark is: 'Moses, after all, has never lacked spokesmen in every town for generations past; he is read in the synagogues sabbath by sabbath.' This remark has proved very puzzling to Christian commentators, but its meaning is surely clear. James is saying, 'There is no need for us to worry about the survival of Judaism. Its future is assured, for the Jewish people are loyal to the law of Moses, whose words they constantly repeat in the synagogues. Therefore, there is no need to look for recruits to Judaism, or to provide reinforcements by insisting on full conversion to Judaism on the part of Gentiles. Let them simply declare their adherence to monotheism by adopting the Noahide code.' James's remark thus implies his own unquestioning adherence to Judaism, and his confidence that Judaism would continue.

There is therefore a tension in our passage between two opposing interpretations of the debate in Jerusalem. One interpretation (evidently that of the author of Acts) is that this debate marked the breakdown of all distinctions between Jews and Gentiles in the Christian movement. The other interpretation (which can be discerned as the substratum of the discussion, and is thus the authentic and original meaning of the incident) is that it was decided that the Jesus movement should consist of two categories of people: Jews, practising the whole Torah; and Gentiles, practising the Noahide laws only. This decision was in one way quite in accordance with normal Judaism; but, in another way, it was unprecedented. It was quite in accordance with Judaism to make a distinction between two kinds of believers in monotheism, Torah-practisers and Noahides. But it was unprecedented that both should be combined in one Messianic movement (see page 137).

The two interpretations of the debate which we find so confusingly intertwined in Acts reflect two interpretations that were felt at the time of the debate itself, though not openly in both cases. For Paul, who travelled to Jerusalem to be present in the debate, came away from it with his own purposes confirmed. As he understood the matter, the conference had given him *carte blanche* to work in the Gentile field without having to impose the demands of the Torah on his converts. This was a great step forward for Paul, even though he well understood that the motives of James in assenting to this policy were quite different from his own. In Paul's mind, the whole distinction between Jews and Gentiles had ceased to be valid, for the revelation at Damascus had convinced him that the spiritual dilemma of mankind could be solved not by Torah or any other kind of moral code, but only through 'faith', i.e. through identification with the cosmic sacrifice of Jesus, conceived as a divine figure. Paul, it appears, did not voice this view at the conference itself. He confined himself to giving an account of his successes in winning over Gentiles to adherence to Jesus. It was the extent of these successes that finally convinced even James that Gentile adherents would have to be given official standing in the movement, rather than being regarded as having merely the status of 'God-fearers' in the periphery of the synagogues. Paul, then, employed cautious tactics at this important conference. He knew that a full disclosure of his position would have aroused strong opposition from James (and Peter, whose views, historically speaking, were the same as those of James), so he went along with the main lines which the discussion followed. He went away with the permission he wanted, to admit Gentile converts without full conversion, and kept his understanding of this permission to himself.

Indeed, the mere fact that Paul obeyed the summons to come to Jerusalem and face the charges made against him shows that at this time he was not revealing openly his full doctrines. For, in reality, Paul did not accept, either in his private thoughts or in his teaching to his Gentile converts, that he was under the authority of the Jerusalem community led by James. On the contrary, he regarded his own authority as higher than theirs, since his doctrines came direct from the risen Christ, while theirs came only from the earthly Jesus. Yet he came meekly to Jerusalem when summoned, and submitted himself to the decision of James, for he did not consider the time ripe for a complete break with Jewish Christianity.

What happened next can be gathered from an interesting account given by Paul in the second chapter of Galatians. First, he presents his own record of the Jerusalem Council discussed above; and then he describes an incident not mentioned in Acts at all, when Peter, some time after the Jerusalem Council, visited Antioch, and serious friction occurred between Paul and Peter. In his version of the Jerusalem Council, Paul (writing for Gentile converts who accepted his valuation of himself as an Apostle superior in inspiration to the Jerusalem leaders) gives himself a much more lofty role than appears from the account in Acts. Instead of being summoned to Jerusalem to answer charges against him, Paul represents himself as having travelled to Jerusalem 'because it had been revealed by God that I should do so'. Instead of concealing his new doctrines and confining himself to the question of whether converts to belief in Jesus' Messiahship should be made into full Jews or left in 'God-fearer' status, Paul represents himself as having fully revealed his new doctrines to the Jerusalem leaders, though only in private. Instead of a tribunal, in which the final decision is delivered by James in his capacity as head of Jesus' movement, Paul gives the impression of a colloquy between leaders, in which he was treated as of equal status with James. The conclusion of this colloquy is expressed as follows:

> But as the men of high reputation (not that their importance matters to me: God does not recognize these personal distinctions) – these men of repute, I say, did not prolong the consultation, but on the contrary acknowledged that I had been entrusted with the Gospel for Gentiles as surely as Peter had been entrusted with the Gospel for Jews. For God whose action made Peter an apostle to the Jews, also made me an apostle to the Gentiles.
>
> Recognizing then the favour thus bestowed upon me, those reputed pillars of our society, James, Cephas [Peter] and John, accepted Barnabas and myself as partners, and shook hands upon it, agreeing that we should go to the Gentiles while they went to the Jews. All that they asked was that we should keep their poor in mind, which was the very thing I made it my business to do. (Galatians 2: 6–10)

This conclusion differs so remarkably from the conclusion recorded in Acts that some scholars have doubted whether it refers to the same conference, while others have adopted the explanation that Paul's account deals with private discussions which took place behind the scenes at the Jerusalem Council, while Acts deals only with the public discussion. Such explanations, however, are unnecessary. Paul's letter to the Galatians was written at a time when his break with the Jerusalem leaders was almost complete. He refers to these leaders with hardly veiled contempt. He still needs to claim their sanction for his own role, however, so he feels free to represent them as having acknowledged his own equal status with them and as having appointed him as 'Apostle to the Gentiles'; though, in fact, as the account in Acts makes clear and as can be gathered from other sources, the Jerusalem leaders by no means gave up their proselytizing activities among the Gentiles, nor did they regard themselves as merely 'apostles to the Jews'. The Jerusalem Council did not hand over the whole Gentile missionary field to Paul. Nor did it ban the conversion of Gentiles to full Judaism; it merely decided that such conversion was not a necessity.

Now comes Paul's account of subsequent events:

> But when Cephas [Peter] came to Antioch, I opposed him to his face, because he was clearly in the wrong. For until certain persons came from James he was taking his meals with gentile Christians; but when they came he drew back and began to hold aloof, because he was afraid of the advocates of circumcision. The other Jewish Christians showed the same lack of principle; even Barnabas was carried away and played false like the rest. But when I saw that their conduct did not square with the truth of the Gospel, I said to Cephas, before the whole congregation, 'If you, a Jew born and bred, live like a Gentile, and not like a Jew, how can you insist that Gentiles must live like Jews?' (Galatians 2: 11–14)

This passage, despite a certain incoherence, is very revealing. (One incoherence, however, arises from the New English Bible translation, 'because he was afraid of the advocates of circumcision'. This should read, as in the Revised Version, 'because he was afraid of those of the circumcision'. No one was 'advocating', at this stage, that all converts to belief in Jesus' Messiahship should be circumcised, i.e. adopt full Judaism. The Jerusalem Council had enacted that this was not a necessity. The Greek simply says 'those of the circumcision', i.e. the Jewish Christians.)

This passage is revealing because it shows that there was much stronger conflict between Paul and the Jewish followers of Jesus than is ever allowed to appear in Acts. Nowhere in Acts is there any criticism of Peter or any suggestion that Paul and Peter did not see eye to eye on all matters. On the contrary, Peter is represented as the link man between Paul and the Jerusalem community, struggling to bring them round to the more enlightened views of Paul. True, Peter is represented in Acts as having to overcome psychological difficulties in performing this transition role: something of the stupidity syndrome attached to the Twelve still clings to him. But the open criticism of Peter by Paul (not followed up by any suggestion of a change of heart by Peter as a result) found in this passage in Galatians is quite alien to the portrayal of Peter in Acts. Galatians must be regarded here as much more historically reliable, not only because it is earlier, but because it reveals a state of affairs that the later Church wished to conceal; it is a passage that goes against the grain. (On the other hand, the previous passage in the chapter in Galatians, in which Paul gives his account of the Jerusalem Council, is *less* historically reliable than the account in Acts, since Paul has such a strong motive to aggrandize his role.)

The actual point of conflict between Paul and Peter, however, is not quite so clear as the fact that serious conflict took place, and that this conflict involved not only Peter but also James (for the emissaries to whom Peter deferred are described unequivocally as 'from James', unlike the previous critics of Paul, whose criticisms led to the Jerusalem Council, Acts 15: 1). It seems, at first, that the issue is whether Jewish followers of Jesus should take their meals together with Gentile followers of Jesus; but Paul's last remark seems to shift the issue to the question of whether Gentile followers should observe the Jewish dietary laws. To clarify this matter, the following points should be borne in mind:

By the decision of the Jerusalem Council, Gentile followers of Jesus were *not* obliged to keep the Jewish dietary laws, but only to refrain from the meat of 'strangled animals'. This means that they were allowed to eat the meat of animals forbidden to Jews, e.g. pig and rabbit, but were still obliged to kill the animals by the Jewish method, by which the blood was drained away.

This means that Jewish followers of Jesus would still not be able to share the food eaten by Gentile followers if this food consisted of meat forbidden to Jews but permitted to Gentile 'God-fearers'.

On the other hand, this did not mean that Jewish followers of Jesus were necessarily forbidden to share the same *table* as Gentile followers. Provided that the food on the table was such as could be eaten by Jews and Gentiles alike (e.g. vegetarian food, or meat from animals permitted to Jews, or fish of the varieties permitted to Jews), there was no reason why Jews and Gentiles should not share the same table.

As far as 'food sacrificed to idols' was concerned, this was forbidden both to Jewish and Gentile followers of Jesus, so did not constitute any difficulty in fellowship at table.

Even if food forbidden to Jews was served to Gentiles at the table, while permitted food was served at the same table to Jews, this would not infringe any essential law, though pious Jews might look askance at this arrangement, feeling that there might be some danger of getting permitted food mixed up with forbidden food.

148

In view of the above points, one may ask what exactly Peter was doing when he shared meals with Gentile followers of Jesus. Commentators have assumed that he was actually sharing forbidden foods, such as pig, with the Gentile believers. This would mean that he had, by this time, adopted Paul's view that the Torah was obsolete, having been supplanted by the salvation doctrine of identification with the sacrifice of Jesus and his resurrection. On this view, Peter, having made this radical transition from observant Pharisee to pork-eating Christian, suddenly had cold feet when some emissaries from James arrived and pusillanimously removed himself from the table of the Gentile converts and started acting like an observant Jew again. Upon this, Paul upbraided him, not for this vacillating behaviour, but for 'insisting that Gentiles must live like Jews'. Such an insistence had been renounced by the Jerusalem Council, and had, in any case, never formed part of Jewish doctrine, so it is extremely puzzling that this now should be made the issue. The explanation to which commentators are forced is that the Jerusalem elders, led by James, had changed their minds and reversed the decision of the Jerusalem Council, and were now sending emissaries to insist that, after all, Gentile believers in Jesus' Messiahship must undergo full conversion to Judaism.

This whole exegesis is confused and improbable. If Peter had crossed the gulf from Torah observance to salvation religion, he would not have slipped back into observance with such ease. In any case, the evidence is that Peter never renounced adherence to the Torah. The probable explanation of the incident is as follows. Peter arrived in Antioch believing that Paul was adhering to the terms of the Jerusalem Council, by which Gentile converts would refrain from food offered to idols and from meat containing blood. In this belief, Peter had no hesitation in sharing meals with Gentiles, who, he was confident, would not offer him anything forbidden to a Jew and would themselves not eat anything forbidden by reason of idolatry or blood. Then, however, emissaries arrived from James who informed Peter that his confidence was misplaced. Information had reached James that Paul was not adhering to the Jerusalem decision, but was allowing Gentile converts to eat everything without restriction, including food offered to idols (see I Corinthians 8, where Paul declares that this prohibition applies only to the 'weak' people who cannot distinguish the food from its idolatrous uses[2]). For Paul no longer adhered to the distinction between the Torah and the Laws of the Sons of Noah, because he regarded all law as outmoded and as irrelevant to salvation.

On receiving this information from James, Peter withdrew from fellowship at table with Paul's Gentile converts, since he no longer trusted them to keep the Noahide dietary laws or to respect his own adherence to the Torah dietary laws – they might well put before him food which they knew was forbidden to an observant Jew. This withdrawal of Peter from fellowship at table with Paul's Gentile converts was no weak vacillation but a climactic act of withdrawal from Paul himself, and a decisive break between the Pauline movement and the Jerusalem community. It marked the rejection by Peter of Paul's new doctrines, which demolished the whole distinction between Jews and Gentiles within the movement; or rather (since there was never any question of Peter adopting such a doctrine) it marked the recognition by Peter that Paul had indeed adopted such a doctrine, which put him beyond the pale of Judaism and made it impossible for any follower of James to associate with him or his converts.

Paul's alleged reproof of Peter was thus never delivered to Peter in person, but was an afterthought inserted by Paul in his account of the break. What this afterthought amounts to is this: 'Peter, when you consented to share a table with my Gentile converts, you were accepting the abolition of the distinction between Gentiles and Jews. Now, however, you are insisting on the old requirements by which Gentiles must keep a law of their own, and if they want to achieve full fellowship with the people of God, they must adopt the whole Torah.' However, the inconsistency of which Paul is accusing Peter did not really exist, for Peter, when he shared a table with the Gentiles, was not conceding any point essential to Judaism, since he thought that they were adhering to the Jerusalem resolution.

So far, the break between Paul and the Jerusalem leadership was only on the personal level of a quarrel between Paul and Peter. Later came the final and decisive break, in which Paul was officially repudiated by the Jerusalem movement as a whole.

There is ample evidence in Paul's Epistle to the Galatians, and also in his two Epistles to the Corinthians, that in the years following his quarrel with Peter, he had to face continual opposition from emissaries of the 'Jerusalem Church', who were sent out by James and Peter to counteract Paul's teaching about the abrogation of the Torah. Moreover, it appears that Paul had to defend himself frequently from the charge of being without true authority in his teaching, since he had no direct personal link with the historical Jesus, but relied only on visions, which were of doubtful validity. However, this uneasy situation did not yet lead to a complete schism. On the one hand, the Jerusalem leaders, while deeply suspicious of Paul, were not yet sure that he was actually preaching against the Torah. Paul's missionary activities were almost entirely among Gentiles, who were not required to observe the Torah. Consequently, his teaching to them could always be plausibly represented by Paul, when enquiry was made from Jerusalem, as not contravening any essential Jewish doctrine. He seems to have been quite willing to use a considerable amount of deception in his relations with Jerusalem, and to have done his best to reassure Jerusalem of his loyalty to Judaism, while at the same time, as his Epistles show clearly, teaching his new converts that the Torah was now entirely obsolete. Paul himself proclaims his policy of adapting his tone to his audience, and hiding his anti-Torah beliefs from those who were loyal to the Torah:

> To Jews I became like a Jew, to win Jews; as they are subject to the law of Moses, I put myself under that law to win them, although I am not myself subject to it. To win Gentiles, who are outside the Law, I made myself like one of them, although I am not in truth outside God's law, being under the law of Christ. To the weak I became weak, to win the weak. Indeed, I have become everything in turn to men of every sort, so that in one way or another I may save some. (1 Corinthians 9: 20–22)

This passage ostensibly describes only his policy in winning converts to belief in Jesus, whether Jews or Gentiles: but if Paul could pretend to be an adherent to the Torah when approaching Jewish prospective converts, he could easily use the same deception when reporting his doings to the central body of the Jesus movement in Jerusalem. In fact, we have, in Acts, in an episode to be considered shortly, a vivid description of Paul's effort to convince the Jerusalem leaders of his orthodoxy by the performance of an elaborate ritual act; this episode shows how far Paul would go to disguise his true beliefs about the Torah from the Jerusalem leaders.

It may be asked, on the other hand, why Paul went to such lengths to avoid a break with the Jerusalem leadership. Why did he not simply found a Church of his own, since his views differed so radically from those of James and Peter? Paul, in his three great missionary journeys, had founded many Gentile communities of Christians, and, if he had broken his links with Jerusalem altogether, could have set up a Gentile Christian Church under his own leadership; this, indeed, is what happened in later years, after Paul's death. But Paul, apparently, could not envisage such a drastic step. The authority of Jerusalem still remained paramount for him, just as the authority of the Old Testament never lost its hold over him, compelling him to reinterpret it in weird, unpredictable ways, but never allowing him to cut himself loose from it, in the way adopted by the more logical Paulinist of the next century, Marcion. Through the Jerusalem leadership, Paul saw himself as linked to the whole history of Israel, from Abraham onwards; to detach himself would be to sink into the forlorn status of being a Gentile again, without past or future. To transform Judaism was his aim, not to abandon it. The masters of Pharisaism were to come to him for instruction; and this could only happen if they occupied the same arena.

Meanwhile, he was prepared to adopt devious tactics in order to maintain the links between himself and the Jerusalem leadership. The first crisis had been successfully surmounted by the decision of the Jerusalem Council, by which Paul was given a free hand and was able to keep his new doctrines to himself. A second crisis, however, now arrived. Paul was summoned to Jerusalem once more to give an account of himself. This time the charges were more serious and the prospect of some ingenious compromise more unlikely. This might have been the moment to refuse to come and thus precipitate a complete break. Instead, Paul accepted the summons. He still hoped to lull the suspicions felt against him by the Jerusalem leaders; and he also felt that he had a strong means of appeasing them by bringing them a substantial sum of money collected by him for the upkeep of the Jerusalem community.

This culminating scene of Paul's relations with the Jerusalem Nazarenes is described in muted terms in chapter 21 of Acts. As in the case of the Jerusalem Council (about five years before), the author of Acts is much concerned to play down the conflict, so that it will not appear that Paul was the true founder of Christianity rather than Jesus and his immediate disciples. Yet even the author of Acts has difficulty in disguising the bitter conflict of this scene:

So we reached Jerusalem, where the brotherhood welcomed us gladly.

Next day Paul paid a visit to James; we were with him, and all the elders attended. He greeted them, and then described in detail all that God had done among the Gentiles through his ministry. When they heard this, they gave praise to God. Then they said to Paul: 'You see, brother, how many thousands of converts we have among the Jews, all of them staunch upholders of the Law. Now they have been given certain information about you: it is said that you teach all the Jews in the gentile world to turn their backs on Moses, telling them to give up circumcising their children and following our way of life. What is the position, then? They are sure to hear that you have arrived. You must therefore do as we tell you. We have four men here who are under a vow; take them with you and go through the ritual of purification with them, paying their expenses, after which they may shave their heads. Then everyone will know that there is nothing in the stories they were told about you, but that you are a practising Jew and keep the Law yourself. As for the gentile converts, we sent them our decision that they must abstain from meat offered to idols, from blood, from anything that has been strangled, and from fornication.' So Paul took the four men, and next day, after going through the ritual of purification with them, he went into the Temple to give notice of the date when the period of purification would end and the offering be made for each one of them. (Acts 21: 18–26)

It is clear that the author of Acts has much softened the tone of the discussion here recorded between Paul and the elders of the Jerusalem community. It is stated that he was greeted warmly on his arrival, and congratulated on his achievements among the Gentiles. Then the elders mention, as if incidentally, that, though the elders themselves believe Paul to be a fully observant Jew, some thousands of their followers are doubtful about this, and need to be reassured by an elaborate demonstration of loyalty to the Torah. Otherwise, there will be trouble of some unspecified kind ('They are sure to hear that you have arrived').

This is a most unlikely tone for the elders to adopt. If the reports of Paul's abandonment of the Torah were so insistent (and indeed they were perfectly true), the elders themselves, who were no less 'staunch upholders of the Law' than any of their flock, would have been thoroughly concerned, especially as Peter (who, strangely enough, is not mentioned specifically as present on this occasion) will have told them about his own rift with Paul and the reasons for it. It is much more likely that this incident was in the nature of an official enquiry or even a trial, and that Paul had been officially summoned to attend it in order to answer, once and for all, the charges now being made against him on all hands. If he failed to attend or failed to satisfy the elders having attended, he would be formally ejected from the Nazarene movement. It seems that, in the course of this enquiry, Paul refused to admit that he had advocated the abandonment of the Torah in his teaching. Consequently, James and the other elders had decided to put him to the test or rather to devise a procedure by which he would publicly repudiate any teaching that he might have given against the continuing validity of the Torah.[3] The news of this public repudiation by Paul of his former views would quickly reach his converts, and thus strengthen the hands of the emissaries from Jerusalem who were working to correct Paul's teaching. The elders were probably convinced that Paul had

153

indeed spread an anti-Torah doctrine, but they hoped to counteract the effect of this by an exhibition of repentance on Paul's part.

Paul had thus failed to find any compromise formula to save his face, as he did at the previous Jerusalem Council. He was forced to capitulate and to agree to a public humiliation and retraction.

Commentators have strangely forborne to comment on this abject behaviour of Paul's. Since he had proclaimed in his Epistles that the Torah was dead, that circumcision was no more than a mutilation, and that observance of the Torah was of no effect towards salvation, which could only be obtained through the sacrifice of Jesus, one would have thought that this was an excellent occasion to give witness to these views, which were for him all important. Instead, he consented meekly to an action that reinstated the Torah, and thus relegated Jesus to the status of a Jewish Messiah figure with no aim of salvation, but only of liberation – the freeing of the people of God from foreign domination so that they could devote themselves more fully to the study and practice of the Torah.

Paul must have been overawed by James on this occasion. Probably (though this is not mentioned in the account in Acts), Peter too took a prominent part in the enquiry, and the third leader, John (who receives only passing mention in Acts), must have been a formidable character as well. Though Paul could convince himself, when not in their presence, that he was their equal or even superior, he could not sustain this attitude to their faces. Some of the grandeur which must have surrounded James can be felt even in the record of Acts, but Peter is turned into an almost comic figure by the exigencies of *tendenz*, which require the author of Acts to find the roots of Paulinism in the so-called 'Jerusalem Church', and therefore force Peter into the mould of a groping transition figure, half in the old Jewish world and half in the new world of Christianity. In reality, these men had the gravity and presence of the great Pharisee teachers (such as Hillel and Gamaliel), and the parvenu Paul could not withstand them in their own milieu; he succumbed, and consented to what was in effect a recantation.

Quite apart from the awesomeness of the Jerusalem leaders, however, there were strong factors compelling Paul to adopt un-palatable emergency policies while in Jerusalem. He was surrounded by enemies, some of whom threatened physical danger. To comply with the demands of one set of enemies meant to offend another. All of Paul's considerable pliancy and powers of adaptability were called for in order to escape the situation into which he had plunged by obeying the summons to Jerusalem. In the next chapter we shall be examining and attempting to unravel the complicated manoeuvres which now ensued. It will be a test of the formulations advanced in this book, explaining the various stances of the 'Jerusalem Church', the High Priest and of Paul himself, if light can be thrown on this most puzzling period in Paul's career.

CHAPTER 14

THE TRIAL OF PAUL

When Paul consented to make a public demonstration of loyalty to the Torah in the Temple, he hoped that this would be the end of opposition to him on the part of the Nazarenes of Jerusalem, who, like their leader, James, were loyal adherents of the Torah. In the event, however, as the story is told in Acts, he met with serious trouble from another quarter: from 'Jews from the province of Asia', who recognized him while he was in the Temple and raised a riot against him, from which he was lucky to escape with his life. The incident is described as follows:

> But when the seven days were nearly ended, the Asian Jews caught sight of Paul in the temple, and they stirred up the whole crowd, and laid hands upon him, shouting: 'Come and help, Israelites! Here is the man who teaches all men everywhere against the people, the Law, and this place; moreover he has brought Greeks into the temple and defiled this holy place.' For they had earlier seen Trophimus of Ephesus with him outside in the city, and they thought that Paul had brought him into the temple. So the whole city was roused, and a crowd gathered. They seized Paul and dragged him out of the temple, and at once the doors were shut. While they tried to kill him [or: were clamouring for his death] a report was made to the tribune of the cohort: 'The whole of Jerusalem is in an uproar.' (Acts 21: 27–31)

Who were the 'Jews from Asia'? Why were they so violently opposed to Paul? If what Paul himself says about his preaching to Jews on his missionary journeys is correct, they had no reason to believe him to be an apostate from Judaism, for Paul's method when approaching Jews is described by him as: 'To Jews I became like a Jew, to win Jews; as they are subject to the Law of Moses, I put myself under that Law to win them, although I am not myself subject to it' (1 Corinthians 9: 20–22). It was only to his Gentile converts that Paul revealed that he regarded the Torah as obsolete; and he may have revealed this also to Jewish converts to Christianity, when he considered that their progress in

156

understanding had reached such a level that they would be receptive to anti-Torah teaching. The news of his abandonment of the Torah was thus confined to the Jesus movement itself, where it had caused such anxiety that Jewish Christian emissaries had been sent out to combat his teaching, and Paul himself had been summoned twice to Jerusalem to answer charges before the supreme tribunal of the Nazarenes.

As far as Jews in general were concerned, the Jesus movement was a resistance movement against the Romans, pious and extremist. They did not know enough about the internal politics of this movement to distinguish Paul from its other leading figures. Whenever they came across Paul in his missionary travels, he seemed to be preaching pious Judaism, combined with belief in Jesus as a Messiah figure. The opposition which Paul met from Jews on his travels was not on the grounds of heresy or apostasy, but on the political grounds that Paul, like his fellow Nazarenes of Jerusalem, was stirring up trouble with the Roman Empire and thus endangering their comfortable settlements in the Jewish Diaspora. This is explicitly stated in relation to the Jews of Thessalonica, who denounced Paul to the local magistrates in these terms: 'The men who have made trouble all over the world have now come here; and Jason has harboured them. They all flout the Emperor's laws, and assert that there is a rival king, Jesus' (Acts 17: 6–7). Here we get a whiff of political reality for once. In other passages, to be sure, the opposition of Diaspora Jews to Paul preaching against the Jewish religion is expressed in doctrinal terms; but this is part of the depoliticizing approach of the author of Acts, which he neglected to apply in the case of the Jews of Thessalonica.

Paul's main interest, in any case, was not in converting Jews, but in converting Gentiles, in accordance with his self-description as the 'apostle to the Gentiles'. It is in his Epistles to his Gentile converts, which have been preserved in the New Testament, that he pours out his real thoughts and expresses his view that salvation does not come from observance of the Torah. These thoughts became known to the Jewish adherents of Jesus in the natural course of events, but the Jews as a whole would have no means of learning about them.

The strong probability, then, is that the 'Asian Jews' who dragged Paul out of the Temple and denounced him to their fellow Jews as an opponent of the Torah, Israel and the Temple were in fact Jewish Christians who had been in conflict with Paul in his Asian missionary activities, in Galatia, for example. (Asia means Asia Minor.) It was against the possible violence of these Jewish Christians that James had already given Paul a warning:

> You see, brother, how many thousands of converts we have among the Jews, all of them staunch upholders of the Law. Now they have been given certain information about you: it is said that you teach all the Jews of the gentile world to turn their backs on Moses, telling them to give up circumcising their children and following our way of life. What is the position, then? They are sure to hear that you have arrived. (Acts 21: 20–22)

In certain early manuscripts of the New Testament, the last portion of this passage reads: '. . . the multitude must needs come together: for they will hear that thou art come' (Revised Version rendering). This is probably the correct reading, and it is much more menacing than the reading adopted by the New English Bible, though even that has a menacing undertone. James is warning Paul that there may be mob violence, and the mob of which he is talking is the rank and file of the Jewish Christians of Jerusalem (whom he reckons in 'thousands', though, in fact, the Greek word here is *myriades*, which means 'tens of thousands'). It seems that the Nazarenes led by James had made great advances in Jerusalem, and a significant proportion of the population now adhered to them. These were the people from whom Paul had to fear violence, for they were in touch with the Jewish Christians of the Diaspora and were thus familiar with Paul's personality and teaching, which they regarded with hostility. Some of these Nazarenes belonged to the extreme wing, which, as argued earlier (p. 79), had previously been led by Stephen and were activists, participating in the resistance against the Roman occupation. Such zealots (who indeed had much in common with the Zealot party founded by Judas of Galilee) would be particularly likely to resort to violence against someone like Paul, who was reported to have given up Jewish patriotism as well as reverence for the Torah. Incidentally, when James said to Paul that he is reported to have been telling 'all the Jews of the Gentile world' to abandon the Torah, he must be referring to the Jewish Christians only, or is perhaps reporting an exaggerated rumour which has spread among the Nazarenes of Jerusalem. For, as we have seen, Paul was careful, when talking to unconverted Jews, not to say anything against the validity of the Torah: 'To Jews, I became like a Jew.'

Why, then, has the author of Acts disguised this matter by representing the people who attacked Paul, dragged him out of the Temple, beat him and called for his execution, as 'Jews', not as Jewish Christians? The obvious answer to this is that the author of Acts wishes to minimize the opposition to Paul in the Jerusalem movement, to which he always attempts to attribute Pauline doctrines. Yet there is an obvious discrepancy between this picture and the speech of James to

Paul, in which it is clearly revealed that James fears for Paul's physical safety because of the hostility felt towards him by 'tens of thousands' of members of the Nazarene community. This discrepancy was felt so keenly by the editor of the Anchor Bible edition of Acts that he proposed to emend James's speech drastically so that James would be referring here to Jews, not to Jewish Christians. Otherwise, he says, 'James is revealed as a bad Christian and an unreliable and cowardly leader of the Church', since he had failed to convince his followers of the validity of Paul's work and attitude.

Having been attacked by the Jewish Christians, Paul was rescued by the Roman police, who had some difficulty in finding out why he had become the centre of a disturbance, but gathered that he had been guilty of some offence which had angered the crowd and so arrested him. Some of the details now added in chapter 22 of Acts are not credible. Thus the Roman commandant is said to have asked Paul whether he was 'the Egyptian who started a revolt some time ago'. Such a question is hardly likely about a man who was so obviously unpopular with the Jewish masses that they were calling for his execution. A Messianic leader such as 'the Egyptian' (about whom details are given in Josephus[1]) would be much more likely to be popular with the Jerusalem crowd, though he would be regarded as a dangerous nuisance by the High Priest and his followers. It is likely that Luke, the author of Acts, has simply inserted the 'Egyptian' here because he had read about this character in Josephus, and wished to add a further touch of drama to the story: Paul is not only hated by the hostile Jews but is also suspected of insurrection by the Romans.

Even more unlikely is the account inserted by the author here that Paul was allowed by the Roman police officer to harangue the crowd from the steps of the police barracks. Luke was evidently an avid reader of Greek historical works, which never lost an opportunity to insert some edifying speech into the mouth of an admired historical character, sometimes in circumstances when a lengthy oration was no more historically likely than a full-throated aria from a dying character in an opera.

The next sequence of events reported in Acts, however, supplies some historical insight:

. . . the commandant ordered him to be brought into the barracks and gave instruction to examine him by flogging, and find out what reason there was for such an outcry against him. But when they tied him up for the lash, Paul said to the centurion who was standing there, 'Can you legally flog a man who is a Roman citizen, and moreover has not been found guilty?' When the

159

centurion heard this, he went and reported it to the commandant. 'What do you mean to do?' he said. 'This man is a Roman citizen.' The commandant came to Paul. 'Tell me, are you a Roman citizen?' 'Yes', said he. The commandant rejoined, 'It cost me a large sum to acquire this citizenship.' Paul said, 'But it was mine by birth.' Then those who were about to examine him withdrew hastily, and the commandant himself was alarmed when he realized that Paul was a Roman citizen and that he had put him in irons. (Acts 22: 24–9)

We can now begin to see why Paul, a shrewd man, had done such an apparently foolish thing as to go to Jerusalem at this point in his life. Jerusalem was for him a hornet's nest: he was in danger from enemies on all sides: from the Jewish Christians who were incensed at reports of his strange and idolatrous teachings about Jesus, and also, as we shall see, from his former associates, the High Priest's party, at the other end of the politico-religious spectrum. But Paul had much to gain by going to Jerusalem: he could perhaps do what he had done before, at the time of the Jerusalem Council, and gain a compromise solution by which he could avoid the painful break that he dreaded. If the worst came to the worst and he was beset by enemies, he could play his trump card, of which his enemies were unaware, that he was a Roman citizen. He could invoke the protection of the Roman authorities, and so escape from Jerusalem unharmed.

It seems likely, indeed, that the Roman police did not arrive on the scene simply because a hubbub arose, as in the account given by Acts, but that Paul had previously arranged that they should be sent for in case of trouble, for Paul was not quite alone in Jerusalem. It appears that he had a Gentile supporter called Trophimus at hand, and we also know that his nephew was in Jerusalem and was active in helping him out of difficulties (Acts 23: 16). His emergency plan was thus put into operation, and one of his supporters alerted the police. Support for this probability comes from the letter sent by the commandant, Claudius Lysias, reporting on the affair to the Governor, Felix, in which he says: 'This man was seized by the Jews and was on the point of being murdered when I intervened with the troops and removed him, because I discovered that he was a Roman citizen' (Acts 23: 27). From this report by the commandant, it appears that he was informed of Paul's Roman citizenship *before* he intervened. Otherwise, he probably would not have intervened at all, since the Romans were not so conscientious in their duties as police as to be much concerned whether some Jew was killed or beaten in a religious squabble. The author of Acts, however, does not wish to give such an impression of conscious planning by Paul, and thus postpones Paul's revelation of his Roman citizenship until he was about to be lashed (but then forgets to alter the commandant's letter accordingly).

According to Acts, Paul had only once before invoked his Roman citizenship when in trouble. This was during his second missionary journey when he was at Philippi, in Greece, when Paul and his companion Silas incurred the wrath of certain Gentile idolaters who denounced them to the magistrates, who ordered them to be beaten (Acts 16: 19ff). On that occasion, both Paul and Silas claimed to be Roman citizens, but strangely enough, said nothing until *after* they had been beaten. There is thus some doubt about the historicity of this episode, especially as it seems incredible that not only Paul, but also Silas, were Roman citizens. It is surprising enough that Paul was a Roman citizen, without his companion Silas being one too. It seems, therefore, that the author of Acts has inserted the claim to Roman citizenship as an afterthought in the story, with the effect that Paul and Silas were not only released from prison but also reduced the magistrates to fear and trembling. The story of Paul's declaration of his Roman citizenship in Jerusalem later was too good not to be used in some earlier context too.

It is also surprising that Paul never invoked his Roman citizenship on other occasions when he was flogged. According to his statement in II Corinthians 11: 25, he was 'beaten with rods' (i.e. by the Roman lictors) three times, and apparently did not protest on these occasions that the punishment was illegal. Nor does Paul mention anywhere in his letters that he was a Roman citizen, though such a mention might have been expected.

These considerations would seem to point to the possibility that Paul acquired his Roman citizenship only shortly before he travelled to Jerusalem. This was a time in his life when he had a large amount of money at his disposal, for he had made a special effort to collect a huge sum to bring with him to Jerusalem (see I Corinthians 16: 1–4). This was in fulfilment of his promise at the Council of Jerusalem to make a substantial contribution from his new Gentile converts to the expenses of the central organization of the Jesus movement in Jerusalem. James had demanded this not as an act of charity (as Acts depicts it), but as a gesture of submission to his own authority as head of the Nazarenes. Paul, therefore, on the eve of his fateful visit to Jerusalem, when his loyalty to James and to the Torah would be questioned, felt it imperative to fulfil this pledge. But while in possession of such large sums, it would be natural for him to think of some method of insurance by which he could prepare a mode of escape, if things went wrong in Jerusalem. An excellent plan in this regard was to purchase Roman citizenship for himself; by this means he could call upon Roman help in an emergency.

Paul would not consider it dishonest to use funds collected for the 'Jerusalem Church' for the purpose of acquiring Roman citizenship for himself, because this was not just a matter of personal advantage, but of high policy, affecting the whole future of Christianity. If negotiations in Jerusalem broke down, his own survival was essential for the continuance of the doctrines which he held dear, and on which, he believed, the salvation of all humanity depended. Moreover, these funds belonged to Jerusalem only if circumstances made possible the continuance of his own loyalty and submission to the Jerusalem leadership as the official centre of the Jesus movement. If matters came to a schism, then Paul himself, instead of the Jerusalem leadership, would become the central authority of a Gentile Christian Church whose funds it would be his duty to administer. So he was merely putting aside a contingency fund, in case the schism actually took place. It is likely that he held back a considerable sum, in addition to the money he spent on purchasing Roman citizenship, in case it was needed to found his own Church.

Some corroboration of this is to be found in a detail that the author of Acts lets slip. This is that Felix, the Roman Governor, 'had hopes of a bribe from Paul; and for this reason he sent for him very often and talked with him' (Acts 24: 26). This happened while Paul was Felix's prisoner, awaiting settlement of his case. Now a Roman Governor would not expect any paltry sum as a bribe, so he must have thought that Paul had considerable amounts at his disposal. Indeed, Paul had previously gone out of his way to hint as much (verse 17). It seems, then, that Paul had not handed over to James all the money which he had brought from the Gentile churches of Asia Minor and Greece; he still had a financial base which he could use for bargaining purposes.

The above considerations throw a poignant light on the conversation already quoted between Paul and the commandant, Claudius Lysias:

But when they tied him up for the lash, Paul said to the centurion who was standing there, 'Can you legally flog a man who is a Roman citizen, and moreover has not been found guilty?' When the centurion heard this, he went and reported it to the commandant. 'What do you mean to do?' he said. 'This man is a Roman citizen.' The commandant came to Paul. 'Tell me, are you a Roman citizen?' he asked. 'Yes', said he. The commandant rejoined, 'It cost me a large sum to acquire this citizenship.' Paul said, 'But it was mine by birth.' Then those who were about to examine him withdrew hastily, and the commandant himself was alarmed when he realized that Paul was a Roman citizen and that he had put him in irons. (Acts 22: 25–9)

This whole conversation is spurious, as argued before, since Paul had really been known to be a Roman citizen before he was rescued by the Roman commandant, and otherwise would not have been rescued at all. So what is the purpose of the insertion of this conversation? It is as if the author of Acts is going out of his way to tell us that Paul did not purchase his Roman citizenship, a possibility which might not otherwise have occurred to us. There is an element of 'protesting too much' in this fictional insertion. It should be remembered that this alleged assertion of Paul's, 'But it was mine by birth,' is the *only* evidence in existence that Paul was born a Roman citizen, which is *prima facie* unlikely.

When Paul declared himself a Roman citizen, this was the end of his uneasy association with the 'Jerusalem Church'. The announcement would have come to James and the other Jerusalem leaders as a great shock. The Jesus movement was essentially an anti-Roman movement. Its aim was the freeing of the Jewish people from bondage to Rome. None of its members, therefore, would have sought Roman citizenship. But Paul's new interpretation of the life and death of Jesus had severed Paul from adherence to Jewish patriotism or to politics in general. He no longer thought of Jesus as the Messiah, in the Jewish sense, who would restore the House of David and Jewish independence, but as a cosmic figure who had come to provide a way of salvation for all mankind by his death on the cross. This 'salvation' was not a matter of political liberation; it was a personal, individual matter that transcended all politics, and indeed made politics irrelevant. To Paul, it did not matter whether a person was physically enslaved, since this did not affect his spiritual salvation. Thus he urged his disciples to obey Rome, whose power was 'ordained of God', and he also urged slaves to be contented with their lot and not to strive for freedom.[2] This contempt for politics was in fact a political attitude – an acquiescence in the political *status quo*. Consequently, the Pauline Christian doctrine was fitted from the start to become the official religion of the Roman Empire. Nothing is more welcome to a military empire than a religious doctrine that counsels obedience and acquiescence. That Paul, the creator of the doctrine that eventually became the official Roman religion, made himself into a Roman citizen is symptomatic.

At the same time, the leaders of the Nazarene community in Jerusalem, knowing that Paul's Roman citizenship must have been purchased for a large sum of money, would immediately know how

Paul had come into the possession of such a substantial amount – by his collection of contributions for the 'Jerusalem Church'. This again would have put him beyond the pale as far as they were concerned; to them, the matter would appear as plain dishonesty and embezzlement, though to Paul himself, as we have seen, the use of these funds for the preservation of what he regarded as the true Christianity would have seemed quite justified.

Having saved himself from a dangerous situation at the hands of the Jewish Christian crowd, and finding himself apparently safe in the hands of the Romans, Paul, ironically enough, now experienced danger from quite a different quarter. For Paul found himself in contact with the last person he wanted to encounter, the High Priest. The Roman commandant, Claudius Lysias, decided to bring Paul before the Sanhedrin, of which the High Priest was the chairman, in order to discover why Paul had fallen foul of the Jerusalem crowd: whether this was a purely internal Jewish religious quarrel (in which case he need not take any further interest), or whether there was some danger to the Roman occupation.

This was an extremely awkward situation for Paul, not so much because of having to appear before the Sanhedrin, but because of having to make an appearance before the High Priest personally. For the High Priest had good reason to think bitterly of Paul, who had been a mainstay of the regime at one time, but had suddenly and unaccountably defected during an important mission. As far as the High Priest was concerned, Paul was indeed a person who constituted a danger to the Roman occupation and to his own quisling regime, since he was a member of a revolutionary organization, the Nazarenes. Even though this movement had been politically quiescent for some years, waiting for the return of Jesus, there was known to be one wing of the party which was more activist, and wished to pursue Jesus' aims even in his temporary absence. Paul, for all the High Priest knew, belonged to this extremist wing; and, in any case, the High Priest had strong reasons for resenting Paul's defection at a crucial juncture of an official operation.

The drama of Paul's confrontation with the High Priest at this time has been entirely missed by commentators, who do not seem to have borne in mind Paul's previous relations with the High Priesthood. True, it was now a different High Priest from the one served by Saul; but even so, the bureaucratic memory is not short, and Paul would certainly be remembered as the high-ranking police officer who fouled up the Damascus operation so spectacularly and actually defected to the dissidents.

The High Priest was thus Paul's personal enemy and the ensuing events made him even more of one, for Paul, finding himself before the Sanhedrin and knowing that this body had a majority of Pharisees which had on a previous occasion rescued Peter from the High Priest, decided, with great presence of mind, but with a distinct lack of scruple, to play on this situation to escape condemnation. This tactic involved appealing to the opponents of the High Priest in the Sanhedrin, which would not endear Paul further to him. But the alternative course, which was to declare his loyalty to Rome, would not work with the High Priest, who remembered him only as the employee who had once proved conspicuously disloyal to the pro-Roman regime.

So Paul decided to play for all he was worth the role of a Nazarene of the type of James or Peter, knowing that this kind of person would receive sympathetic treatment from the Pharisee majority of the Sanhedrin. The proceedings are described in Acts:

> Paul fixed his eyes on the Council and said, 'My brothers, I have lived all my life, and still live today, with a perfectly clear conscience before God.' At this the High Priest Ananias ordered his attendants to strike him on the mouth. Paul retorted, 'God will strike you, you whitewashed wall! You sit there to judge me in accordance with the Law; and then in defiance of the Law you order me to be struck!' The attendants said, 'Would you insult God's High Priest?' 'My brothers,' said Paul, 'I had no idea that he was High Priest; Scripture, I know, says: "You must not abuse the ruler of your people." '
>
> Now Paul was well aware that one section of them were Sadducees and the other Pharisees, so he called out in the Council, 'My brothers, I am a Pharisee, a Pharisee born and bred; and the true issue in this trial is our hope of the resurrection of the dead.' At these words the Pharisees and Sadducees fell out among themselves, and the assembly was divided. [The Sadducees deny that there is any resurrection, or angel or spirit, but the Pharisees accept them.] So a great uproar broke out; and some of the doctors of the law belonging to the Pharisaic party openly took sides and declared, 'We can find no fault with this man; perhaps an angel or spirit has spoken to him.' The dissension was mounting, and the commandant was afraid that Paul would be torn in pieces, so he ordered the troops to go down, pull him out of the crowd, and bring him into the barracks. (Acts 23: 1-10)

Many of the details of this account are manifestly unhistorical. The Sanhedrin was a dignified body, not an unruly mob, and conducted its affairs with great decorum, in accordance with the provisions of the law: it is extraordinary how the New Testament, while complaining that the Jews and particularly the Pharisees showed over-zealous attachment to the law, portrays them on occasion as flouting it outrageously. We may extract certain things from the account, however, as historically true: that the High Priest showed personal hostility to Paul; that Paul appealed to the Pharisees, declaring himself to be a Pharisee and a believer in the doctrine of resurrection, as especially exemplified in the resurrection of Jesus; and that when the matter came to a vote, the Pharisees, as they had done in the case of Peter, voted for Paul's acquittal, arguing that to be a Nazarene was no offence against the law, and that the Nazarenes (as Gamaliel had argued) were quite possibly the recipients of a revelation from God. In the case of Peter and Gamaliel, the author of Acts preserved something of the atmosphere of debate in the Sanhedrin; but in the present passage, while forced to admit that Paul was saved by the Pharisees, he tries to deprive them of all credit by ascribing their attitude to mere factiousness, degenerating into ludicrous brawling.

Nevertheless, this incident gives further support to the picture of the Pharisees put forward in the present book. The Pharisees were not opposed to the Jesus movement, which was indeed a Pharisee movement. It was the Pauline Christian movement that blackened the name of the Pharisees by distorting their image in the New Testament, the scripture of Paulinism. In the four trials described in the New Testament – those of Jesus, Stephen, Peter and Paul – all purporting to be before the Sanhedrin, only two, those of Peter and of Paul, can be regarded as genuine Sanhedrin trials, and in both of these the Pharisees were on the side of humanity and tolerance.

Furthermore, the trial of Paul proves conclusively the unacceptability of the idea proposed earlier in Acts, that Paul was an object of hatred to pious Jews as a whole. It was only within the Nazarene movement that Paul's new doctrines about Jesus were known. To the main body of Jews, Paul, if known at all, was thought of as simply a member of the Nazarene movement, and was presumed to hold the same doctrines as James and Peter. It was easy, therefore, for Paul to pose before the Sanhedrin as a pious Pharisee and Nazarene, and thus enlist the support of the Pharisees.

Most commentators seem to gloss over Paul's duplicity on this occasion. His claim to be still a Pharisee was simply a lie, and if his real views had been known, the Pharisees would certainly not have supported him. His policy of being all things to all men might have had some justification in terms of winning converts to belief in Jesus' Messiahship, but here the issue was simply to save his skin. In the fictitious story of Stephen, much is made of Stephen's alleged disregard for his own life when he testified to his beliefs; why then should Paul's refusal to testify to his beliefs, or rather his deliberate misrepresentation of his beliefs, be regarded as so free from question? We have to admit that Paul was no martyr and was not even notably truthful; he was first and foremost a survivor. Despite his undoubted belief in the genuineness of his vision at Damascus and subsequent visions, he was in some respects unscrupulous, especially when he felt that the Lord's cause required a policy of deception. In the light of Paul's behaviour at his trial, we need not feel amazed that he told lies in less urgent circumstances too: for example, when he claimed to be descended from the tribe of Benjamin, or that he had been born a Pharisee and the son of Pharisees, or that he had been born a Roman citizen (though, to be sure, he may never have claimed the latter, since the claim is only attributed to him by Luke, the author of Acts, and is not found in Paul's letters).

His subterfuge at his trial was most successful, and he was acquitted and discharged. The representation of Acts that he had to be rescued from the meeting of the Sanhedrin by Roman troops, because the rioting Sanhedrin members were endangering Paul's life, is unhistorical. The letter written by Claudius Lysias to Felix, the Governor, makes no mention of any riot in the Sanhedrin but simply says that, as a result of the Sanhedrin enquiry, 'I found that the accusation had to do with controversial matters in their law, but there was no charge against him meriting death or imprisonment' (Acts 23: 29). The author of Acts no doubt found this letter in the archives and transcribed it, without reflecting that it refuted several of his own statements.

As far as Claudius Lysias was concerned, Paul was now free to go. The Sanhedrin had refused to condemn him, and since Paul had proved that he was a Roman citizen (presumably he had documents to prove this), it did not occur to the commandant that Paul might be guilty of sedition against Rome – a conclusion which might otherwise have been held to follow from Paul's connection with the Nazarenes. It was probably felt that Paul must belong to the quietist wing of the Nazarenes, and was no political threat, and had even taken great pains to prove himself friendly to Rome by becoming a Roman citizen.

But Paul was by no means out of the woods, for what happened next was a determined attempt to assassinate him. In Acts, of course, this attempt is blamed on 'the Jews'. It is not explained who these 'Jews' were, but there is no need of an explanation, for in the New Testament generally it is taken as understood that 'the Jews' are the enemies of the Light and are always eager to murder any person who is of the party of Jesus. Thus it was 'the Jews' who attacked Paul before and from whom

167

the Romans rescued him, though we have seen reason to suppose that these attackers were actually Jewish Christians. Certainly it would be hard to explain why Paul, having been acquitted by the Sanhedrin, would still be an object of hatred to ordinary pious Jews, who were adherents of the Pharisees and followed their rulings. Who then were these 'Jews' who wished to kill Paul?

We cannot come to the same conclusion as before and say that these 'Jews' were Jewish Christians, for, despite certain attempts to indicate that the previous attack was an attempted lynching, it is in fact clear that it was, on the contrary, an attempt to bring Paul to trial. The Jewish Christians were not murderers or a lynch-mob, but pious Jews, with whom it was a point of civilized behaviour that no one could be killed without a trial according to law. The present incident, however, was a plain assassination plot:

> When day broke, the Jews banded together and took an oath not to eat or drink until they had killed Paul. There were more than forty in this conspiracy. They came to the chief priests and elders and said, 'We have bound ourselves by a solemn oath not to taste food until we have killed Paul. It is now for you, acting with the Council, to apply to the commandant to bring him down to you, on the pretext of a closer investigation of his case; and we have arranged to do away with him before he arrives.' (Acts 23: 12–15)

These conspirators cannot have been Jewish Christians, not only because of their murderousness, but also because of their closeness to the 'chief priests', i.e. to the High Priest and his entourage. The clue to the whole incident is the involvement of the High Priest. Paul had succeeded in escaping from the Jewish Christians, from the Sanhedrin, and from the Romans. He still had one enemy to reckon with, the most deadly of all, the High Priest, who, as Paul well knew from personal acquaintance, had a body of ruffians at his command who were accustomed to perform lynchings and assassinations in order to uphold his position as *Gauleiter* for the Romans. The High Priest was not willing to let Paul escape scot free after his defection nearly twenty years before; he therefore arranged to have him eliminated.

Of course, the author of Acts, in characteristic fashion, obfuscates the issue by associating with the High Priest in this plot the 'elders' and the 'Council'. In view of the fact that he has just described the acquittal of Paul by these very 'elders' and this very 'Council', one would have thought that he would have balked at including them in the ensuing conspiracy; but consistency or logic is not his strong point.

Paul, however, was again too clever for the High Priest. He learned of the plot and was able to avoid it. The informant was his nephew, but no doubt Paul was aware of danger from the High Priest, knowing his methods so well, and instructed his friends to spy out the land for him and report to him any threatening rumours. Paul then prevailed on the Roman commandant, no doubt using his status as Roman citizen again, to remove him from danger by transporting him under armed guard from Jerusalem to Caesarea.

Even in Caesarea, however, Paul had not quite escaped from the High Priest, who took the matter seriously enough to pursue him there to lay charges against him:

> Five days later the High Priest Ananias came down, accompanied by some of the elders and an advocate named Tertullus, and they laid an information against Paul before the Governor. When the prisoner was called, Tertullus opened the case.
>
> 'Your Excellency,' he said, 'we owe it to you that we enjoy unbroken peace. It is due to your provident care that, in all kinds of ways and in all sorts of places, improvements are being made for the good of this province. We welcome this, sir, most gratefully. And now, not to take up too much of your time, I crave your indulgence for a brief statement of our case. We have found this man to be a perfect pest, a fomenter of discord among the Jews all over the world, a ringleader of the sect of the Nazarenes. He even made an attempt to profane the temple; and then we arrested him. If you will examine him yourself you can ascertain from him the truth of all the charges we bring.' The Jews supported the attack, alleging that the facts were as stated. (Acts 24: 1–9)

It is clear enough that the High Priest's charge against Paul was a political, not a religious one, consisting of an allegation that Paul was a danger to Roman rule, the benefits of which are depicted by the High Priest's representative in sycophantic style. Nevertheless, the author of Acts cannot resist involving the 'elders' (though he has the grace this time to say only 'some' of the elders) and, finally, the 'Jews' once more. The use of the blanket term 'the Jews' in Acts (exceeded in this respect only by the Gospel of John) is a major contribution to the general anti-Semitic effect of the book, despite the fact that many details, if closely examined, contradict the author's intention. There would be no reason for the 'elders' of the Sanhedrin to be involved in the case at all at this stage, since the Sanhedrin had cleared Paul of all religious charges. Who the 'Jews' are here is even less clear than usual (the Jews of Caesarea?), and they have evidently been included only to add to the general anti-Semitic indictment.

Though the High Priest is bringing a political charge (even to the extent of employing a Roman advocate in the case), he also adds, as an afterthought, the religious charge that Paul has 'made an attempt to profane the temple'. This charge was first raised, also as a kind of afterthought, by the 'Asian Jews' who first denounced Paul in the Temple grounds (Acts 21: 28). Remarkably, however, this charge is not mentioned during the proceedings before the Sanhedrin. It seems likely, therefore, that this charge was actually first raised by the High Priest in Caesarea, and was only afterwards inserted by the author of Acts into the denunciation by the 'Asian Jews' (with the awkward explanation that they had seen Paul walking around Jerusalem with a Gentile called Trophimus, and wrongly thought that Paul had brought this Gentile into the Temple area forbidden to Gentiles). The High Priest, in accusing Paul of being a troublemaker, adds that Paul has offended not only against the Roman jurisdiction, but also against his own authority in the Temple in some way. This too, as the Roman Governor would understand it, would be an aspect of troublemaking rather than of religious opinion. It may be that we have here an echo of the charge made against Jesus and later against Stephen that they had spoken against the Temple, by declaring that it was destined to be destroyed and rebuilt, a prophecy typical of Messianic movements. The High Priest adds this detail only to complete his picture of Paul as a prominent figure in a dangerous Messianic movement of dissidence and rebellion.

Thus the High Priest's charge confirms that he is pursuing a personal vendetta against Paul because of the latter's defection from the pro-Roman camp. It does not occur to the High Priest that Paul is in fact still pro-Roman, since Paul's peculiar variety of belief in Jesus is divorced from all politics and does not require any implementation on Earth in the form of an independent Judaea. The High Priest thinks of all Nazarenes as political nuisances, and this particular Nazarene as the most obnoxious of all, since he is a deserter from the collaborationist side to the resistance. This speech of the High Priest is valuable further evidence of the standpoint of the Nazarene movement, as argued in this book, showing that the Jerusalem Jesus movement had strong political aims.

The Governor, however, decided to keep an eye on Paul, rather than hand him over to the High Priest, partly because of Paul's Roman citizenship, and partly because he scented that Paul had large funds at his disposal of which he hoped to obtain a slice. It may well be that Paul did in fact give Felix a bribe, and so was enabled to live unmolested in Caesarea until the governorship of Felix ended two years later.

When the new Governor, Festus, arrived, the High Priest renewed his charges against Paul, and pressed them so vigorously that Paul was forced to a new recourse: he appealed for a trial in Rome before Caesar, to which he was entitled as a Roman citizen.

Now follows in Acts a set piece in which Paul is brought before the Jewish King, Herod Agrippa II, and states his views so eloquently that the King is full of admiration and seems to hover on the brink of becoming a Christian. This whole episode has the atmosphere of fiction, and is full of unhistorical aspects. Thus Herod Agrippa II, whose father, Herod Agrippa I, had executed the Nazarene leader James, son of Zebedee, could not have been totally unaware of the political aspects of the Nazarene movement, which threatened his own regime (since the Nazarenes did not recognize the Herodian dynasty as rightful kings). Yet he raises no objection to Paul's non-political account of the aims of the Jesus movement, according to which its aim was merely to call Israel to repentance, in line with the wishes of Jesus, portrayed as a non-Messianic figure. Luke, the author of Acts, was something of a novelist and could not resist introducing the colourful characters of Herod and his sister Berenice, and giving his hero Paul an opportunity to harangue them and win their respectful attention.

Paul was thus sent to Rome, as he had requested, to answer a charge, preferred by the High Priest, of disloyalty to Rome. The charge was certainly not one of offences against the Jewish religion, since the Roman Emperor would have had no interest in hearing such a charge. Yet the author of Acts, despite his clear portrayal of the High Priest's charges as political in chapter 24, goes back to describing them as religious in chapter 25: 18 and chapter 28: 20. Otherwise, it would not be possible to involve the 'elders' and the 'Jews', who were to be held responsible for Paul's troubles, just as they were blamed for Jesus' troubles.

What happened to Paul in Rome we do not know. It is probable that he was able to persuade the Roman authorities that he had severed all connection with the seditious Nazarene movement centred on Jerusalem. On the other hand, his grave dereliction of pro-Roman duty at Damascus may have weighed heavily against him. His Roman citizenship would have helped to confirm his continued attachment to Rome, despite that aberration. According to Church legend, Paul was martyred in Rome, but no reliance can be placed on this story. It is quite possible that he lived on to a ripe old age, building up the Gentile Christian Church which he had created, and for the sake of which he had brought to bear such ingenuity and resource.

171

CHAPTER 15

THE EVIDENCE OF
THE EBIONITES

In the preceding chapters we have built up, from the evidence of the New Testament itself, a picture of Paul that is very different from the conventional one. We have seen that Paul, in describing himself as deeply learned in Pharisaism, was not telling the truth. On the contrary, we have reason to think that Paul reacted to his failure to acquire Pharisee status by creating a synthesis of Judaism with paganism; and that the paganism so deeply embedded in his conception of Jesus argues a Gentile, rather than a Jewish, provenance. We have seen, further, that the impression of unity between Paul and the leaders of the Jerusalem Jesus movement, so sedulously cultivated by the author of Acts, is a sham and that there is much evidence, both in Acts itself and in Paul's Epistles, that there was serious conflict between the Pauline and the Jerusalem interpretations of Jesus' message. This conflict, after simmering for years, finally led to a complete break, by which the Pauline Christian Church was founded, comprising in effect a new religion, separated from Judaism; while the Jerusalem Nazarenes did not sever their links with Judaism, but regarded themselves as essentially believers in Judaism who also believed in the resurrection of Jesus, a human Messiah figure.

Scholars have not been able to deny that the Jerusalem Church, under the leadership of James, consisted of practising Jews, loyal to the Torah, but they have attempted to explain this fact by the concept of 're-Judaization', i.e. a tendency to slip back into Judaism, despite the contrary teaching of Jesus. We have seen that attempts to by-pass the Jerusalem Nazarenes by constructing a different tradition linking Jesus to Paul (through the 'Hellenists' and Stephen) fail under examination. Similarly, scholars have attempted to explain away all the evidence in the Gospels that Jesus himself was a loyal adherent of the Torah by the same concept of 're-Judaization': when, for example, Jesus is represented in Matthew as saying, 'If any man therefore sets aside even the least of the Law's demands, and teaches others to do the same, he will have the lowest place in the kingdom of Heaven, whereas anyone who keeps the Law and teaches others so, will stand high in the kingdom of Heaven' (Matthew 5: 19), this is explained as not something that Jesus said, but something that was inserted into the text of Matthew by a 're-Judaizer'. Since the Gospel of Matthew contains quite a number of such sayings, the Gospel as a whole has been characterized as a re-Judaizing Gospel, written specifically for a Jewish Christian community.

Several scholars, however, in recent years, have come to see that this position is untenable.[1] For the main tendency and standpoint of the Gospel of Matthew is far from supporting the continuing validity of Judaism or of the Jews as the chosen people of God. Passages such as the parable of the vineyard (Matthew 21: 33–43) preach the incorrigible sinfulness of the Jews and their supersession by the Gentiles. It is Matthew that stresses, perhaps more than any other Gospel, the alleged curse that has come upon the Jews because of their crime of deicide: e.g. Matthew 23: 33–6, 'on you will fall the guilt of all the innocent blood spilt on the ground', and Matthew 27: 26, ' "His blood be on us, and on our children." ' Such anathematization of the Jews is hardly consistent with loyalty to the Torah, which declares the Jews to be God's priestly nation for ever. No Jewish Christian community would assent to the statements quoted.

Consequently, if the Gospel of Matthew contains assertions by Jesus about the validity of the Torah, this is strong evidence that Jesus actually made these assertions, for only a persistent and unquenchable tradition that Jesus said these things would have induced the author of the Gospel to include such recalcitrant material, going against the grain of his own narrative and standpoint.

If Jesus himself was an adherent of the Torah, there was no need for re-Judaization on the part of the Nazarenes in Jerusalem, who were simply continuing the attitudes of Jesus. But, in any case, several scholars have now come to think that the loyalty of the Jerusalem movement to the Torah is itself strong evidence that Jesus was similarly loyal. It is, after all, implausible, to say the least, that the close followers of Jesus, his companions during his lifetime, led by his brother, should have so misunderstood him that they reversed his views immediately after his death. The 'stupidity' motif characterizing the disciples in the

Gospels is best understood as a Pauline attempt to explain away the attachment of the 'Jerusalem Church' to Judaism, rather than as historical obtuseness.

Though the concept of re-Judaization has become distinctly suspect in relation to the Gospels and to the Jerusalem followers of Jesus, it does not appear to have occurred to scholars to reconsider it in relation to certain groups for whom our evidence is later. We know of a number of Jewish Christian groups or sects which existed in the first four centuries of the Christian era, the best known being the Ebionites. The evidence about these groups is scanty and sometimes contradictory; but our understanding of Jewish Christianity may be furthered by a willingness to criticize the assumption that they were essentially and invariably re-Judaizing sects, falling away from Pauline Christianity and 're-lapsing' into Judaism. It may well be that some, at least, of these groups were genuine historical continuations of the Nazarene community led by James and Peter, and were thus closer in spirit to Jesus than the official Catholic Church based on the teachings of Paul. If so, we may be inclined to listen to what they had to say about the background and life of Paul with more attention, since they may have had access, through their unbroken tradition, with the origins of the Christian religion and its earliest conflicts.

The 'Jerusalem Church' itself has a sad history. This has been obscured by the Church legend, found in Eusebius and later in Epiphanius, that before the Jewish War against Rome broke out in AD 66 the whole Nazarene community, warned by an oracle, left Jerusalem and went to Pella in Transjordania. That this story is merely a legend has been well demonstrated by S. F. G. Brandon[2], and confirmed by later research.[3] The Jerusalem Nazarenes never left the city at the time of the Jewish War; they stayed there and played their part, as loyal Jews, in the fight against Rome. When the Jews were broken by the Romans and their Temple destroyed in AD 70, the Jewish Christians shared in the horrors of the defeat, and the Jerusalem Nazarenes were dispersed to Caesarea and other cities, even as far as Alexandria in Egypt. Its power and influence as the Mother Church and centre of the Jesus movement was ended; and the Pauline Christian movement, which up to AD 66 had been struggling to survive against the strong disapproval of Jerusalem, now began to make great headway. It was not until nearly seventy years later that a Christian Church was reconstituted in Jerusalem, after the city had been devastated by the Romans for the second time (after the Bar Kokhba revolt) and rebuilt as a Gentile city called Aelia Capitolina. This new

Christian Church had no continuity with the early 'Jerusalem Church' led by James. Its members were Gentiles, as Eusebius testifies, and its doctrines were those of Pauline Christianity.[4] It attempted, however, to claim continuity with the early 'Jerusalem Church', in accordance with the Pauline policy (evinced in the New Testament book of Acts) of denying the rift between Paul and the Jerusalem elders. The Pella legend was developed in order to give colour to this alleged continuity, since some of the members of the new Church had come from Pella. Jerusalem, however, never regained its former centrality. In the now dominant Pauline Christian Church, the centre was Rome; while the descendants of the former proud 'Jerusalem Church', now scattered and poor (for which reason, probably, they acquired the nickname of 'Ebionites', from the Hebrew *evyonim*, meaning 'poor men') were despised as heretics, since they refused to accept the doctrines of Paul.

Another name by which these later Jewish Christians were known, according to the Church historians, was 'Nazarenes'. This name goes back to very early times, for it is found in the New Testament itself, not only applying to Jesus ('Jesus the Nazarene') but also (Acts 24: 5) to the members of the 'Jerusalem Church', in the denunciation by the High Priest. It seems, then, that 'Nazarenes' was the original name for the followers of Jesus; the name 'Christians' was a later development, not in Jerusalem but in Antioch (Acts 11: 26). In the Jewish rabbinical writings, the name used for Jesus' followers is similar to 'Nazarenes', i.e. *notzerim*. Whether this name is derived from Jesus' place of birth, Nazareth, or from some other source, is a matter of scholarly debate. But it is clear that the survival of this name in sects of the third and fourth centuries points to continuity between these sects and the original followers of Jesus in Jerusalem. Various theories have been put forward as to why some Jewish Christian sects were called Nazarenes, while others were called Ebionites. The best solution seems to be that the original name was Nazarenes, but at some point they were given the name Ebionites, as a derogatory nickname, which, however, some of them adopted with pride, since its meaning, 'poor men', was a reminder of Jesus' saying, 'Blessed are the poor,' and also of his and James's sayings against the rich.

Nevertheless, it does seem from the rather confused accounts given by the Church historians that the Jewish Christians, as time went on, split into various sects, some of which strayed far from the tenets of the original Nazarenes. Thus we read of certain Gnostic Ebionites, of whom the founding father was Cerinthus, who combined belief in the humanity of Jesus and in the validity of the Torah with a Gnostic belief

175

in a Demiurge ('creator') and a High God.[5] We also read of certain Nazarenes who believed in the Torah, but also believed in the virgin birth of Jesus and in his divine nature. These sects, however, arose by attrition of the original beliefs of the Nazarenes; for the isolation of the Nazarenes from both Christianity and Judaism subjected them to pressures which could give rise to some strange mixed or synthetic forms.

In general, however, the Nazarenes or Ebionites held fast to their original beliefs which we find mentioned again and again in our Christian sources: that Jesus was a human being, born by natural process from Joseph and Mary; that he was given prophetic powers by God; that he was an observant Jew, loyal to the Torah, which he did not abrogate and which was, therefore, still fully valid; and that his message had been distorted and perverted by Paul, whose visions were deluded, and who had falsely represented Jesus as having abrogated the Torah.

In view of the thesis, argued earlier, that the Nazarenes were a monarchical movement of which James was the Prince Regent and Jesus the awaited King, we may ask whether there is evidence that the Nazarenes or Ebionites of later times looked upon Jesus as their King. Most of our Christian sources do not mention this aspect. Instead, they stress that the Ebionites, while insisting that Jesus was no more than a man, achieved prophetic status by the descent of the Holy Spirit upon him, which was identical with 'the Christ', a divine power. Of course, the Gentile Christian historians who wrote these accounts were strongly affected by the Pauline Christian definition of the word 'Christ', by which it lost its original Jewish monarchical meaning and became a divine title (partly because it became assimilated, in the Hellenistic mind, to the Greek word *chrestos*, meaning 'good', which was a common appellation of divine figures in the mystery religions). Apart from this inauthentic use of the word 'Christ', the accounts ring true; for the idea that prophecy is attained by the descent upon a human being of a divine force (called in the Jewish sources 'the Holy Spirit' or *ru'ah ha-qodesh*, or sometimes the *shekhinah* or indwelling presence of God) is common in Judaism, and must have been shared by the Ebionites. But the monarchical overtones of the word 'Christ' (Hebrew *Messiah*) are lost in most of these Christian accounts. Where the monarchical aspect reappears, however, is in the occasional mention of the millenarian or chiliastic beliefs of the Ebionites, who believed that Jesus, on his return, would reign for a thousand years on Earth.[6] Here the concept of Jesus as King of the Jews (and by virtue of the priest role of the Jewish nation) spiritual King of the whole world is clear, and the Ebionites are shown to regard Jesus as the successor of David and Solomon. The thousand-year reign does not point to a concept of Jesus as a supernatural being, but reflects the common idea that human longevity in Messianic times would recover its antediluvian dimension.

Of course, millenarian beliefs are not entirely lacking in Pauline Christianity, too, where they have a curiously subterranean role. The Book of Revelation, originally a Jewish Christian work but much edited, was included in the New Testament canon, and from this stemmed millenarian beliefs which are somewhat hard to reconcile with Pauline Christology. The belief in the thousand-year earthly reign of a kingly Jesus at the end of days inspired many movements of political revolt within Christendom and often threatened the domination of the Pope and the Emperor, for inherent in these beliefs was the notion that justice is attainable on Earth and that the kingdom of God is an earthly Utopia, not an other-worldly condition of blessedness. The role of Antichrist, the earthly power opposed to Jesus *redivivus*, was usually assigned to the Jews, so that populist millenarian movements were often viciously anti-Semitic;[7] but occasionally, the Antichrist was identified instead as the real oppressors of the poor and on these occasions the political aspirations derived from Judaism and from Jewish Christianity threatened to perform a role of liberation in Christendom, in contrast to the other-worldly Paulinist theology which always worked on the side of the powers that be. It is not surprising that Popes and Emperors have always deprecated millenarianism, despite its New Testament authority, and excluded it from official Christian doctrine.[8] In the beliefs of the Ebionites, however, it plays a natural and integral part, and helps to characterize Ebionitism as continuous with Judaism, as well as with the 'Jerusalem Church' led by James, the brother of Jesus.

The prophetic role assigned to Jesus by the Ebionites also deserves some comment. Even in the New Testament, there is much evidence that Jesus, in his own eyes and in those of his followers, had the status of a prophet. Thus some of his followers regarded him as the reincarnation of the prophet Elijah[9], with whom John the Baptist had also been identified. Jesus saw himself, at first, as a prophet foretelling the coming of the Messiah, and it was only at a fairly late stage of his career that he had came to the conviction that he was himself the Messiah whom he had been prophesying. Jesus then combined the roles of prophet and Messiah. This was not unprecedented, for his ancestors David and Solomon were also regarded in Jewish tradition as endowed

177

with the Holy Spirit, which had enabled them to write inspired works (David being regarded as the author of most of the Psalms, and Solomon of the canonical works, Proverbs, Ecclesiastes and the Song of Songs). Nevertheless, these works were not regarded as having the highest degree of inspiration, and were included in the section of the Bible known as the 'Writings', not that known as the 'Prophets'. Jesus was not the author of inspired writings, but he belonged, in his own eyes, to the ranks of the non-literary, wonder-working prophets such as Elijah and Elisha. Such a prophet had never before combined his prophetic office with the position Messiah or King, but there was nothing heretical about the idea that the Messiah could be a prophet too. Such a possibility is envisaged in the eleventh chapter of Isaiah, where the Messiah is described as an inspired person and as having miraculous powers, like a prophet. This assumption of a prophetic role distinguished Jesus from the more humdrum Messiah figures of his period such as Judas of Galilee or, later, Bar Kokhba (though it seems that Theudas also sought to combine the two roles). Thus the Ebionite belief that Jesus had the status of a prophet was not at all inconsistent with their belief that he was the King of Israel, who would restore the Jewish monarchy on his return. To be both king and prophet meant that Jesus was not just an interim Messiah, like Bar Kokhba, sent to deliver the Jews from another wave of Gentile oppression, but the final, culminating Messiah, who would inaugurate the kingdom of God on Earth, as envisaged by the Hebrew prophets, a time of worldwide peace and justice, when the knowledge of God would cover the Earth 'as the waters cover the sea' (Isaiah 11: 9).

On the other hand, this belief in Jesus as an inspired prophet is what ultimately cut off the Ebionites from the main body of Judaism. As long as Jesus was alive his claim to prophetic and Messianic status was not in any way heretical; Pharisee leaders such as Gamaliel were prepared to see how Jesus' claims would turn out in actuality and meanwhile would suspend judgment: in Gamaliel's phrase, 'if this idea of theirs or its execution is of human origin, it will collapse; but if it is from God, you will never be able to put them down, and you risk finding yourselves at war with God' (Acts 5: 39). Even after Jesus' death, for some considerable time, the Pharisees, in view of the Nazarene claim that Jesus' movement had not yet 'collapsed', Jesus being still alive and on the point of return, would be prepared to suspend judgment, as evidenced by Gamaliel, who was speaking after the death of Jesus. But as time went on, these Nazarene claims would wear very thin as far as the main body of the Jewish community was concerned. How long did one have to wait in order to reach a decision that the Nazarene movement had collapsed? Jesus had failed by being crucified, and the assurance by the Nazarenes that he would return had not been fulfilled. The conclusion reached by most Jews, therefore, was that Jesus was just another failed Messiah. As for his alleged prophetic powers, these must have been delusions. He was not after all a genuine prophet or his prophecies about himself would have been fulfilled. The Ebionites, however, still refused to accept this conclusion; though no doubt some of them, weary of waiting for Jesus' return, went back to the fold of normative Judaism and gave up their belief in Jesus as Messiah and prophet. The remaining Ebionites, while still loyal to the Torah, built up an additional scripture or gospel (unfortunately now lost, having been suppressed by the Pauline Christian Church together with the other Ebionite writings), in which they set down the sayings of Jesus, who, to them, was just as inspired as Isaiah or Jeremiah and therefore deserved to be included in the canon. This new scripture, for the main body of the Jews, was a heretical addition to the canon of holy writ, and its appearance marked out the Ebionites as a heretical Jewish sect, like the Samaritans and the Sadducees. Moreover, since the Ebionites thought that the age of prophecy had returned in the person of Jesus, they cannot have been willing to accept the authority of the Pharisee sages who built up a corpus of teachings after Jesus' death, on the assumption that the age of prophecy was over, having ceased with the last of the biblical prophets, Malachi. Thus the Ebionites, by their continued belief in Jesus as prophet and Messiah, were increasingly cut off from the developing activity of rabbinical Judaism. Yet it was probably not until about AD 135[10] that the Ebionites were finally declared heretics by the Pharisee rabbis. This decision was no doubt influenced by the awareness of the rabbis that the Gentile branch of Christianity, following the teachings of Paul, had abrogated the Torah and developed anti-Semitic attitudes. This was the conclusive proof that Jesus' claim to Messiahship had not been 'from God'. Gentile Christianity, however, unlike Ebionite Christianity, was never declared heretical, since it was too far removed from Judaism to be regarded as a heretical form of it.

The Ebionites were thus in the unhappy position of being ostracized both by what was now the main body of Christians, the Catholic Church, and by the Jews. The pressure to join one or other of these two religions was enormous, and by the fourth century the Ebionites had ceased to be a discernible separate community. Consequently, they have tended to be disregarded and despised by historians. Yet what

179

remains of their testimony about the origins of Christianity is of unique importance, for, unlike the Catholic Church, they were directly linked to the 'Jerusalem Church' and thus to Jesus himself. Their testimony about Paul and the circumstances in which he broke with the 'Jerusalem Church' deserves to be treated with respect, not with the usual scornful dismissal.

The testimony of the Ebionites has been preserved in two forms. Firstly, there are the summaries, already mentioned, of Ebionite beliefs found in the writings of the Church authors Justin Martyr (second century), Irenaeus, Hippolytus and Tertullian (end of the second century and the first half of the third), Origen (middle of the third century), and Epiphanius and Jerome (fourth century). These all confirm that the Ebionites opposed Paul as a false apostle.

The second type of testimony is more indirect, depending on the detective work of modern scholars, yet it is very convincing. Certain texts which have been handed down from the ancient world and the early middle ages are ostensibly not writings of the Ebionites, but of other religious groups; but the painstaking analysis of scholars has shown that embedded in each of these works is a stratum written by an Ebionite author, which has been taken over and adapted by a non-Ebionite author. The two examples that are most pertinent here (since they show how the Ebionites thought of Paul) are the following.

The Pseudo-Clementine writings. These writings were preserved as orthodox patristic works because they were falsely attributed to the authorship of Pope Clement I, who was popularly supposed to have been a disciple of Peter himself. In fact, the core of these writings, as was pointed out by F. C. Baur in the nineteenth century and as most scholars now agree (after an interim of dispute and denigration of Baur's work), is Jewish Christian or Ebionite, stemming from second-century Syria. This core shows a staunch adherence to the Torah, and contains an impassioned attack on those who attributed anti-Torah views to Peter. Paul is not mentioned by name, but he is strongly hinted at as the supreme enemy under the disguise of 'Simon Magus', against whom Peter is represented as polemicizing. Peter's attack on this lightly disguised Paul is on the grounds that he is a false prophet, that he has spread lies about Peter and, most telling of all, that he knows nothing about the true teachings of Jesus, since he never met him in the flesh and bases his ideas of Jesus on delusive visions. That this 'Simon Magus' is really Paul is now accepted by scholars, despite many desperate attempts to resist this conclusion made by critics of Baur who realized how profound would be the consequences of such an admission. For it shows that Paul, far from being a unanimously accepted pillar of the Church, like Peter, was a controversial figure, whose role in the founding of Christianity was a subject of great contention.

The Arabic manuscript discovered by Shlomo Pines. Some interesting evidence of the views of the Jewish Christian community of Syria at a later date, probably the fifth century, was discovered by the Israeli scholar Shlomo Pines. While studying a tenth-century Arabic work by 'Abd al-Jabbar in a manuscript in Istanbul, he was able to prove that one section of this work had actually been incorporated from a Jewish Christian source. The standpoint of this incorporated section is that of the Ebionites: belief in the continuing validity of the Torah, insistence on the human status of Jesus as a prophet, and strong opposition to Paul as the falsifier of Jesus' teachings. According to this source, Paul abandoned the observance of the Torah mainly in order to obtain the backing of Rome and achieve power and influence for himself. Paul is even held responsible for the destruction of the Temple by the Romans, since his anti-Jewish propaganda inflamed the Romans against the Jews. His Christianity, says this source, was 'Romanism'; instead of converting Romans into Christians, he converted Christians into Romans.

This Jewish Christian source also contains some acute criticism of the Gospels, which it declares to be untrustworthy and self-contradictory. The only trustworthy Gospel, it declares, was the original one written in Hebrew, yet it is doubtful whether the community which produced this source still possessed a copy of this original Gospel. One of the source's remarks on the Gospel stories of Jesus' alleged abrogation of the laws of the Torah is of special interest. It relates to the corn-plucking incident, which it explains as a case of dire emergency due to the state of starvation of the disciples; and the technical phrase in Arabic used to explain the legality of the corn-plucking is a direct translation of the Hebrew *piqquah nefesh* ('the saving of a soul'), used in the Talmud in connection with the abrogation of the sabbath law in cases of danger to human life.

In general, the picture emerging from this text is of a Jewish Christian community, in the fifth century, out of touch in many ways with its own sources and barely managing to preserve an underground existence, yet still clinging to elements of belief deriving from centuries earlier and, at certain points, still linked to the earliest Jewish Christians of all, the Jerusalem Nazarene community of James and Peter.

The Ebionites did not survive for the simple reason that they were persecuted out of existence by the Catholic Church. When this oppression was lifted for any reason (for example, when an area changed from Christian to Muslim rule), they sometimes came out of hiding and resumed an open existence. There is even evidence, from the works of the Jewish philosopher Saadia,[11] that this happened as late as the tenth century. Mostly, however, the Ebionites were forced to assume a protective disguise of orthodoxy, and in time this led to complete assimilation. Yet, while they still retained their clandestine beliefs, they often had a profound influence on Christianity in general; there is reason to believe that many Judaizing heresies in Christian history, including Arianism, derived from underground Ebionite groups. Their influence was in the direction of humanism and this-worldly concern, and against the meek acceptance of slavery and oppression, and they had a restraining influence on Christian anti-Semitism. They represented an alternative tradition in Christianity that never quite died out.

The Ebionites are thus by no means a negligible or derisory group. Their claim to represent the original teaching of Jesus has to be taken seriously. It is quite wrong, therefore, to dismiss what they had to say about Paul as unworthy of attention.

Let us look, then, more carefully at the earliest extant formulation of the Ebionite view of Paul, found in the works of Epiphanius (fourth century). 'They declare that he was a Greek ... He went up to Jerusalem, they say, and when he had spent some time there, he was seized with a passion to marry the daughter of the priest. For this reason he became a proselyte and was circumcised. Then, when he failed to get the girl, he flew into a rage and wrote against circumcision and against the sabbath and the Law' (Epiphanius, *Panarion*, 30.16. 6–9). This account, of course, is not history. It is what Epiphanius declares the Ebionites were saying in the fourth century and is coloured both by Epiphanius's hostility to the Ebionites and by the Ebionites' hostility to Paul. Nevertheless, there is a core here that may well be true.

Two elements in particular in the story have been shown in our previous discussions to be important: that Paul was a 'Greek' (i.e. a Hellenistic Gentile), and that he was involved with the High Priest (here simply called 'the priest'). A third authentic element may be detected: a failure by Paul to achieve an ambition, and his consequent desertion of the High Priest and involvement with the Jesus movement.

The picture of Paul as a disappointed lover is a typical creation of the folk imagination, yet it is not entirely off the mark. Paul was indeed in love, not with the High Priest's daughter, but with Judaism, of which the High Priest was the symbol (if not the exponent). It was Paul's frustrated love-affair with Judaism that created Pauline Christianity.

On the more realistic level, the High Priest was indeed the key person in Paul's life: his employer when he harassed the Nazarenes, his enemy when he abandoned his attachment to the High Priest's collaborationist regime by his defection at Damascus, and again his deadly enemy when he escaped from the hostility of the Nazarenes into the custody of the Roman police.

Epiphanius's account is clearly incomplete, for it contains no reference to Paul's relations with the Jerusalem Nazarenes. The Ebionites of Epiphanius's day must have had some view about how Paul stood with James and Peter.

Yet, incomplete and romanticized as Epiphanius' account is, it is in several respects more accurate than the account of Paul that was handed down by the Catholic Church or even than the account that Paul gives of himself in his Epistles. Instead of the respectable Pharisee of unimpeachable Jewish descent, the friend and peer of James and Peter, we can sense through Epiphanius's garbled account something of the real Paul – the tormented adventurer, threading his way by guile through a series of stormy episodes, and setting up a form of religion that was his own individual creation.

CHAPTER 16

THE MYTHMAKER

Books on Paul generally end with a chapter on Paul's theology, in which the authors try to tease out Paul's position on such matters as predestination, original sin, the trinity, soteriology and eschatology. It generally emerges that Paul has no sustained philosophical position on these abstract matters, though he provides much material for later more professional thinkers. Paul was not primarily a thinker, but he had a religious imagination of a high order. It seems more fruitful, therefore, to consider Paul as mythologist, rather than as theologian. No religion is based primarily on a theology. First comes the story; and later, when the imaginative fires have died down and the mythmaking faculty has ceased, along come the theologians to try to turn the story into a system. What, then, was the new story that Paul created? For the commonly held picture of Paul as the theorist who spun an intellectual framework for the simple teachings of Jesus will not do. This picture assumes that Jesus was the founder of Christianity, and Paul was the intellectualizing epigone. The truth, however, as we have seen, is that Jesus did not found a new religion at all, but simply sought to play an accepted role in the story of an existing religion, Judaism. It was Paul who founded Christianity, and he did so by creating a new story, one sufficiently powerful and gripping to launch a new world religion. In this new story Jesus was given a leading role, but this does not make him the creator of Christianity, any more than Hamlet wrote the plays of Shakespeare. The Jesus of Paul's story was a fictional character, just as Shakespeare breathed new imaginative life into the bones of the historical figure of Hamlet the Dane.

The basic theme in the Pauline myth can be summed up in one phrase: the descent of the divine saviour. Everything in the so-called theology stems from this; for since salvation or rescue comes from above, no efficacy can be ascribed to the action or initiative of man.

Thus some kind of doctrine of predestination follows: when the divine rescuer descends, he does not look to see who *deserves* to be rescued, because this would be to ascribe some kind of saving efficacy to something that man does by his own effort, whatever he does that comprises deservingness. How, then, do we know who will be rescued? We do not. Those will be rescued whom the saviour has decided to rescue. What, then, can we do to be rescued? Nothing, except to have *faith*. What does this mean? It means to rely entirely on the descending saviour, and to abandon every other hope of rescue. But surely even to have an attitude of faith requires some kind of effort, and, if so, not everything is contributed by the saviour. This kind of conundrum engages the attention of later theologians, and helps to fill the libraries of Christian theology, but the basic thing is still the story: rescue has come from above.

The descent of the divine saviour implies other narrative elements. It means that there are two realms, Above and Below. Above is the region of Light, and Below is the region of Darkness, the dark prison from which we need to be rescued and from which no one belonging to Below can release us. Thus no Below-type act of liberation can do us any good, no transfer from one area of Below to another, such as from Egypt to Palestine or from slavery to freedom. What imprisons us is the human condition, which is one of bondage to the powers of Evil. From this aspect of the story comes what theologians call the doctrine of Original Sin, a re-reading by Paul of the Hebrew story about the ejection of Adam and Eve from the Garden of Eden, which in the story itself, and its traditional Jewish exegesis, did not have this radical connotation.

So far the story is the same as that found in the type of religion known as Gnosticism. Recent discoveries have shown that, contrary to what was previously argued, Gnosticism existed before Christianity, though it later took Christian forms.[1] The essence of the Gnostic myth was that this world is in the grip of evil, and that therefore a visitor (or a series of visitors) is necessary from the world of Light, in order to impart the secret knowledge (*gnosis*) by which some privileged souls may escape from the thrall of this world. In Gnosticism, this world is regarded as so evil that it cannot have been created by God. It was created by a limited or evil power called the Demiurge ('creator'). The true High God lives in a region beyond the skies, but he has pity on humanity and sends them an emissary to teach them how to free themselves from the Demiurge. In some Gnostic sects the Demiurge is identified with the God of the Jews, and it was thought that the Jewish scripture, the Torah, was given by this evil deity. The Jews were therefore regarded

185

by these sects as the special people of the Demiurge and as having the role in history of obstructing the saving work of the emissaries of the High God. While anti-Semitism (in the sense of intense dislike of Jews) was not uncommon in the ancient world, it was probably among the Gnostic sects that the most radical form of anti-Semitism originated – the view that the Jews are the representatives of cosmic evil, the people of the Devil.

Paul's Epistles show a form of Gnosticism which is worth isolating, though it is combined with other, non-Gnostic mythological elements to which we shall come later. The basic perception of Gnosticism is certainly present in Paul: that this world is so sunk in evil that rescue from above is a necessity. But the mythological details are modified. Paul does not think that the world was actually created by an evil power; he accepts the account of Genesis that the world was created by God. But he believes that the world has come under the control and lordship of an evil power; the Earth is captured territory. This is why there can be no hope of salvation except from outside.

The importance of the concept of an evil power or the Devil in Paul's thought, or rather mythology, cannot be overestimated. When referring to this power or powers, he generally uses expressions derived from Gnosticism rather than from Judaism. Thus, he gives a picture of the assault of cosmic evil powers on Jesus in these words: 'None of this world's rulers knew this wisdom; for if they had known it, they would not have crucified the glorious Lord' (1 Corinthians 2: 8). The expression 'this world's rulers' (*archonton tou aionos toutou*) does not refer to earthly rulers such as the Romans or the High Priest, but to supernatural powers who rule over 'this world' in the sense of 'this cosmic era'. Similarly, he uses the expression 'principalities and powers' and other such expressions with Gnostic connections to refer to the supernatural forces that oppose Jesus and himself (e.g. Romans 8: 38). On one occasion, he even calls the supreme evil force a 'god' (II Corinthians 4: 4).

Paul thus thinks of the forces of evil as organized in a hierarchy and as having power independent of God, at least for a period in cosmic history. It was primarily to break the power of these forces that Jesus came to the world; though the earthly power that opposed him, that of the Jews, seemed to be his main enemies, this was only on the surface, for he was engaged, in reality, in a vast cosmic struggle in which his earthly antagonists were the pawns of evil supernatural forces.

Even in Iranian religion, from which the dualism of the Gnostics was ultimately derived, the evil supernatural power was regarded as

186

inferior to the good power in that good would ultimately prevail. So Paul's dualism is hardly less extreme than that of Iranian or Gnostic religion. It has been argued recently that Paul derived this dualism from Jewish, not Hellenistic, sources since the Jewish Apocryphal and Pseudepigraphical books do give an important role to Satan; and the Qumran writings (the Dead Sea Scrolls) also ascribe much of the evil in the world to the activities of an evil angel called Belial. These writings, of course, were excluded from the canon of scripture by the Pharisees, who strongly opposed dualism and regarded Satan as merely one of God's angels, who did not rebel against Him, but obeys his orders, whether as the Angel of Death or as prosecutor of human beings in the divine court. Even in purely Jewish terms, Paul's dualism would exclude him from the Pharisee mode of thought. But, in any case, there is a great difference between Paul's dualism and that of the Jewish writings mentioned, which, though affected by despair, never descend to the depths out of which Paul's writings spring. Though the Jewish Pseudepigrapha and Qumran writings have a sense of cosmic evil, they still believe in the efficacy of the Torah and of the election of Israel; they do not require a saviour from the upper world in order to make human life viable. It is through the practice of the Torah that the power of evil is eventually broken; and this means that the exercise of the human will to good is still the most important factor in history. The scene of the battle between good and evil is still within the human psyche, not removed to the skies with humans as helpless and passive reflections of the conflict. On the contrary, the battle that goes on between supernatural powers is a reflection of the battle on Earth; and the outcome of the battle will be a transformation of the Earth, not an organized escape from it.

No plausible Jewish model can be found for Paul's type of dualism; the only contemporary parallel is in Gnosticism. There are some differences, of course, but even in the differences we note a basic similarity; and here we must bear in mind that there were many varieties of Gnosticism, and that the central doctrines of the evil of this world and the need for extraterrestrial salvation could receive an almost infinitely varied mythological elaboration. Paul's variety does not include the notions that the evil power created the world and the Torah; but it contains notions that perform the same kind of function.

Paul belongs to the kind of Gnosticism that was fascinated by the Jews and Judaism, and sought to weave them both into its pattern, usually with anti-Semitic effect. The Torah, in this kind of scheme, is acknowledged to be of supernatural origin, but it comes from the wrong supernatural source. Yet the Torah, for this kind of Gnostic, contains a secret message: despite itself, it gives information about the tradition of the true *gnosis*. Over and against the official tradition contained in the Hebrew Bible there are hints of an alternative tradition, by-passing the authority of the Jews and Judaism. Thus we find the .Gnostics concentrating on figures in the Bible who are not Jews, but who nevertheless seem to have authority: such as Seth, the son of Adam born after the murder of Abel by Cain; or Enoch, reputed to have been taken alive into heaven; or Melchizedek, the priest of the Most High who was not of the Jewish Levitical priesthood. On figures such as these it was possible to construct the fantasy of an alternative tradition, stemming not from the Jewish God, but from the High God above whose message far transcended Judaism.

Some Gnostic sects, indeed, went much further than this and, instead of constructing an alternative tradition out of non-Jewish figures mentioned with respect in the Bible, they reversed the values of the Bible altogether, and constructed their alternative tradition out of figures regarded by the Bible as evil. Thus the Cainites revered Cain, and all the other villains of Bible stories. Yet even this is a kind of tribute to the power of the Bible saga; only by a parasitic feeding on the Bible could the Gnostics supply their myth with content. The Gnostics of this type were actuated by an ambivalent feeling towards Judaism. They felt the pull of Judaism and especially its vast canvas of human history, but could not accept it, since the pride of Hellenistic culture prevented them from accepting a 'barbarian' religion; and also the basic optimism of Judaism, with its gratitude to God for the gift of this world, was repugnant to them.

Paul, as we have seen, did not adopt the Gnostic myth of the creation of the world by the Demiurge; but he adopted the almost equivalent myth of the 'ruler of this age', the evil power who has taken over the world, though he did not create it. Similarly, Paul did not adopt the Gnostic myth that the Torah was given by an evil power and was thus an evil work; instead, he introduced the view that the Torah was a work of limited authority. Giving mythical expression to this view, he asserted that the Torah was given, not by God, but by angels. This demotion of the status of the Torah is expressed as follows: 'It was a temporary measure pending the arrival of the "issue" to whom the promise was made. It was promulgated through angels, and there was an intermediary; but an intermediary is not needed for one party acting alone, and God is one' (Galatians 3: 19–20). Various scholars have tried to argue that the Jewish sources contain the notion that the Torah was given by angels, not by God, and that therefore Paul was not saying anything startling or new in this passage. Note that the New English Bible translation, quoted above, rather disguises the starkness of Paul's statement by translating the Greek word '*diatageis*' as 'promulgated' instead of the correct translation (found in the Revised Version) 'ordained'. If the Torah was 'ordained' by angels that means that they originated it, while if they only 'promulgated' it, it may have originated from God. Paul is saying quite definitely that the angels were the authors of the Torah, not God. Despite the convoluted arguments of scholars, there is no parallel to this in Jewish sources, which all insist that God was the sole author of the Torah and that it was God Himself, not angels, whose voice was heard on Mount Sinai 'giving' the Torah.[2]

The only parallel to Paul's statement is to be found in the Gnostic literature, which states that the Torah was given by an inferior power, the Demiurge. Paul is thus adapting the Gnostic doctrine of the inferiority of the Torah: instead of being ordained by an inferior and also evil power, it is ordained by inferior but beneficent powers. This is in accordance with Paul's view of the Torah as merely temporary and as foreshadowing something greater that would supersede it, the advent of the saviour. The other two references to the angels as authors of the Torah in the New Testament (Acts 7: 53 and Hebrews 2: 2) are simply based on Paul's statement here. Paul was the sole creator of this myth about the angels fathering the Torah. Here again we encounter the pressure that exists in the Christian tradition and scholarship to deprive Paul of his originality as the inventor of Christianity.

The 'intermediary' to whom Paul refers is Moses, but his remark that 'an intermediary is not needed for one party acting alone, and God is one' is somewhat cryptic. The best explanation seems to be that Paul is pointing out that the Torah constitutes a covenant or contract between two parties, God and Israel. God's pronouncement of blessings to Abraham, on the other hand, was one-sided, with Abraham as passive recipient, required only to have 'faith': consequently no 'intermediary' was needed. This one-sided conferring of blessing is, for Paul, a far superior and more immediate form of communication between man and God, reflecting the helpless state of man, utterly dependent on salvation from above. Paul thus rejects as inferior the Jewish concept of the dignity of human nature, by which the Torah constitutes a covenant and agreement between two partners, God and Israel.

Paul's use of Abraham in his discussion in Galatians and elsewhere is interesting in the context of our consideration of his affinity to

Gnosticism. We have seen that the Gnostics used non-Jewish biblical characters such as Seth, Enoch and Melchizedek as alleged representatives of an alternative tradition of *gnosis*. Paul uses Abraham in just the same way. Abraham, though the ancestor of the Israelites, was also the ancestor of other nations and was a pre-Mosaic figure not involved with the Torah. Paul therefore treats him as an exponent of the way of 'faith', foreshadowing the obsolescence of the Torah even before it was given. This trend is developed in the Epistle to the Hebrews (written by a later disciple of Paul, though wrongly attributed to Paul himself by Church tradition), where the figure of Melchizedek is used in the same way, to show that there is an alternative priesthood, superior to that of the Jewish Aaronites.

This use of non-Jewish figures from the Bible, so reminiscent of Gnosticism, is not, however, the main strategy of Paul and of the Pauline Church with regard to the Hebrew Bible. The Gnostics regarded themselves as outsiders and therefore constructed an 'outsider' tradition from biblical materials, rejecting the main line of the biblical story as concerned with the people of the Demiurge and thus contaminated by worldly dross. Paul, however, and the Christian tradition that followed him, adopted a much bolder line. He asserted that all the main prophets of the Hebrew Bible were proto-Christians. None of them (not even Moses) had regarded the Torah as permanently binding; all of them had looked forward to the advent of the saviour who would abrogate the Torah and show the true way of faith and salvation.

This amounted to a wholesale usurpation of the Jewish religio-historical scheme. Something very similar happened six centuries later, when Islam performed the same operation of usurpation on both Judaism and Christianity, declaring that Abraham, Moses and Jesus had all been proto-Muslims. Islam, however, did not adopt the Jewish and Christian scriptures into its own canon; it was able, therefore, to alter the details freely, for example substituting Ishmael[3] (thought to be the ancestor of the Arabs) for Isaac in the story of the *akedah* or Binding of Isaac. Alterations of this kind were not open to Paul, who accepted the Old Testament in full as the word of God, but instead he imported his own meanings into it, and turned it into a coded message of the Pauline mythology. In this way, the succession of Hebrew prophets was put into the place of the succession of 'outsiders' bearing *gnosis*, envisaged by the Gnostic exegetes of the Bible. The prophets were now the outsiders, because they knew the Christian meaning of their message, which was rejected by the Jews, who insisted on the permanence of the Torah and treated the prophets as they later treated Jesus. The division between Jews and outsiders is retained, as in Gnosticism, but the lines are differently drawn, with the result that Pauline Christianity, instead of opposing prophetic Judaism, appropriated it for its own purposes.

Paul's attitude to the Torah must now be examined in order to show his affinity to Gnostic antinomianism. It is the essence of Paul's religious stance that law cannot save; for if so, as he says, what need would there be for the sacrifice of Jesus? In Judaism, these alternatives are not even intelligible, since in Judaism the issue is not salvation at all, for one is saved merely by being in the covenant, and the issue is then to work together with God by implementing the Torah. For the Jew, only outrageously wilful behaviour can jeopardize his condition of being 'saved', and thus the expression 'saved' is not even part of the Jewish religious vocabulary. For Paul, however, the human condition is desperate, and the only issue is salvation. Thus law is irrelevant, for it is useless to talk to a drowning man about how he should behave; instead, one should throw him a rope. The purpose of the law or Torah, says Paul in Galatians and elsewhere,[4] is not to teach us how to behave, but to convince us of the desperate nature of our moral situation. By giving us a model of what good behaviour would be, it shows us how incapable we are of such behaviour in the evil state of human nature, and therefore impels us to seek a way of acquiring a new nature. The human condition must be changed, for as it is, it is not viable.

This attitude to law corresponds to that of Gnosticism. For in Gnosticism, too, the issue is not instruction about how to behave, but salvation. On the other hand, there are some differences between the antinomianism of Paul and that of Gnosticism. The Gnostics did not merely despair of law, as Paul did; they actually despised law, as something essentially inferior to *gnosis*. For law was indissolubly connected with the activities of the body, as opposed to the spirit (*pneuma*). The spiritual being, the 'pneumatic', was above the operation of the moral law or, in the phrase of a modern thinker with some affinity to the Gnostics, Nietzsche, 'beyond good and evil'. Like Nietzsche, the Gnostics were led by this attitude to develop a human typology, by which only a minority of humanity was capable of true spirituality; most human beings were irretrievably bound to the body and materialism. Paul too uses the expression 'spirit' (*pneuma*) in ways analogous to the usage of the Gnostics; thus at times he suggests that only those already predisposed to the 'spirit' can benefit by the sacrifice of Jesus, and here the tendency towards predestination inherent in

Pauline doctrines is reinforced by a destiny of personality and character. Yet Paul's attitude towards law itself is not straight-forwardly Gnostic. At times, at any rate, he sees law, as supremely embodied in the Torah, as the ultimate goal, but one that cannot be realized except through 'salvation' and rebirth. Only the reborn personality can achieve the goal of observing the Torah.

It has been argued that here Paul is merely echoing the thought of rabbinical Judaism, which envisaged that in the 'world to come', God would obliterate the 'evil inclination', and mankind would be able to observe the Torah without psychological impediment or struggle. This is the concept formulated by the prophet Ezekiel: 'I will give them a different heart and put a new spirit into them; I will take the heart of stone out of their bodies and give them a heart of flesh' (Ezekiel 11: 19). The only difference between Paul and the rabbis, it is argued, is that Paul believed that the world to come had already arrived, with the advent of Jesus. By having 'faith' in Jesus and sharing in his crucifixion, Paul believed, the 'heart of stone' would be removed, and the Torah could be observed at last. This, however, is to misunderstand the subtlety of the rabbinical attitude in this matter. The rabbis did believe that the 'evil inclination' would be obliterated finally, but this would be as a reward to humanity for its long struggle against evil. It was not the solution to the problem of sin, which was the task of this world and of humanity; it was the removal of the problem in order to reward mankind with a state of blessedness. Thus the rabbis say in the Mishnah: 'Better is one hour of repentance and good works in this world than the whole life of the world to come; and better is one hour of bliss in the world to come than the whole life of this world' (Mishnah, Avot 4: 17). This is an attitude that Paul could not understand. It shows a subtlety and maturity that contrasts strongly with Paul's adolescent despair and impatience for perfection. For rabbis, the point of life is in the struggle, rather than in the reward. For Paul, the reward has become the indispensable substitute for the struggle, which he regards as hopeless and, therefore, pointless.

Thus, even when Paul is in the mood to take the Torah to be the true standard of moral behaviour, he destroys its efficacy: in a fallen state humanity cannot implement it, while in a 'saved' state humanity does not need it, since its provisions then become second nature and are automatically obeyed. But Paul does not adopt this comparatively respectful attitude to the Torah consistently. Sometimes (especially when combating the influence of the Jerusalem Jesus movement) he takes up an attitude of hostility to the Torah, berating it as materialistic and unspiritual, quite in the Gnostic vein. Thus he declares that those who wish to keep the sabbaths and festivals of the Torah are subservient to 'the mean and beggarly spirits of the elements' (Galatians 4: 9), a Gnostic expression for the lower forces of nature. At times he seems to be saying that there is now a new law, called 'the law of Christ', which has superseded the old law of the Torah, which has been abrogated and was always imperfect. But this is not just a matter of reform, for the new 'law of Christ' operates in a different way, being based on grace and faith, not on works. Nor is it a matter of simply dropping the ceremonial provisions of the old law, while retaining its moral provisions, for Paul introduces new ceremonies such as the Eucharist and Pauline Christianity has been, if anything, more fully equipped with ritual than Judaism ever was.

The fact is that Paul, like all the Gnostics, is unable to fit law into his scheme of things intelligibly, and yet he has to try to do so, because law simply will not go away. All Gnostics wish to abolish law and to substitute for it some kind of instinctive, 'saved' behaviour that will fulfil all the demands of law without the necessity of having a law. But in practice things never work out in this way. People who are supposed to be 'saved' behave, unaccountably, just as badly as before they were saved, so that law has to be reintroduced to restrain them. Also, there are always logically minded people to say that if they are 'saved', all their behaviour *must* be correct, so they can indulge in any kind of behaviour that happens to appeal to them (such as sexual orgies or murder) in the confidence that nothing they do can be wrong. In other words, by being 'saved', people may behave worse instead of better. Paul had to cope with this 'saved' libertinism, and could only use the methods of moral exhortation that were supposed to have been made obsolete by faith and the transition from 'works' to 'grace'. The same problem was felt throughout Gnosticism, as is shown by the Gnostic libertine sects such as the Carpocratians.

Thus Paul's attitude of partly admitting the validity of law, under pressure, does not exclude him from the category of Gnosticism, as some have argued, for this compulsion to do something, however unwillingly, about fitting law into the scheme is common to all the Gnostic sects, each of which dealt with the matter in its own way. It is interesting to compare Valentinian Gnosticism, for example, with Pauline Christianity. Each, on the level of basic theory, is antinomian, but each provides a place for law out of practical necessity. This led to the ironic result, in Christianity, of the building up, eventually, of a huge body of canon law in a religion which began as a revolt against law. The new law was supposed to be fundamentally different from the old law of the Torah, being a law of grace, but in fact it was administered in exactly the same way, except that it lacked the humanity and sophistication which centuries of rabbinical development had given to the Torah. For example, all the safeguards for the position of women which had been developed in Pharisee law were jettisoned by the new Pauline law.[5] Starting from scratch, Christian law had to rediscover painfully insights that Pharisee law had long taken for granted. For example, Pharisee law regarded all evidence extorted by compulsion as invalid. Christian law was still torturing people to obtain evidence, regarded as legally valid, sixteen centuries after Paul scrapped the Torah and instituted the 'law of Christ'. The paradox of an antinomian religion with a complicated legal system led constantly to attempts in Christian history to restore pristine antinomian attitudes; the Reformation was the most massive instance. But the Reformation churches soon found themselves in precisely the same dilemma and developed systems of canon law of their own. The dichotomy between an antinomian core and an outer shell of law is not conducive to the best kind of development of law, but rather leads to a desiccated form, very different from the warmth and enthusiasm found in Jewish law. It is ironic that the best exemplification of the dry 'Pharisees' of Christian myth is to be found among Christian religious lawyers.

Paul, by adopting the Gnostic myth of the descending saviour, produced doctrines typical of Gnosticism in his dualism, his anti-Jewish use of the Jewish scriptures and his antinomianism, though in each case, the more extreme forms of Gnosticism are excluded by Paul's acceptance of the Hebrew Bible as the word of God. He emerges from this examination as a moderate Gnostic, but a Gnostic none the less. He does not represent the world as the creation of an evil God; nor does he say that the Torah emanated from an evil God; nor does he say that law is to be utterly condemned as a mere prescription for the body; but he has doctrines which are analogues of all these, adding up to a Gnostic system of salvation by a heavenly visitant.

Why, then, did the Pauline Christian Church treat those Gnostic groups that attached themselves to Christianity as heretical? This fact alone has led many scholars to argue that Pauline Christianity cannot be regarded as owing anything to Gnosticism. This conclusion, however, does not follow. For Pauline Christianity did not consist of Gnosticism alone, but contained other important ingredients which the Gnostic Christians were not prepared to accept. It is the fusion of these other elements with Gnosticism that constitutes the uniqueness of Paul's mythology. Paul did not invent any of the elements that went to make his mythology; what he did invent was the way in which all the elements were combined to make a new and powerful myth.

The chief non-Gnostic element was derived from the mystery religions. It was from the latter that Paul derived his idea of Jesus as a dying and resurrected god, who confers salvation and immortality through a mystic sharing in his death and resurrection. In the Gnostic myth, the bearer of *gnosis* may encounter hostility from the unspiritual followers of the Demiurge, and he may even be killed by them, but this is not the main purpose of his coming. His chief purpose is to bring the *gnosis*, which is the secret knowledge of a mystic or magical nature, by which the initiate can undertake the spiritual journey that takes him away from the domination of the lower powers. There is thus no *sacrificial* motif in Gnosticism. The saviour does not come to Earth to act as a sacrifice for mankind, but to bring them knowledge, if they are fit to receive it.

In Pauline Christianity, on the other hand, the *gnosis* which the saviour brings is nothing but the knowledge of the saving power of his own death. He functions as a sacrifice, but only if the initiate is aware of his sacrificial power and shares, by 'faith', in the saviour's sacrificial experience. This idea is derived wholly from the mystery cults, in which precisely the same mystery of sharing in the death and resurrection of the deity was central.

This explains why the Gnostic Christians were condemned as heretics, for they could never accept this sacrificial aspect of Pauline salvation doctrine, the aspect derived from the mystery cults. For them, Christ was a bringer of secret knowledge, not a sacrificial figure. They therefore denied that he ever died on the cross, saying that this was mere appearance; consequently, their heresy was known as 'Docetism', from a Greek word meaning 'to appear' or 'to seem'. The Gnostics, with their radical opposition between spirit and matter, could not accept that Christ was material enough to undergo a sacrificial experience; that would argue that he had truly become flesh, for only the flesh could undergo such real suffering. But for Paul, it was essential that Christ should be a real sacrifice, not just a seeming one. Otherwise, the burden of sin, for which all mankind deserved death, could not be rolled away. Consequently, Christ had to be made sufficiently material to undergo such a death. The descent into matter of the divine saviour was part of both myths; but for the Gnostics, this descent was sacrifice enough and was undertaken only because the imparting of *gnosis* would be

195

impossible without it. But for Paul, with his mind full of sacrificial imagery, with his conviction of the saving power of the shedding of blood and the undergoing of torture (derived from his youthful experience of the horrific Attis cult), such bloodless imparting of secrets was unsatisfying. There had to be a cosmic agony to answer to the agony of his own soul. He therefore turned from the sophistication and intellectuality of the Gnostics to the primitive imagery of the mystery cults, derived from prehistoric rites of human sacrifice.[6]

There was thus a real amalgamation in Paul's mind between Gnosticism and mystery religion, and this was unprecedented. From Gnosticism came the picture of a world in hellish darkness, yearning for salvation, into which a figure descends from the world of light. This figure walks through the world dispensing cryptic saving wisdom, attracting a few, but surrounded by the baying forces of evil. From mystery religion comes the story of the death of the saviour: overwhelmed by the forces of evil, he suffers a cruel death, but this very death is the source of salvation, far more than anything he has taught (and what he has taught turns out to be only the saving efficacy of his coming death).

From mystery religion, too, comes the paradox of sacrificial salvation: that it is the result of the success of evil. Only because the forces of evil succeed in overwhelming the saviour does salvation come to the world; because death must precede resurrection, and without death there can be no atonement for mankind, which can provide from its own number no person worthy of such a sacrificial function. So, in mystery religion, the dying and resurrected god has an evil opponent – Set against Osiris, Mot against Baal, Loki against Balder – who is essential to the story, because without him there would be no salvation, though his lot is to be accursed and damned; he is the Evil Christ, who bears the sin of killing the Good Christ.

It must be emphasized that neither Gnosticism alone, nor mystery religion alone, could have produced this powerful myth. For Gnosticism, as we have seen, is without the concept of the divine sacrifice. Mystery religion, on the other hand, is without several ingredients of the Pauline myth. It does not conceive the world as a dark hell into which the god descends, nor does it conceive the salvation it offers as a rescue from hellish damnation.[7] Typically, mystery religion offers immortality as a kind of bonus for initiates; those who are not initiates are not regarded as damned, but simply as having missed an extra benefit. It is the admixture of Gnosticism that adds urgency to the mystery religion initiation, giving the sense of escape from a terrible

196

doom. Thus the element of incarnation is unimportant in mystery religion, though not entirely absent.[8] Sometimes the god undergoes death (like Balder) without incarnation or descent to Earth. This is not because Pauline Christianity values the flesh more than mystery religion (as some Christian apologists have argued) but because the Gnostic descent into vile matter is essential to Paul in order that the sacrifice should be complete. It is because the world is a hell which has to be harrowed that Christ descends into it, not because the flesh has to be beatified. Similarly, the insistence of Paul that Christ has to be really crucified, not apparently crucified as the Gnostics would have it, does not argue a higher valuation of the flesh by Paul, but rather a concern that the flesh should be thoroughly tortured and thus exorcised on behalf of mankind, whose own sufferings are not sufficient and who cannot be saved by mere enlightenment.

The Pauline myth is not, however, composed merely of Gnosticism and mystery religion; a third ingredient was necessary to make it the most compelling myth known to mankind, and that is the ingredient of Judaism. It was from Judaism that Paul added to his concoction the dimension of history. Judaism contains a vast panorama of history from the creation of the world until the last days, and part of the impressiveness of Judaism to observers in the ancient world was its purposive scheme of history, quite different from the annalistic approach of Greek historians. Mystery religion was completely ahistorical; its offer of salvation was for the individual alone. Gnosticism, on the other hand, did have a historical scheme of a kind, parasitic on the Jewish scheme; the succession of outsiders, beginning with Seth, which provided a tradition of *gnosis*. But this was again individualistic, and provided little sense of the development of a community – indeed the only well-formulated community in the Gnostic scheme was that of the Demiurge, the Jews. Gnostic history was a kind of anti-history. Paul, however, boldly took over the whole Jewish scheme of history from Adam to the last days, as a framework for his story of salvation, which he conceived as working itself out through various epochs. The actual content of this historical framework, however, was not derived from Judaism. The Jewish myth of a liberated nation leaving Egypt and crossing the desert to the Promised Land – a paradigm of the political and social Utopianism of Judaism – did not touch Paul at all; instead, he converted it into a parable of his own scheme of salvation for the individual through the sacrifice of Christ. Yet his early admiration for Judaism prevented him from sinking into the quest for mere individual salvation; he conceived of the

Church as a community moving through history, and to this end he incorporated the Jewish 'promises' to Abraham as the rationale of a new 'Israel' taking over the function of a chosen people. The incorporation of the Old Testament into the Christian canon ensured the future of Pauline Christianity as a solidly based human institution, as opposed to the evanescent Gnostic sects and the mystery cult secret societies.

This threefold synthesis of Judaism, Gnosticism and mystery religion was not constructed consciously by Paul, but, as argued in a previous chapter, sprang ready made into Paul's psyche on the road to Damascus, as the solution to his hitherto unsuccessful spiritual quest. It was an imaginative creation of tremendous poetic power, and its progress in the Greco-Roman world is not to be wondered at. Its chief ingredients are indeed Greco-Roman rather than Jewish, and its appeal was to the world-weary Hellenists, yearning for escape from disorientation and despair, not to the Jews, energetically working out the implications of their own very different myth and world view. Pauline Christianity, despite its effort to anchor itself in Judaism by usurping the Jewish religio-historical scheme, is far from Judaism in tone. Its basic world attitude is that of Gnosticism, reinforced by powerful sado-masochistic elements derived from mystery religion, evoking echoes of primitive sacrifice.

An important feature of the Gnostic tone of Paul's religious attitude is his negative view of sex. A relevant passage is the following:

> It is a good thing for a man to have nothing to do with women; but because there is so much immorality, let each man have his own wife and each woman her own husband. . . . All this I say by way of concession, not command. I should like you all to be as I am myself; but everyone has the gift God has granted him, one this gift and another that. To the unmarried and to widows I say this: it is a good thing if they stay as I am myself; but if they cannot control themselves, they should marry. Better be married than burn with vain desire. To the married I give this ruling, which is not mine but the Lord's: a wife must not separate herself from her husband; if she does, she must either remain unmarried or be reconciled to her husband; and the husband must not divorce his wife. (1 Corinthians 7: 1–11)

This passage shows that Paul regarded sexual activity as unspiritual, but regarded the 'gift' of chastity as somewhat rare and therefore did not enjoin chastity on all. This passage and others like it have led to the institution of celibate orders in Christendom and in general to the Christian admiration of celibacy and virginity as ideals; thus Jesus himself is portrayed in the Gospels as sexless or celibate, and his birth is described as miraculously unsexual. Further, Paul, in order to emphasize the grudging nature of his permission of sexual activity in those who lack his 'gift', hedges round even permitted sexual activity with prohibitions: he forbids divorce and remarriage. This prohibition too was institutionalized in Pauline Christianity.

Nothing of this is derived from Judaism. Unmarried people, in Jewish tradition, are regarded with pity, not admiration. It was regarded as a duty to marry. Rabbis were all expected to be married, and the few exceptions were regarded as lacking in full humanity. The cult of the Virgin Mary is entirely alien to Judaism, and Paul's reference to a 'gift' of chastity would be regarded as unintelligible. Jewish mysticism (based on the biblical Song of Songs) regards sexual intercourse as of high mystical significance, and as the earthly analogue of the bliss of the Godhead.

Divorce and remarriage are permitted in Judaism. It is often said wrongly that divorce is permitted only to husbands, not to wives. This is true only in a technical sense; when the ceremony of divorce takes place, the husband hands the bill of divorce, which he has signed, to the wife. But a wife, in rabbinical law, can sue the courts for divorce, and the courts can compel the husband to give a divorce. Grounds for divorce are liberal: a wife can sue for divorce, for example, on the ground that her husband wishes to move to a place where she does not want to live. If it is the husband who wants a divorce, the wife's rights are protected: any property which she brought into the marriage must be returned to her, and she is entitled to a sum of alimony. Though divorce, in Jewish law, is easy, this has not led to an attitude of levity towards marriage; Jewish marriages are notoriously stable. The Jewish attitude to divorce, however, is relaxed and uncensorious. Such an attitude to divorce is generally associated with a positive view of sex, in which the cruelty of condemning people to a sexually unhappy life is fully appreciated.

Attitudes of hostility to sex were not uncommon, however, in the Hellenistic world, and were particularly marked in the Gnostic sects, which, on the whole, associated sex with the contamination of the body, and regarded sexual activity as affecting adversely the spiritual progress of the initiate. In a few Gnostic sects, the attempt to exorcise sex produced, instead of the usual abstinence, a wild, indiscriminate incontinence. This phenomenon is well known in ascetic mystical groups. Paul's attitude of sexual asceticism would have been well understood in the Gnostic sects, some of which (the Valentinians, for example) showed exactly the same tolerance as Paul towards the

199

weaker brethren, who did not have the 'gift'. Thus this aspect of Paul's teaching, in view of his general affinity to Gnostic outlooks, should be ascribed to the influence of Gnosticism, and is certainly strongly opposed to the outlook of Judaism.

Paul's attitude to women, however, has often been ascribed to the influence of Judaism. A common formulation is the following: Jesus showed a new attitude of respect for women, as opposed to Judaism, in which 'women had no rights'; Paul, however, relapsed into the attitude of rabbinical Judaism and regarded women with contempt. This formulation is misconceived. Jesus had women disciples, and imparted his sayings to women as well as men. In having women disciples Jesus was not departing from Judaism, but following the well-known prophetic pattern, shown in the stories in the Hebrew Bible about Elijah and Elisha. In imparting his teachings to women as well as men, Jesus was following not only the prophetic but also the rabbinical pattern, for the preaching of the rabbis, still preserved in the voluminous Midrashic writings, was performed in the presence of both men and women. As for the allegation that in Judaism 'women had no rights', this shows a steadfast ignorance of the rabbinical legislation about women, which gave women rights which they later entirely lost in Christendom, because the abolition of Pharisaic law, instead of producing a new era of spontaneous saintly behaviour, as Paul intended, simply led to a legal vacuum, in which women were without legal protection.

Paul's attitude to women was actually somewhat complex, and cannot be deduced in any simple way from his negative attitude to sex. Indeed, an anti-sex attitude can often lead to a doctrine of the equality of women, since the obliteration of sex also brings about the obliteration of sex differences, so that all human beings are regarded as belonging to a neuter sex. This was the case in some of the Gnostic groups in which sex was regarded as having been overcome, so that women could be regarded as asexual human beings, or even as men, or beings indistinguishable from men.[9]

Many pro-feminist details and remarks can be collected from the writings of Paul. For example, he says, 'There are no such things as Jew and Greek, slave and freeman, male and female; for you are all one person in Christ Jesus' (Galatians 3: 28). Paul's letters show that he was friendly with many women, who were prominent helpers in his work as missionary and apostle.

On the other hand, the following passage shows considerable anti-feminism: 'As in all congregations of God's people, women should not address the meeting. They have no licence to speak, and should keep their place as the law directs. If there is something they want to know, they can ask their own husbands at home. It is a shocking thing that a woman should address the congregation' (1 Corinthians 14: 34–5). The usual explanation given of this passage is that here Paul is relapsing into Pharisaic Judaism, which, it is assumed, gave women an inferior position in the synagogue. Thus when Paul supports his remarks by appeal to the 'law' ('as the law directs'), what he had in mind, according to this unthinking but widespread view, was Pharisaic law. As Paul has devoted so much of his energy in his letters to explaining that this law is no longer in force, this explanation is, to say the least, open to objection.

If, however, Paul, as some have argued, is referring to scripture when he says 'as the law directs', what passage of scripture does he have in mind? It has been suggested that he was thinking of Genesis 3: 16: '. . . and thy desire shall be to thy husband, and he shall rule over thee.' If indeed Paul was thinking of this verse, he was applying it in a new way, for nowhere in Pharisee law do we find this verse used as a basis for anti-feminist legislation. It was regarded as a narrative part of the Bible, not a legal part. It was a kind of 'Just-so Story', explaining how women came to be subjected to men, though in an unfallen state they were men's equals. Pharisee legislation was based on the avowedly legal parts of the Bible, not on its narratives. So if Paul was using this passage to derive a new 'law' about how women should behave in church, this was not Pharisaic law, but the 'law of Christ' to which he refers at times: a new Christian system of *halakhah* which, he claims, he derived partly from personal revelations given to him by the heavenly Christ, and partly from his own human decisions which his position as Apostle entitled him to make.

Moreover, if Paul had turned to the Hebrew Bible for guidance in this matter, he would have found much to contradict his ruling that women must not speak up in a religious context. The Bible contains many vocal women: for example, the prophetesses Miriam, Deborah and Hulda, and the 'wise women' who take a leading role at various points and were evidently an institution in biblical times.[10]

Furthermore, the assumption that Pharisaic religion gave a downtrodden role to women in the synagogue is not correct. Recent research has shown that it was considerably later than the time of Paul that, for example, women were confined to a separate gallery in the synagogue. Women, as excavated inscriptions show, were given the title of *archisynagogissa* ('head of the synagogue') and *presbytera* ('elder').

Whereas the general organization of Jewish society was undoubtedly patriarchal, this did not exclude women of special talent from rising to positions of high influence in a religious context, and there was no blanket prohibition to prevent this, such as Paul is here proposing.[11]

It is indeed rather puzzling that Paul gives such an illiberal ruling in view of other evidence about the position of women in the early Christian Church. The Book of Acts refers to women with the gift of prophecy; for example, the four daughters of the evangelist Philip (Acts 21: 9). Would Paul's prohibition on women speaking in church apply to them too? The gift of 'speaking in tongues' evidently belonged to men and women alike (Acts 2: 18–19).

The answer seems to be that at first licence was given to women as well as to men to speak in church meetings just as the spirit moved them. In theory this was supposed to produce spontaneous and ecstatic worship, but in practice, as in other areas of Pauline antinomianism, the result tended to be chaos. A perusal of the passage in 1 Corinthians leading up to Paul's outburst against women shows that he was concerned with the problem of disorder in church due to spontaneous 'speaking in tongues'. As often happens in antinomian movements, a reaction against chaos produces repressive legislation – far more repressive than is found in communities that value law in the first place. Thus Paul moved from an initial position in which no distinction was made between the sexes in worship to a final repressive position made in the interests of order.

The explanation that he 'relapsed into Pharisaism' is thus incorrect. Where Paul actually was influenced by Pharisaism is in some of his more liberal and humane remarks about relations between the sexes. For example: '. . . the husband cannot claim his body as his own; it is his wife's' (1 Corinthians 7: 4), which corresponds to the Pharisaic concept that a husband must not withhold intercourse from his wife, who is entitled to divorce if intercourse is withheld or irregularly performed ('irregularity' being defined according to the circumstances and profession of the husband).[12] Similarly, the precept, 'Each of you must love his wife as his very self' (Ephesians 5: 33) can be paralleled in many rabbinical sayings; but, unfortunately, the Epistle to the Ephesians was probably not written by Paul.

Paul's attitude to women was thus not wholly consistent. His friendships with women helpers do not tally with his later illiberal view that it is shocking for women to speak up. A possible explanation lies in the context of proselytizing. Many women of aristocratic birth were attracted to Judaism and became converted; and as converts, their high rank gave them a status not enjoyed by native Jewish women. The same phenomenon no doubt occurred in Paul's missionary work, and accounts for the high consideration in which some of his women converts were held. Also the Gnostic influence no doubt made itself felt: the obliteration of sex made women, especially those who chose chastity as their way of life, into neuter beings. Finally, the prophetic model, which had influenced Jesus himself, gave women a special status as the helpers of a prophet figure (as in the case of Elijah and Elisha), and Paul, as a prophet, may have felt this influence. It is hard to say which of these models was most important for Paul.

We thus find in Paul's attitudes towards women the pressures and difficulties of founding a new movement, giving rise to contradictions.

An important aspect of Paul's mythology is the strong potential for anti-Semitism which it shares with Gnosticism. If Paul was the creator of the Christian myth, he was also the creator of the anti-Semitism which has been inseparable from that myth, and which eventually produced the medieval diabolization of the Jews, evinced in the stories of the 'blood libel' and the alleged desecration of the Host.

Even if the most explicit outburst against the Jews in Paul's Epistles (1 Thessalonians 2: 15–16) is regarded as a later interpolation (and this is by no means proved), there is quite sufficient in his more moderate expressions about the Jews and in the general configuration of his myth to give rise to anti-Semitism. It is he who first assigns to the Jews the role of the 'sacred executioner', the figure fated to bring about the death of the Saviour. He says that the Jews 'are treated as God's enemies for your sake' (Romans 11: 28), a phrase that sums up the role of the Jews in the Christian myth as the Black Christ who assumes the burden of guilt for the bloody deed without which there would be no salvation.

The responsibility of Paul for Christian anti-Semitism has been overlooked because of the settled prejudice that Paul came from a highly Jewish background. It seemed impossible that a 'Hebrew of the Hebrews', a descendant of the tribe of Benjamin, and a Pharisee of standing could be the originator of anti-Semitic attitudes. (The solution, put forward at times, that Paul was a self-hating Jew is anachronistic. Self-hating Jews, such as Otto Weininger, were produced by many centuries of Christian contempt, which, in the case of some individual Jews under intolerable pressure, was introjected. In the ancient world, there was no such pressure of universal contempt and there were no self-hating Jews.)

But the picture of Paul that has emerged from the present study makes it understandable that he was the originator of Christian anti-

Semitism. He belonged to the fringes surrounding Judaism, of people who were impressed and attracted by Judaism, but had to fight against their upbringing and emotional make-up when they attempted a closer approach. Often such people would succeed in overcoming all difficulties and would become fully attached to Judaism either as 'God-fearers' or as proselytes; such people, as the Talmud says, became the best Jews of all.[13] But occasionally the influence of childhood culture was too strong; they might fall back into paganism or, alternatively, they might concoct weird religious fantasies, partly derived from Judaism and partly from Hellenism, in which the Jews tended to figure as the villains, rather than as the heroes. A certain feeling of failure or rejection lies behind these fantasies.

Paul was the greatest fantasist of all. He created the Christian myth by deifying Jesus, a Jewish Messiah figure whose real aims were on the plane of Jewish political Utopianism. Paul transformed Jesus' death into a cosmic sacrifice in which the powers of evil sought to overwhelm the power of good, but, against their will, only succeeded in bringing about a salvific event. This also transforms the Jews, as Paul's writings indicate, into the unwitting agents of salvation, whose malice in bringing about the death of Jesus is turned to good because this death is the very thing needed for the salvation of sinful mankind. The combination of malice and blindness described here is the exact analogue of the myth of Balder, in Norse mythology, in which malice is personified by the wicked god Loki and blindness by the blind god Hother, and both together bring about the salvific death which alone guarantees a good crop and salvation from death by famine.

Paul took the cosmic drama of good and evil from Gnosticism, and so took over also the dramatization of the Jews as the representatives of cosmic evil. But, by combining the myth of Gnosticism with the myth of the mystery cults (which were not themselves anti-Semitic), Paul sharpened and intensified the anti-Semitism already present in Gnosticism. The Jews became not just the opponents of the figure descended from the world of light, but the performers of the cosmic sacrifice by which the heavenly visitant brings salvation. The Jews thus become identified as the dark figure which in myths of the deaths of gods brings about the saving death – Set, Mot, Loki; and the stage is prepared for the long career of the Jews in the Christian imagination as the people of the Devil. The elements which Paul took over from Judaism to embellish his myth – the religio-historical element which set the death of Jesus in a panorama of world history – only intensified the resultant anti-Semitism, because there was now an aspect of usurpation in the Pauline myth, an incentive to blacken the Jewish record in order to justify the Christian take-over of the Abrahamic 'promises'. The career of the Jews in history began to be seen as a prefiguring of their central role, the murder of the divine sacrifice;[14] they were separated from their prophets, now regarded as proto-Christs, hounded, like Jesus, by the Jews.

The myth adumbrated by Paul was then brought into full imaginative life in the Gospels, which were written under the influence of Paul's ideas and for the use of the Pauline Christian Church. A fully rounded narrative of mythological dimensions is now elaborated on the basis of historical materials, which are adapted to provide a melodrama of good and evil. The powerful image of Judas Iscariot is created: a person fated and even designated by his victim, Jesus, to perform the evil deed, possessed by Satan and carrying out his evil role by compulsion, yet suffering the fate of the accursed – a perfect embodiment of the role of the sacred executioner, deputed to perform the deed of blood, yet execrated for performing it.[14] While Judas performs the role on the personal level, the Jewish people, in the Gospel myth, perform it on the communal level: actuated by blindness and malice in alternation, calling for Jesus' crucifixion in the climactic Barabbas scene and accepting responsibility for the sacrifice by saying, 'His blood be on us and on our children' (Matthew 27: 25). What in Paul's letters was only the outline of a myth has become definite and replete with narrative quality, an instrument for cultural indoctrination and the conveyor of indelible impressions to children who are told the tale.

The myth created by Paul was thus launched on its career in the world: a story that has brought mankind comfort in its despair, but has also produced plentiful evil.

Out of his own despair and agony, Paul created his myth. His belief that he received the myth from the heavenly Jesus himself has obscured Paul's own role in creating it. The misunderstandings which he fostered about his own background have prevented readers of the New Testament from disentangling Paul's myth from the historical facts about Jesus, the so-called Jerusalem Church, and Paul's own adventures and clashes with his contemporaries. Paul's character was much more colourful than Christian piety portrays it; his real life was more like a picaresque novel than the conventional life of a saint. But out of the religious influences that jostled in his mind, he created an imaginative synthesis that, for good or ill, became the basis of Western culture.

NOTE ON METHOD

The history of New Testament scholarship may be summarized as follows. Though some sporadic efforts had been made (by Jewish scholars in the Middle Ages and by English and German Deists in the eighteenth century) to apply scientific principles to the study of the New Testament, this was begun in a massive way only in the nineteenth century. The religious dogma of scriptural infallibility was abandoned, and it was fully acknowledged that contradictions and inconsistencies in the narratives should not be 'harmonized' away, but should be treated as the outcome of human fallibility. It was recognized that the books of the New Testament were derived from various sources, stitched together as best the editors could manage, and that the editors had been much affected by considerations of bias and propaganda in their work, suppressing or altering what did not suit their religious standpoint in the controversies of the early Church.

The tendency of all this work was to uncover the fact that Jesus himself and his earliest followers in the 'Jerusalem Church' were very Jewish figures, who knew nothing of the doctrines which later became characteristic of the Christian Church (the divinity of Jesus, the abolition of the Torah, and the Crucifixion as a means of salvation and atonement taking the place of the Torah). As Julius Wellhausen said, 'Jesus was not a Christian.' The analysis of the editorial work in the Gospels showed that it consisted of the foisting on the original material (still discernible under the editorial revisions) of the later standpoint of the Church. The intensely Jewish standpoint of the early 'Jerusalem Church' (who did not regard themselves as having separated from Judaism) was disguised in order to cover up the fact that there had been a catastrophic split. It was F. C. Baur (1792–1860) and his followers of the 'Tübingen school' who stressed the Jewishness of the Jerusalem Church, though they did not fully realize the implications of this as far as Jesus himself was concerned.

In the twentieth century, however, an ingenious way was found to halt this unpalatable trend. This was to cast doubt on whether the New Testament contains any material of historical value at all. The school of 'form criticism', of which Rudolf Bultmann became the leading exponent, denied that there was any underlying historical layer in the New Testament at all, since the narrative framework was merely a device for linking together items which served various functions in the life of the Church of the late first century and second century. This intensified scepticism served a pious purpose, for, by removing Jesus from historical enquiry, it was possible to prevent him from assuming too Jewish an outline. Instead of defending the traditional Jesus by attempting to reassert the editorial standpoint of the Gospels (a trap into which nineteenth-century apologists had fallen) it was now possible to defend an orthodox standpoint through the ultra-scepticism of declaring the quest for the historical Jesus to be impossible. All the evidence of Jesus' Jewishness in the Gospels could simply be ascribed to a phase of 're-Judaization' in the history of the Church: this too served a Church function. Though the historical Jesus was beyond a historical approach, he could still be reverently guessed at through faith; and the guess generally made was that he must have had some affinity with the doctrines at which the Church eventually arrived. So, by a *tour de force*, the ultra-sceptics found themselves thankfully back at square one.

Bultmann himself, in his earlier work, had taken a slightly different standpoint: namely, that the historical Jesus may indeed have been a figure of wholly Jewish import (a Messiah figure raising a banner of revolt against Rome). This could not be proved or disproved, but, in any case, it did not matter, because Christianity was based not on the historical Jesus, who lived and died in Palestine, but on the mythical Jesus, who was resurrected like the gods of the mystery cults and brought salvation through his resurrection. This Hellenistic myth removed Jesus from his historical connections, whatever they may have been, and turned him into a totally mythical figure of far greater spiritual importance, since religion is built on myth, not on fact. Later Bultmann abandoned this radical position (much to the disgust of Jaspers, who reproached him for forsaking his own main insight) and resorted to the strategy outlined in the last paragraph, by which a denial of the quest for the historical Jesus on the scholarly plane could be combined with a fairly orthodox guess about what he must have been like.

It is from the early Bultmann, however, that we may derive a very interesting and important phenomenon in twentieth-century New

Testament scholarship, the work of S. G. F. Brandon. Since Bultmann had declared the historical Jesus to be of no theological importance, the way was open to someone like Brandon, who did not agree that 'the quest for the historical Jesus' was impossible (but, on the contrary, that the Gospels are full of clues about the historical Jesus) to search for him purely as a historian, without any theological axe to grind. Bultmann's very insistence on the insignificance of the historical Jesus released Brandon to build up a picture of him from the evidence of the Gospels without the theological worries which had always attended such a search, and which had prompted Bultmann's dismissal of the significance of the historical Jesus in the first place. Brandon's theological views, as can be gathered from various remarks scattered through his writings, were similar to Bultmann's: he thought that the mythological scheme of Paul was far superior, spiritually, to that of the Jerusalem Nazarenes and indeed to that of Jesus, which he regarded as identical to that of the Jerusalem Nazarenes. Here I personally part company with Brandon. As will be seen from the present book, I am not at all inclined to think that Paul's scheme of mythology was a spiritual improvement on Judaism, the faith of both Jesus and of the Jerusalem Nazarenes. But I am grateful for Brandon's magnificent remodelling of the Tübingen insights, freeing them from philosophical and methodological irrelevancies, and establishing them on a sound basis of twentieth-century historical and textual enquiry.

Thus, though my views coincide in many ways with those of the Tübingen school and Brandon, I do not count myself a member of that school, but rather of the school of what has been called 'the Jewish view of Jesus'. An interesting and scholarly, though hostile, account of this school is given in David Catchpole's The Trial of Jesus (1971), which shows that over 300 authors (some of them non-Jewish) have contributed to it since the eighteenth century. Catchpole does not mention, however, that the first contributions were made by Jewish authors in the Middle Ages, notably Joseph Kimchi, Profiat Duran and Isaac Troki. Prominent contributors in the twentieth century have been Joseph Klausner, Robert Eisler, Solomon Zeitlin, Samuel Sandmel, Paul Winter, Hugh J. Schonfield, Haim Cohn, David Flusser, Geza Vermes, Robert Graves with Joshua Podro, Joel Carmichael, and H. J. Schoeps. Though all these writers have their individual approaches, it is characteristic of the school as a whole to use the Talmud to show that Jesus' life and teaching are entirely understandable in terms of the Judaism of his time, particularly rabbinical or Pharisaic Judaism. The corollary is that, since Jesus did not conflict with Judaism, his death took place for political reasons, later camouflaged as religious by the Christian Church in its anxiety to cover up the fact that Jesus was a rebel against Rome.

Where, then, does the 'Jewish position' put Paul? Unfortunately, many adherents of the 'Jewish position', such as Klausner and Schoeps, have thought it only natural and proper, after demonstrating the Jewishness of Jesus, to go on to 'prove' the Jewishness of Paul. This, however, leaves unexplained the break with Judaism that produced the Christian Church and its motivation to feign a split between Jesus and Judaism. Not all 'Jewish position' adherents have taken this false step: Kaufmann Kohler, for example, the distinguished Talmudic scholar and editor of the Jewish Encyclopaedia, wrote in 1902 that 'nothing in Paul's writings showed that he had any acquaintance with rabbinical learning' – a judgment with which I entirely concur (see chapter 7). The trouble is that well-meaning eirenic or oecumenical considerations have interfered with perception of the facts. Many Jews (and many non-Jews, W. D. Davies, for example) have considered themselves to be building a bridge between Jews and Christians by asserting the rabbinical Jewishness of Paul (though in earlier times, Paul's alleged 'rabbinical Jewishness' had been held against him by scholars such as Renan, who held the 'Romantic liberal' conception of Jesus, and deplored the complications introduced into the sweet simplicity of Jesus' message by the tortuous Paul).

Among Christian scholars in general the Bultmannite approach is still the most influential, and the 'Jewish position' is combated by the assertion that the historical Jesus is a chimera, and that all attempts to reconstruct the historical Jesus by the use of Gospel texts are naive, since they fail to take into account the sophistications of 'form criticism'. This approach has even been welcomed by some Jewish scholars (e.g. Trude Weiss-Rosmarin), who hope that the disappearance of the historical Jesus will also mark the disappearance of Christian anti-Semitism, overlooking the fact that a mythical Jesus hounded to death by mythical Jews can cause just as much anti-Semitism as a historical Jesus hounded by historical Jews (how much anti-Semitism has been fostered by admitted fictions such as *The Merchant of Venice*?).

On the other hand, a growing body of Christian scholars in recent years has rebelled against the Bultmannite approach and has re-asserted the historical Jesus, while at the same time explicitly seeing its task as the dismantling of the 'Jewish view of Jesus'. The definitive volumes of this 'backlash' movement, as I have called it, are David

Catchpole's *The Trial of Jesus* (mentioned above), and *Jesus and the Politics of his Day*, edited by Ernst Bammel and C. F. D. Moule (1984).

The 'backlash' movement has the merit of taking the 'Jewish view of Jesus' seriously as its most formidable opponent, instead of dismissing it, as the Bultmannites do (with the exception of Brandon who was a theological rather than a methodological Bultmannite), as failing to employ the ultra-professional mysteries of 'form criticism'. On the contrary, the 'backlash' scholars (K. Schubert, for example) tend to point out the shortcomings of 'form criticism', particularly its frequent subjectivism and dogmatism, masquerading as the minute application of an unimpeachable methodology. In this stance, I am happy to regard myself as in line with 'backlash' scholarship, as also with their conviction that the historical Jesus cannot be banished from the scene as easily as form critics would like. On the other hand, in the 'backlash' attempts to outdo the adherents of the 'Jewish view' by applying Talmudic knowledge, but with an opposite result, I find great incompetence and prejudice, comparable to the shortcomings of early German critics of Pharisaic Judaism such as Billerbeck and Schürer. Also the stance of ultra-professionalism is just as marked in the 'backlash' as in the form critics, and equally phoney. Though the 'backlash' scholars eschew form criticism itself, they employ assumptions strongly associated with form criticism, notably the assumption of re-Judaization, wherever the evidence seems to point to strong Jewishness in the earliest layers of Christianity and in the teaching of Jesus. To support this assumption, recourse is had to minutiae of source criticism which, despite their air of formidable science, are just as subjective and debateable as the minutiae of form criticism. For example, great play is made of stylistic criteria, which in fact prove nothing, because a later writer copying out a passage from an early source is quite likely to import features of his own style in the course of copying out: such stylistic features thus do not disprove the earliness of the *content* of a passage, even if the stylistic analysis is valid, which is frequently doubtful because of the paucity of material for statistical analysis.

In the present work, the main principles of New Testament study are employed, without recourse to pseudo-scientific minutiae. These principals are the detection of bias or *tendenz*, and the isolation of passages which contradict the *tendenz* and can thus be identified as belonging to an earlier stratum, since they could not have been added when the *tendenz* was fully established. In this research, the dating of the main sources is important, especially the priority of Mark, since without such dating, it would not be possible to chart the growth of the *tendenz* or arrive, by extrapolation, at the situation before the composition of the Gospels. While twentieth-century scholarship has made great progress in many areas, especially the dating of the main documents, it has often lost sight of basic principles of *tendenz* criticism, despite the splendid beginning made in the nineteenth century. The main reason for this myopia has been programmatic, i.e. theological: the reluctance to face the consequences of research into the Jewishness of Jesus and the 'Jerusalem Church', and the consequent elaboration of ever more sophisticated methods of escape.

This is not to say that the present work does not require supplementation. It has been my aim to make the book fully intelligible to the non-specialist reader, and this has meant that certain aspects have been presented in a somewhat simplified form. Those readers who would like to see a more academic treatment of these aspects are referred to my forthcoming book (written under the auspices of the International Centre for the Study of Anti-Semitism, the Hebrew University of Jerusalem), entitled *Paul, Pharisaism and Gnosticism*.

NOTES

Chapter 1: The Problem of Paul

1 See Maccoby (1982: 1).

Chapter 3: The Pharisees

1 For a fuller treatment of the subject-matter of the present chapter and the following two chapters, see Maccoby (1980).
2 See Moore (1927), Herford (1924), Parkes (1960), Sanders (1977), Sanders (1985).
3 *Antiquities*, XIII. 294.
4 Babylonian Talmud, Bava Metzi'a, 59b.
5 Mishnah, Avot, 5: 23.
6 Rabbi Hillel (not the famous Hillel the Elder). See Babylonian Talmud, Sanhedrin, 99a.
7 Mishnah, Horayot, 3: 8.
8 For example, Deuteronomy 4: 9; 6: 7; 11: 19; Psalms 78: 4–6.
9 *Antiquities*, XVII. 41.
10 Josephus (*Antiquities*, XIII. 372) describes an occasion when the people showed indignation against a Sadducee High Priest. The incident is further explained, in terms of Pharisee law, in Mishnah, Sukkah 4: 9. See also Tosefta, Sukkah 3: 1, and Babylonian Talmud, Sukkah 43b. In these passages, the people (*ammei ha-'aretz*) are shown in alliance with the Pharisees against the Sadducees, which demonstrates the falsity of the picture often drawn of enmity between the people and the Pharisees, based mainly on the Gospels, but also on certain Talmudic passages taken out of context.
11 See Baumgarten (1980).

Chapter 4: Was Jesus a Pharisee?

1 Babylonian Talmud, Berakhot 13b.
2 Babylonian Talmud, Shabbat 31a, where the principle of love of

neighbour is expressed in the form of the Golden Rule: 'What is hateful to you, do not to your fellow creature.'

3 Sifra 89b, Genesis Rabbah 24: 7. 'Rabbi Akiba said, "Thou shalt love thy neighbour as thyself" is the greatest principle in the Law.'

4 See Acts 5: 36, and Josephus, *Antiquities*, xx. 97, for Theudas. See Acts 21: 38, and Josephus, *Antiquities*, xx. 167, for 'the Egyptian'.

5 See Maccoby (1980), pp 139–49.

6 For example, the prayer of Mar bar Ravina (Babylonian Talmud, Berakhot 17a), 'To those who curse me may my soul be dumb,' which has been incorporated into the Jewish liturgy (Singer, p. 110, etc.).

7 Babylonian Talmud, Yoma, 85b, where Rabbi Jonathan ben Joseph derives it from the scriptural expression, 'For it is holy *for you*' (Exodus, 31: 14).

8 Babylonian Talmud, Menahot 96a.

9 'One may violate all laws in order to save life, except idolatry, incest, or murder.' Palestinian Talmud, Sheviit, 4: 2 (35a); Babylonian Talmud, Sanhedrin 74a.

10 Because of the difficulty of finding their victims to make restitution. The solution of giving money to charity or public works is offered in Tosefta, Bava Metzi'a, 8: 26.

Chapter 5: Why Was Jesus Crucified?

1 Vermes (1973).
2 Grant (1977).
3 See, however, Freyne (1980), who warns against exaggerations of this aspect.

Chapter 6: Was Paul a Pharisee?

1 Some of Theudas's followers were killed too, and some were taken prisoner (*Antiquities*, xx. 97). Jesus' followers, however, according to the Gospel accounts, were allowed to escape. From this, Sanders argues that Jesus cannot have had political aims (Sanders, 1985, p. 231) and could not have been regarded as posing a political threat to the Romans. However, the aim of the Gospels to depoliticize Jesus and his movement accounts sufficiently for the omission of details of the arrest of Jesus' followers. Nevertheless, some traces remain showing that Jesus was not the only person to be arrested. He was crucified between two 'robbers' (Greek, *lestai*, a word often used to designate rebels), and the probability is that they were members of his movement (as against the late legends concerning them). Moreover, the mystery of the relationship between Jesus and Barabbas has led several commentators to postulate that they were part of the same movement, or linked movements (see Brandon, 1968, p. 102). See Maccoby (1980) for the view that Jesus and Barabbas

were the same man, Barabbas being the split-off embodiment of the political aspects of Jesus.

2 See Townsend (1968), Haaker (1971–2), Hübner (1973).

3 See Büchler (1902), Mantel (1965), pp 54–101.

4 For example, Mark 7: 13, '. . . making the word of God of none effect through your tradition'. See Maccoby (1980), p. 108. The contrast between the 'word of God' (i.e. the Bible) and 'tradition' is typical of the Sadducees and, taken seriously, would nullify all the reforms by which the Pharisees had made scriptural law less severe.

5 Munck (1967).

Chapter 7: Alleged Rabbinical Style in Paul's Epistles

1 The term 'lord', of course, could be used in its human sense without giving any offence. See Vermes (1973), pp 103–28. In Hebrew, the two senses are distinguished, *adon* meaning 'human lord' and *adonai*, Divine Lord.

2 For example, 1 Corinthians 1: 23, Galatians 5: 11.

3 It may be said that we do not *know* what Pharisaism was like in Paul's day, since all the Pharisee or rabbinical writings come from a later period (for this agnostic view see Sandmel, 1970, pp 14–15, and 44–6). As against this, see Vermes (1983), showing the folly of ignoring the rabbinical data relevant to the time of Jesus and Paul on purist grounds. The agnostic view at least acknowledges that Paul shows little sign of Pharisaism in the rabbinical sense, but seeks to substitute the view that Paul was a Pharisee in some other (unprovable) sense. The real point of this argument is that, if we cannot prove whether Paul was a Pharisee or not from the evidence of his writings, we must fall back on his own assertion that he was one. This is at least an advance on the dogmatic view that Paul's writings show him to be a typical rabbi.

4 See Guggenheimer (1967), pp 181–5, for an excellent discussion by a professional logician. In the Mishnah (Bava Qamma 2: 5), an argument between the sages and Rabbi Tarfon turns on the question of *dayo*. It is clear, however, that even Rabbi Tarfon does not dissent from the principle of *dayo*, but thinks that a certain well-defined type of *a fortiori* argument may be exempt from it (see Gemara, *ad loc.*).

5 Tosefta, Sanhedrin 9: 5, 'Those who are put to death by the court have a share in the world to come.'

6 Rabbi Meir's explanation, Babylonian Talmud, Sanhedrin 46b. The Mishnah (Sanhedrin 6: 4) gives another interpretation: that this punishment is given only in a case of blasphemy, when the accused has 'cursed God's name' (the translation is thus, 'He is hanged *because of* a curse against God'). This interpretation too involves no curse on the executed man, who expiates his sin by his death.

7 Joseph Klausner (1942, pp 453–4) states roundly, 'It would be difficult to

find more typically Talmudic expositions of scripture than those in the Epistles of Paul.' Among six unconvincing examples, he includes the example discussed here, concluding, 'Could there be a more unnatural interpretation than this? Truly only Paul the Jew could have based his entire teaching on radical reinterpretations of Torah like these.' Klausner here comes close to saying that Paul must have been a Pharisee because only a Pharisee could have used such nonsensical arguments. In fact, rabbinical arguments are never guilty of logical confusions, though their assumptions may often be questioned.

8 Paul's attempt at legal argument is swamped by his imaginative obsession with death and rebirth. Thus he produces a muddled poem, instead of a legal argument. Various attempts have been made to defend his argument on the ground of its 'poetic truth', but such analysis has no tendency to confirm the picture of Paul as a rabbinical thinker.

9 In I Corinthians 15: 33, he quotes a line from Menander, 'Bad company corrupts good habits' (*Thais*, 218). The line has been traced further back, however, to a fragment of Euripides (1024).

10 This is not in the Epistles, but in the report of Paul's speech in Acts 17: 28, 'For we also are his offspring.' This is from the Stoic poet Aratus (c. 270 BC), *Phaenomena*, line 5. The words also contained in Paul's speech, 'In him we live, move and have our being,' come from Epimenides, a poet and prophet of the sixth century BC, as quoted by Diogenes Laertius (*Lives of Philosophers*, i. 112), with slight alteration. The second line of the quatrain is quoted by Paul in Titus 1: 12, 'Cretans were always liars, vicious brutes, lazy gluttons,' so Luke was certainly correct in portraying Paul as familiar with these lines.

11 It has been argued that Paul deliberately used the Septuagint rather than the Hebrew text because he was writing for Greek-speakers who had no access to the Hebrew. Alternatively, it has been argued that Paul used the Septuagint to save himself the trouble of retranslating from the Hebrew (Klausner, 1942, p. 305). Both these arguments fail to take into account the importance of the canonical Hebrew text to Palestinian scholars, who would never base any argument on a reading found in the Greek but not in the Hebrew. The use of the Septuagint thus stamps Paul as at the very least a Hellenistic Jew of the type of Philo, as Sandmel argued (Sandmel, 1970), and as definitely not in the rabbinical mould. Another line of argument is that Paul did use the Hebrew text, but later editors altered his quotations in accordance with the Septuagint, though traces of his use of the Hebrew text remain. For a sustained attempt to establish this view, see O'Neill (1975). For criticism of this view, see my forthcoming *Paul, Pharisaism and Gnosticism*, where the earlier attempt by Puukko to establish Paul's use of the Hebrew text (Puukko, 1928, pp 34–63) is also criticized.

12 See Pseudo-Philo, 12C and 13A.

Chapter 8: Paul and Stephen

1 See Maccoby (1980), pp 135–6. See also now Sanders (1985), pp 71–6. Sanders argues correctly that Jesus' threatened destruction and rebuilding of the Temple was an inevitable feature of his hopes of eschatological 'restoration'. Later, however, he argues inconsistently (p. 270) that the majority of Jews would have found Jesus' threat against the Temple 'offensive'. Only those who were sure that Jesus was *not* the Messiah would have resented such Messianic behaviour; most would have been doubtful but hopeful, like Gamaliel. Note also that the description by Ezekiel of the eschatological Temple made it heretical *not* to believe that there would be a new Temple in the Last Days.

2 See Cadbury (1933), Hengel (1983), pp 1–29.

3 Eusebius, quoting Justin Martyr, *Ecclesiastical History*, IV, 8. Also, Latin version, Hadrian's Year 17.

Chapter 9: The Road to Damascus

1 Gaston (1970), Stendhal (1976), Gaston (1979), Gager (1983).

2 Gaston (1979), pp 56–8, attempts to prove that before Maimonides (!) the Noahide laws had nothing to do with salvation/covenant for Gentiles, but were simply a code for Gentiles resident in Israel. 'The point of this legislation is only to keep the land from being polluted' (p. 57). He ignores the evidence from the Book of Jubilees, which shows that the idea of a Gentile code was current from at least the second century BC (Jubilees 7: 20–39). Earlier, the biblical book of Jonah already shows that Gentiles (the inhabitants of Nineveh) could achieve God's grace by repentance without conversion to Judaism. Yet Gaston argues that the idea of repentance by Gentiles was unknown before Paul!

3 At the time of the return from Babylon (536 BC), the returned exiles still distinguished between Judah and Benjamin (Ezra : 5, Nehemiah 11: 7, 31–6, and Nehemiah 7: 6), and even settled in their old territories. However, later the distinction was lost (Babylonian Talmud, Berakhot 16b, '. . . we do not know whether we are descended from Rachel or Leah'). In the Apocrypha, there is no indication that Benjamites were distinct (in II Maccabees 3: 4, 'Benjamin' is a copyist's error for *miniamin*; see Jewish Encyclopaedia, s.v. 'Benjamin'). Only one passage has been cited to support the survival of Benjamites in Paul's period: the ascription of Benjamite origin to Hillel in Genesis Rabbah 33: 3. This cannot be regarded as historically authentic. Klausner (1942, p. 304) acknowledges this, but it does not occur to him that Paul's claim to be a Pharisee may be in the same category as his claim to be a Benjamite.

4 The most probable theory is that he adopted the name 'Paul' as a token of respect to his patron and convert, Sergius Paulus, Governor of Cyprus. See Acts 13, where we encounter the name 'Paul' for the first time in the

context of Cyprus.

5 The Peshitta (Syriac translation of the New Testament) translates as 'harness-worker' (using a word which is a transliteration of the Latin *lorarius*). Chrysostom, Theodoret and Origen all called Paul a 'leather-worker'. This evidence suggests that the Greek word *skenopoios* used of Paul in Acts 18: 1–3 (though literally 'tent-maker') had come to mean 'leather-worker'. The earliest Latin translation calls Paul *lectarius*, which means literally a 'maker of beds' or 'bedsteads', but could also mean a 'maker of leather cushions'. See *IDB*, s.v. 'Tentmaker'.

Chapter 11: Paul and the Eucharist

1 See Petuchowski (1978).
2 See Higgins (1952), p. 25. The alternative preposition *para* has been held to be more appropriate for *direct* derivation, but *apo* is found elsewhere in this sense too (e.g. Colossians 1: 7). Loisy (1908), ii, p. 532, n. 1, accepts that Paul is speaking here of a direct revelation. Lietzmann (1955), p 255, argues that 'Paul, by emphasizing the atoning death of Christ, was the real originator of a type of Eucharist which differed from the so-called Jerusalem type.'
3 An example in modern times is the Soviet rewriting of the history of the Russian Revolution. Despite all the care of Soviet historians to underplay the role of Trotsky and overplay the role of Stalin, inconsistencies remain which would enable a historian of the future to reconstruct the real course of events, even if no other sources of information survived. With a succession of datable textbooks covering a period of forty to fifty years, the task would be much easier, since the trend or *tendenz* would be more easily observable – and this is the case with the four Gospels.

Chapter 12: The 'Jerusalem Church'

1 Derekh Eretz Zutta, 1; Yalqut Shimoni ii, 367. See also Maccoby (1982: 1), p. 129.
2 See, for example, Babylonian Talmud, Hagigah 14b: when Rabbi Eleazar ben Arakh expounded the Work of the Chariot (Ezekiel 1), 'fire came down from the heavens and surrounded all the trees that were in the field.'
3 An instructive later example is the Messianic campaign of the seventeenth-century Messiah figure Sabbatai Sevi. This campaign included both mass repentance and baptism. See Scholem (1973).
4 See Bultmann (1921).
5 See Sanders (1985), p. 268, 'We have again and again returned to the fact that nothing which Jesus said or did which bore on the law led his disciples after his death to disregard it. This great fact, which overrides all others, sets a definite limit to what can be said about Jesus and the law.'
6 A book that is vitiated throughout (despite its apparently scientific stance)

by the assumption of 're-Judaization' is Bammel (1984).

7 This is often obscured by vague translations, e.g. Acts 13: 16, where Paul, in Pisidian Antioch, addresses both Jews and God-fearers explicitly.

8 See Spiro (1980).

9 For full discussion of ritual purity laws, see Maccoby (1986).

10 Babylonian Talmud, Yevamot 24b: 'No proselytes will be accepted in the days of the Messiah. In the same manner, no proselytes were accepted in the days of David or in the days of Solomon.'

11 The status of a resident alien (*ger toshav*) was well defined in Judaism and was respected (see Talmudic Encyclopaedia, s.v. '*Ger*'). Obviously, however, the personal link with the Messiah in the case of a resident alien would not be as strong as in the case of a Jewish national.

12 See Acts 12: 1–3, which says that Herod Agrippa, who ruled from AD 42 to 44, 'beheaded James', adding that 'the Jews approved' (the usual general charge against the Jews in all matters relating to persecution of the Nazarenes). In historical fact, the persecution of the Nazarenes by Herod Agrippa is best explained by Nazarene political oppositon to his reign. The Nazarenes (see p. 79) had become politically quiescent, waiting for the return of Jesus, but the appointment of a Jewish King (by the Romans) would have roused them from their political quiescence into active opposition, since the new King was usurping, in their eyes, the throne of Jesus. Similarly, the Nazarenes opposed the reign of the Messiah figure, Bar Kokhba (see p. 80).

13 See Josephus, *Antiquities*, xx. 197–203. Josephus stresses that this was a Sadducee act of violence, and that it was strongly opposed by the Pharisees ('those who were strict in the observance of the law'), who complained to the Roman Albinus and to the King, with the result that Ananus was deposed from his office. This incident deserves to be placed alongside the trial of Peter and the trial of Paul as evidence of the friendliness of the Pharisees towards the Nazarenes. The Sadducee hostility to the Nazarenes is also shown in all three trials, but it was political, not religious, in character. A later and less reliable account of the death of James is found in Hegesippus (quoted in Eusebius, *Ecclesiastical History*, II, 23: 4–18).

Chapter 13: The Split

1 The existence of divergent exegeses of Genesis 9: 4 is shown by Jubilees 7: 28–31, which, in fact, interprets the verse as prohibiting flesh from which the blood has not been drained, just as in Acts 15. A position intermediate between that of Jubilees and that of the Talmud is found in Tosefta, Avodah Zarah 8: 6, where one authority forbids blood from a *living* animal to Gentiles. The difficulty which led to the Talmudic opinion that Gentiles are forbidden only to eat a limb from a living animal, and are not forbidden to eat flesh undrained of blood, is that Deuteronomy 14: 21 explicitly

permits meat of this kind to Gentiles (i.e. to a resident alien or *ger toshav*). Therefore, the opinion prevailed that Genesis 9: 4 must refer to living flesh.

2 Paul does advocate care in using 'this liberty', in case it should become 'a pitfall for the weak' (verse 9). This means that food consecrated to idols should not be eaten in the presence of one who might thereby be tempted back into idol-worship.

3 The procedure advised was that Paul should pay the expenses of four Nazirites undergoing purification at the end of their vows. This was a not uncommon way of showing piety and charity (see Josephus, *Antiquities*, XIX. 294, and Genesis Rabbah XCI. 3). The further requirement that Paul should undergo purification together with the Nazirites does not mean (as some commentators have said) that Paul was to undertake a Nazirite vow too (for this would have taken a minimum of thirty days), but that Paul should go through the usual purification for one arriving in the Holy Land from abroad, timing this so that he could enter the Temple simultaneously with the Nazirites and offer a free-will offering while they were making their offerings in completion of their vows. See Strack-Billerbeck (1922) a.l.

Chapter 14: The Trial of Paul

1 Josephus, *Antiquities*, XX. 169; *War*, II. 261–3.
2 I Corinthians 7: 20–22. See also Ephesians 6: 5, Titus 2: 9.

Chapter 15: The Evidence of the Ebionites

1 For example, Gager (1983), pp 129, 141.
2 See Brandon (1951), pp 168–73.
3 See Lüdemann (1980).
4 Eusebius, *Ecclesiastical History*, III. v. 2–3. See also Epiphanius, *De Mensuris et Ponderibus*, XV (*Patrologia Graeca*, ed. Migne, t.xliii).
5 See Irenaeus, *Adversus Haereses*, I, xxvi. 1, 2.
6 This feature has been preserved only in connection with Cerinthus (see Irenaeus, I xxvi, Epiphanius, *Haer.* xxviii), but was probably common to all Ebionite groups.
7 See Maccoby (1982: 2), pp 171–5.
8 See Cohn (1957).
9 Matthew 16: 14, Mark 6: 15, Luke 9: 19.
10 The common scholarly opinion that the Nazarenes were excluded from the synagogue in about AD 90 at the 'Synod of Javneh' by the formulation against them of the *birkat ha-minim* has been refuted by Kimelman (1981). The actual exclusion of the Nazarenes did not take place until the time of the Bar Kokhba revolt, in which the Nazarenes refused to take part (see p. 80).

11 Landauer (1880), p. 90. See Pines (1968), p. 276.

Chapter 16: The Mythmaker

1 MacRae (1976), p. 618.
2 The Hebrew Bible states quite plainly that God Himself gave the Torah: e.g. '. . . and the Lord spoke unto you out of the midst of the fire,' (Deuteronomy 4: 12); 'Out of heaven he made thee to hear his voice,' (Deuteronomy 4: 36). Some have cited Deuteronomy 33: 2 and Isaiah 63: 9, which only say that God was accompanied by angels when he gave the Torah, not that the angels gave it. Some cite Josephus, *Antiquities*, xv. 136, but this refers only to the mediation of Moses and other prophets (see W. D. Davies, 1984, pp 85–6). Davies, however, wrongly refers to a 'well-attested tradition that the Law was given by angels'. This so-called tradition has been derived by Christian scholars from Canticles Rabbah 1: 2, which they have misunderstood. This Midrashic passage, in the name of Rabbi Johanan, does not say that the Torah was given or ordained by angels, but only that angels acted as *carriers* of each word from God to each Israelite; a notion that actually *emphasizes* the derivation of each word from God Himself, and also the care of God that each word should be individually received and accepted. Even this idea of Rabbi Johanan's, however, was rejected by the other rabbis, who insisted that each word went directly from God to each individual, without the employment of an angel as carrier.
3 Quran, Sura 37: 100–111. See Torrey (1967), pp 102–4.
4 Romans 3: 19; Galatians 2: 24.
5 For example, the right of women to divorce, and the right of married women to own their own property. See Amram (1897), Kahana (1966), Falk (1973).
6 Of course, there were other factors also leading to the condemnation of the Gnostics as heretics: their rejection of the Old Testament as the work of the Demiurge, their rejection of the divine origin of the world, and, generally, their extreme cosmic dualism. Their Christology, however, was the most obviously heretical consequence of this extreme dualism.
7 Thus, by stressing the differences between Christianity and mystery religion, on the one hand, and Christianity and Gnosticism on the other, Christian apologists try to prove that Christianity was indebted to neither. All the features of Christianity, however (other than those derived from Judaism), can be explained by the postulate of a *fusion* between mystery religion and Gnosticism, and this fusion itself is the only truly original feature of Christianity.
8 Some have argued that Christianity differs fundamentally from the mystery religions in that Jesus was a historical personage. But Osiris too was asserted to have once been a historical personage, a King of Egypt.

Whether this is factually true or not is beside the point; the Egyptian myth includes the concept of the suffering and apotheosis of a historical personage, and all the incarnational consequences that flow from this.

9 See Gospel of Thomas, 114: 'For every woman who will make herself male will enter the Kingdom of Heaven.'

10 For example, 1 Samuel 25: 3–35 (Abigail), 11 Samuel 14: 1–20 (the wise woman of Tekoa), 11 Samuel 20: 16–22 (the wise woman of Abel).

11 See Brooten (1982).

12 See Mishnah, Ketuvot 5: 6.

13 See, for example, Leviticus Rabbah 4: 5, for the parable of 'The King and the Stag', with the message that God loves the proselyte more than born Jews, because of the proselyte's self-sacrifice in leaving his native surroundings to join the people of God.

14 See Maccoby (1982: 2).

15 That the Judas myth had not yet developed in the time of Paul can be seen from 1 Corinthians 15: 5, which speaks of the appearance of the resurrected Jesus to the Twelve Apostles – in later Christian myth, there were only eleven Apostles at this time, Judas having died for his sin. For an analysis of the Judas myth see Maccoby (1982: 2), pp 121–33, and (for a purely literary analysis) Kermode (1980).

BIBLIOGRAPHY

Amram, D. W., *The Jewish Law of Divorce*, London, 1897

Baeck, Leo, *The Pharisees*, New York, 1947

Bammel, E., and Moule, C. F. D. (ed.), *Jesus and the Politics of His Day*, Cambridge, 1984

Bauer, W., *Rechtgläubigkeit und Ketzerei im ältesten Christentum*, 2nd ed., Tübingen, 1964. Eng. tr. *Orthodoxy and Heresy in Earliest Christianity*, Philadelphia, 1971

Baumgarten, Joseph M., 'The Pharisaic-Sadducean Controversies about Purity, and the Qumran Texts', *Journal of Jewish Studies*, XXXI. 2 (Autumn 1980)

Baur, F. C., *Kirchengeschichte*, Tübingen, 1853. Eng. tr. *The Church History of the First Three Centuries*, London, 1878

Birkeland, H., 'The Language of Jesus', Norwegian Academy *Avhandlinger*, 1954–55

Bonsirven, J., *Exégèse Rabbinique et Exégèse Paulinienne*, Paris 1939

Brandon, S. G. F., *The Fall of Jerusalem and the Christian Church*, London, 1951
Jesus and the Zealots, Manchester, 1967
The Trial of Jesus of Nazareth, London, 1968

Braude, William G., *Jewish Proselyting in the First Five Centuries of the Common Era*, Providence, R.I., 1940

Brooten, Bernadette J., *Women Leaders in the Ancient Synagogue*, Chico, 1982

Büchler, Adolf, *Das Synhedrion in Jerusalem und das Grosse Beth-Din in der Quader-Kammer des jerusalemischen Tempels*, Vienna, 1902

Bultmann, Rudolf, *Der Stil der Paulinischen Predigt und die kynischstoische Diatribe*, Göttingen, 1910
Geschichte der Synoptischer Tradition, Göttingen, 1921 Eng. tr. *History of the Synoptic Tradition*, Oxford, 1958
Gnosis, London, 1952
Jesus and the Word, London, 1958
See Jaspers, Karl

Cadbury, H. J., 'The Hellenists', in Lake and Cadbury, 1933, pp 59–74

Carmichael, Joel, *The Death of Jesus*, London, 1963

Catchpole, David, *The Trial of Jesus in Jewish Historiography*, Leiden, 1971

Chilton, Bruce (ed.), *The Kingdom of God*, London, 1984

Cirlot, Felix L., *The Early Eucharist*, London, 1939

Cohn, Haim, *The Trial and Death of Jesus*, London, 1967

Cohn, L., 'An Apocryphal Work ascribed to Philo of Alexandria', *Jewish Quarterly Review*, x, 1898, pp 277–332

Cohn, Norman, *The Pursuit of the Millennium*, London, 1957

Dahl, N. A., 'The Arrogant Archon and the Lewd Sophia: Jewish Traditions in Gnostic Revolt', in Layton, 1982, pp 599–712

Danielou, J., *The Theology of Jewish Christianity*, London, 1964

Daube, David, *The New Testament and Rabbinic Judaism*, London, 1956
'He that Cometh' (lecture), London, 1966

Davies, Alan T. (ed.), *Antisemitism and the Foundations of Christianity*, New York, 1979

Davies, W. D., *Paul and Rabbinic Judaism*, London, 1965
Jewish-Pauline Studies, London, 1984

Dix, Gregory, *The Shape of the Liturgy*, London, 1945

Eckardt, Roy, *Elder and Younger Brothers: the Encounter of Jews and Christians*, New York, 1973

Eisler, Robert, *The Messiah Jesus and John the Baptist*, London, 1931

English, George Bethune, *The Grounds of Christianity*, Boston, 1813

Epiphanius, *Panarion (Refutation of All Heresies)*, in Migne, 1857–66, xlii–xliii

Eusebius, *Ecclesiastical History*, tr. K. Lake (Loeb Classical Library), London and Harvard, 1926

Falk, Z. W., *The Divorce Action by the Wife in Jewish Law*, Jerusalem, 1973

Flusser, D., *Jesus*, New York, 1969

Freyne, S., *Galilee from Alexander the Great to Hadrian*, Notre Dame, 1980

Friedländer, M., *Der vorchristliche jüdische Gnosticismus*, Göttingen, 1898

Gager, John G., *The Origins of Anti-Semitism*, New York/Oxford, 1983

Gardner, P., *The Origin of the Lord's Supper*, London, 1893

Gasparro, G. S., *Soteriology and Mystic Aspects in the Cult of Cybele and Attis*, Leiden, 1985

Gaston, Lloyd, *No Stone on Another: Studies in the Significance of the Fall of Jerusalem in the Synoptic Gospels*, Leiden, 1970
'Paul and the Torah', in Davies, 1979, pp 48–71

Glasson, T. Francis, *Jesus and the End of the World*, Edinburgh, 1980

Goguel, M., *L'Eucharistie des Origines à Justin Martyr*, Paris, 1910

Goosens, W., *Les Origines de l'Eucharistie, Sacrament et Sacrifice*, Paris, 1931

Grant, F. C., *Roman Hellenism and the New Testament*, Edinburgh/London, 1962

Grant, Michael, *Jesus*, London, 1977
Saint Paul, New York, 1976

Graves, Robert, and Podro, Joshua, *The Nazarene Gospel Restored*, London, 1953

Gruenwald, I., 'Aspects of the Jewish-Gnostic Controversy', in Layton, 1982, pp 713–23

'Jewish Merkavah Mysticism and Gnosticism', in *Studies in Jewish Mysticism*, ed. J. Dan and F. Talmage, Cambridge, Mass., 1981, pp 41–55

Guggenheimer, Heinrich, 'Logical Problems in Jewish Tradition', in *Confrontations with Judaism*, ed. Philip Longworth, London, 1967

Haaker, K., 'War Paulus Hillelist?', *Das Institutum Judaicum der Universität Tübingen*, 1971–72, pp 106–20

Harris, H., *The Tübingen School*, Oxford, 1975

Hengel, Martin, *Between Jesus and Paul*, London, 1983

Herford, R. Travers, *The Pharisees*, London, 1924

Higgins, A. J. B., *The Lord's Supper in the New Testament*, London, 1952

Hübner, H., 'Gal. 3,10 und die Herkunft des Paulus', *Kerygma und Dogma*, 19 (1973), pp 215–31

Irenaeus, *Against Heresies*, in *Early Christian Fathers*, tr. and ed. C. C. Richardson, London, 1953

James, William, *The Varieties of Religious Experience*, New York, 1902

Jaspers, Karl, and Bultmann, Rudolf, *Myth and Christianity*, London, 1958

Jeremias, Joachim, *Jerusalem in the Time of Jesus*, London/Philadelphia, 1969

Jonas, H., *The Gnostic Religion*, 2nd ed., Boston, 1963

Philosophical Essays: from Ancient Creed to Technological Man, Englewood Cliffs, 1974

Kahana, K., *The Theory of Marriage in Jewish Law*, London, 1966

Käsemann, E., *Essays on New Testament Themes*, London/Nashville, 1964

Kermode, Frank, *The Genesis of Secrecy*, Harvard, 1980

From Jesus to Paul, London, 1942

Kimelman, Reuven, '*Birkat ha-Minim* and the Lack of Evidence for an Anti-Christian Jewish Prayer in Late Antiquity', in Sanders, 1981, pp 226–44, 391–403

Klausner, Joseph, *Jesus of Nazareth: His Life, Times and Teaching*, London, 1929

Klijn, A. F. J. and Reinink, G. J., *Patristic Evidence for Jewish-Christian Sects*, Leiden, 1973

Kohler, Kaufmann, 'Saul of Tarsus', *Jewish Encyclopaedia*, New York/London, 1905

Kraabel, A. T., 'The Disappearance of the "God-fearers" ', *Numen*, 28, 1981, pp 113–26

Kümmel, W. G., *The New Testament: the History of the Investigation of its Problems*, London, 1972

Introduction to the New Testament, London, 1975

'Eschatological Expectations in the Proclamation of Jesus', in Chilton, 1984

Lake, K., and Cadbury, H. J. (ed.), *The Beginnings of Christianity*, London, 1933

Lange, N. de, *Origen and the Jews*, Cambridge, 1976

Layton, B. (ed.), *The Rediscovery of Gnosticism*, vol. 2, Leiden, 1982

Leaney, A. R. C., *The Jewish and Christian World 200 BC to AD 200*, Cambridge, 1984

Leipoldt, J., *Sterbende und aufstehende Götter*, Leipzig, 1923

Lieberman, Saul, *Hellenism in Jewish Palestine*, New York, 1950
  Greek in Jewish Palestine, New York, 1965
Lietzmann, H., *Messe und Herrenmahl*, 3rd ed., Berlin, 1955
Loisy, A., *Les Evangiles Synoptiques*, Paris, 1908
Longenecker, Richard N., *The Christology of Early Jewish Christianity*, London, 1970
Lüdemann, Gerd, 'The Successors of Pre-70 Jerusalem Christianity: A Critical Evaluation of the Pella-Tradition', in Sanders, 1980, pp 161–73
Maccoby, Hyam, 'The Parting of the Ways' (Cardinal Bea Memorial Lecture), *European Judaism*, 1980 (1)
  Revolution in Judaea, 2nd ed., New York, 1980 (2)
  Judaism on Trial: Jewish-Christian Disputations in the Middle Ages, E. Brunswick/London, 1982 (1)
  The Sacred Executioner, London, 1982 (2)
  'The Washing of Cups', *Journal for the Study of the New Testament*, 14, pp 3–15, 1982 (3)
  Early Rabbinic Writings, Cambridge, 1986
MacGregor, G. H. C., *Eucharistic Origins*, London, 1928
MacRae, G. W., 'The Jewish Background of the Gnostic Sophia Myth', *Novum Testamentum* 12 (1970), pp 86–101
  'Nag Hammadi', *Interpreter's Dictionary of the Bible* (Supplementary Volume), Abingdon, 1976
Maier, J., *Jesus von Nazareth in der talmüdischen Überlieferung*, Darmstadt, 1978
Mantel, Hugo, *Studies in the History of the Sanhedrin*, Cambridge, Mass., 1965
Meeks, W. A. (ed.), *The Writings of St Paul*, New York, 1972
  The First Urban Christians: the Social World of the Apostle Paul, Yale, 1983
Michel, O., *Paulus und seine Bibel*, Gütersloh, 1929
Migne, J. P. (ed.), *Patrologia Graeca*, Paris, 1857–66
  Patrologia Latina, Paris, 1844–64
Montefiore, C. G., 'Rabbinic Judaism and the Epistles of Paul', *Jewish Quarterly Review*, XIII (1901), pp 161 ff
Moore, George Foot, *Judaism in the First Centuries of the Christian Era*, Cambridge, Mass., 1927
Morgan, W., *The Religion and Theology of Paul*, Edinburgh, 1917
Munck, Johannes (ed.), *The Acts of the Apostles* (Anchor Bible). Revised by William F. Albright and C. S. Mann, New York, 1967
Nickelsburg, George W. E., *Jewish Literature Between the Bible and the Mishnah*, London, 1981
Oesterley, W. O. E., *The Jewish Background of the Christian Liturgy*, Oxford, 1925
O'Neill, J. C., *Paul's Letter to the Romans*, Harmondsworth, 1975
Pagels, Elaine, *The Gnostic Paul*, Philadelphia, 1975
  The Gnostic Gospels, New York, 1979
Parkes, James, *The Conflict of the Church and the Synagogue*, London, 1934
  Jesus, Paul and the Jews, London, 1936

The Foundations of Judaism and Christianity, London, 1960

Pearson, B. A., 'Friedlander Revisited: Alexandrian Judaism and Gnostic Origins', *Studia Philonica*, 2 (1973), pp 23–39

'Jewish Sources in Gnostic Literature', in *Jewish Writings of the Second Temple Period*, ed. Michael E. Stone, Assen/Philadelphia, 1984

Perrin, Norman, *Rediscovering the Teaching of Jesus*, London, 1967

Petuchowski, Jakob J., and Brocke, Michael (ed.), *The Lord's Prayer and Jewish Liturgy*, London, 1978

Pines, S., 'The Jewish Christians according to a New Source', *Proceedings of the Israel Academy of Sciences and Humanities*, vol. 2, Jerusalem, 1968

Podro, Joshua, see Graves, Robert

Pseudo-Clementine, *Recognitions*, ed. B. Rehm, Berlin, 1965
Homilies, ed. B. Rehm, Berlin, 1969

Pseudo-Philo, *Liber Antiquitatum Biblicarum*, ed. M. R. James, with Prolegomenon by Louis H. Feldman, New York, 1971

Puukko, A. F., *Paulus und das Judentum*, Helsingfors, 1928

Reinink, G. J., see Klijn, A. F. J.

Reitzenstein, R., *Die Hellenistische Mysterienreligionen*, 3rd ed., Leipzig/Berlin, 1927

Rivkin, Ellis, 'Defining the Pharisees: the Tannaitic Sources', *Hebrew Union College Annual*, 40 (1969–70), pp 234 ff
The Hidden Revolution, London, 1975

Robertson, J. M., *Pagan Christs*, 2nd ed., London, 1911

Robinson, J. M., and Meyer, M. (ed.), *The Nag Hammadi Library in English*, London/San Francisco, 1977

Rowland, Christopher, *The Open Heaven: a Study of Apocalyptic in Judaism and Early Christianity*, London, 1982
Christian Origins, London, 1985

Rudolph, K., *Gnosis* (ed. R. McL. Wilson), Edinburgh/New York, 1983

Ruether, Rosemary, *Faith and Fratricide*, New York, 1974

Safrai, S., and Stern, M., *The Jewish People in the First Christian Century*, Assen, 1974–6

Sanders, E. P., *Paul and Palestinian Judaism*, London, 1977
(ed.), *Jewish and Christian Self-Definition*, volume 1: *The Shaping of Christianity in the Second and Third Centuries*, London, 1980
with Baumgarten, A. I., and Mendelson, Alan, *Jewish and Christian Self-Definition*, volume 2: *Aspects of Judaism in the Graeco-Roman Period*, London, 1981
Paul, the Law and the Jewish People, Philadelphia, 1983
Jesus and Judaism, London, 1985

Sandmel, Samuel, *The Genius of Paul*, New York, 1970

Schiffman, Lawrence H., *Who Was a Jew?*, Hoboken, 1985

Schoeps, H. J., *Theologie und Geschichte des Judenchristentums*, Tübingen, 1949
Paul: the Theology of the Apostle in the Light of Jewish Religious History, London,

1961

Scholem, Gershom, *Major Trends in Jewish Mysticism*, London, 1955
  Jewish Gnosticism, Merkabah Mysticism and Talmudic Tradition, New York, 1960
  Sabbatai Sevi: the Mystical Messiah, 1626–1676, London, 1973
Schonfield, Hugh J., *The Jew of Tarsus*, London, 1946
  Those Incredible Christians, London, 1968
Schwarzchild, Steven S., 'Noachites', *Jewish Quarterly Review*, LII, pp 297–308;
  LIII, pp 30–65, 1961–62
Schweitzer, Albert, *Paul and His Interpreters*, London, 1912
  The Quest of the Historical Jesus, London, 1948
Segal, A. F., *Two Powers in Heaven*, Leiden, 1978
Shepherd, M. H., Junior, 'Lord's Supper', *Interpreter's Dictionary of the Bible*,
  Abingdon, 1968
Sherwin-White, A. N., *Roman Society and Roman Law in the New Testament*,
  Oxford, 1963
Silver, A. H., *A History of Messianic Speculation in Israel*, New York, 1927
Simon, M., *St Stephen and the Hellenists in the Primitive Church*, London, 1958
  Verus Israel, 2nd ed., Paris, 1964
Singer, S. (tr.), *The Authorised Daily Prayer Book*, London, many editions
Smallwood, E. Mary, *The Jews under Roman Rule*, Leiden, 1976
Spiro, Solomon J., 'Who Was the *Haber*? A new Approach to an Ancient
  Institution', *Journal for the Study of Judaism*, 11, 1980, pp 186–216
Stendahl, Krister, *Paul Among Jews and Gentiles*, Philadelphia, 1976
Stern, Menahem, *Greek and Latin Authors on Jews and Judaism*, Leiden, 1974
  See Safrai, S.
Strack, Hermann L., and Billerbeck, Paul, *Kommentar zum Neuen Testament aus
  Talmud und Midrasch*, 4 vols., München, 1922
Strecker, G., *Das Judenchristentum in den Pseudoklementinen*, Berlin, 1958
Stroumsa, G., *Another Seed: Studies in Sethian Gnosticism*, Leiden, 1985
Talmudic Encyclopaedia (Hebrew), Jerusalem, 1947–
Toland, John, *Nazarenus: or Jewish, Gentile and Mahometan Christianity*, London,
  1718
Torrey, C. C., *The Jewish Foundations of Islam*, USA, 1967
Townsend, J. T., '1 Corinthians 3: 15 and the School of Shammai', *Harvard
  Theological Review*, 61, 1968, pp 500–4
Unnik, W. C. van, *Tarsus and Jerusalem*, London, 1962
Vermaseren, M. J., *Cybele and Attis: the Myth and the Cult*, London, 1977
Vermes, Geza, *Jesus the Jew*, London, 1973
  Scripture and Tradition in Judaism, Leiden, 1973
  Jesus and the World of Judaism, London, 1983
Weiss, J., *Earliest Christianity*, 2 vols., New York, 1959
Weiss-Rosmarin, Trude (ed.), *Jewish Expressions on Jesus*, New York, 1977
Wells, G. A., *The Jesus of the Early Christians*, London, 1971
Whiteley, D. E. H., *The Theology of St Paul*, Oxford, 1964

227

Williams, A. L., *Adversus Judaeos*, Cambridge, 1935
Wilson, R. McL., *The Gnostic Problem*, London, 1958
Winter, Paul, *On the Trial of Jesus*, Berlin, 1961
Yadin, Yigael, *Bar-Kokhba*, Jerusalem, 1971
Yamauchi, E. M., *Pre-Christian Gnosticism: A Survey of the Proposed Evidences*, 2nd ed., Grand Rapids, 1983
Zeitlin, S., *The Rise and Fall of the Judaean State*, vol. 2, Philadelphia, 1962

INDEX

229

INDEX OF QUOTATIONS

235

237